Literature as Recreation
in the Later Middle Ages

Literature as Recreation in the Later Middle Ages

GLENDING OLSON

Cornell University Press

ITHACA AND LONDON

Cornell University Press gratefully acknowledges a grant from the Andrew W. Mellon Foundation that aided in bringing this book to publication.

First published 1982 by Cornell University Press.
Published in the United Kingdom by Cornell University Press Ltd.,
Ely House, 37 Dover Street, London W1X 4HQ.

International Standard Book Number 0-8014-1494-6
Library of Congress Catalog Card Number 82-2462
Printed in the United States of America
*Librarians: Library of Congress cataloging information appears
on the last page of the book.*

*The paper in this book is acid-free, and meets the guidelines for permanence and durability
of the Committee on Production Guidelines for Book Longevity of the Council on Library
Resources.*

for my mother and father

A merry heart doeth good like a medicine:
but a broken spirit drieth the bones.

Proverbs 17:22

Contents

Preface

> The comments are not always what we should expect, that is,
> if we cling to the widely disseminated idea . . . that the medi-
> aeval reader, spiritually sharpened by a training in allegory,
> heard nothing but the mystical overtones in Ovid's works,
> such as the *Art of Love.* How disappointing to find that the
> *intentio scribentis* in the *Amores,* according to one of these com-
> mentators of the twelfth century, is—*delectare!* Only this and
> nothing more. What a vista is opened by these few words—a
> vista into the mediaeval mind!—E. K. Rand

This book is intended as a contribution to the history
of medieval literary thought. It deals with an aspect of the
subject that modern scholarship has paid relatively little attention to: that vista of delight which, half a century ago, E. K.
Rand saw in a commentary on Ovid's *Amores.*[1] Most scholarship on medieval literary theory and criticism has dealt with
other matters—narrative structure, rhetorical influence, and,
perhaps most extensively, allegory and typology. In Horatian
terms, it has concentrated on profit rather than pleasure, and
the notion that people in the Middle Ages always read and
wrote allegorically is perhaps even more widely disseminated
now than in Rand's generation. Scholars have applied medieval literary ideas to medieval poetry in many cases, but not
usually to all that nondidactic, principally entertaining material we know existed: Goliardic verse, the fabliaux, trivial
court lyrics, even some work by Chaucer and Boccaccio. Yet
there are medieval explanations and justifications of the value

[1] "The Classics in the Thirteenth Century," *Speculum,* 4 (1929), 252.

of literary pleasure, whether conjoined with profit or not. They are the subject of this book.

Although my focus throughout is on literary thought, I have always tried to see that thought in its social and intellectual context. This perspective has led to fairly extended treatment of some nonliterary matters, such as the medieval idea of emotional health, the secular implications of fourteenth-century hunting manuals, and psychological responses to the Black Death. I hope that these interdisciplinary forays, however limited or inadequate in themselves, will help to place the literary ideas in one of their most important contexts, the increasingly substantial but not fully autonomous secular culture of the later Middle Ages. Although my approach is historical, some of the medieval ideas I treat have modern resonance, and we will see that much of the justification of entertainment in the Middle Ages has affinities with recent holistic approaches to health and well-being.

The first three chapters deal with theory. Chapter 1 surveys the medieval recognition that some literature pleases as well as, or rather than, profits. The next two discuss ideas in the later Middle Ages which justify the offering of pleasure. Chapter 2 presents an essentially medical tradition that regards the emotional response of pleasure, elicited from sources including literature, as physically and mentally healthful. It discusses a few examples of criticism predicated on the hygienic value of entertainment, notably the concept of theatrics in Hugh of St. Victor and later thinkers. Chapter 3 presents a more psychological and ethical approach that views the taking of entertainment as recreation, a necessary part of our lives. The remaining three chapters deal with literature and literary criticism that invoke, in one way or another, these theoretical arguments. Chapter 4 treats a variety of works and genres that claim to recreate or reinvigorate. Chapter 5 discusses a structural pattern central to the *Decameron* and a few other compositions, the movement from plague to pleasure; it returns to medical texts, specifically the plague tracts, to make its point about the therapeutic implications of the pattern. Chapter 6 continues with further analysis of the *Decameron*, the culminating work of medieval literary recreation, and of some early critical opinion about it.

It may be helpful to make clear at the start some of the things this book will not treat. It is not an attempt to prove that people in the Middle Ages enjoyed themselves, or to produce a full inventory of the medieval literature and performance that seem principally for entertainment. I assume, rather than rehearse, the copious documentation concerning entertainment and entertainers by such scholars as E. K. Chambers, Edmond Faral, and Helen Waddell;[2] and when I turn to such texts, some of them well known, for evidence, it is for the sake of literary theory rather than social history. Nor do I discuss the subjects of comedy, humor, or laughter; they are often involved in that literature which pleases rather than profits, but the theories I consider do not usually explore them in much detail. Finally, though I believe (and will state more than once in the course of this book) that the attitudes toward literary delight treated here are relevant to literature that seeks to profit as well as please, I have tended to avoid discussing instances where pleasure appears as part of a work meant primarily for instruction. Much of the material in Ernst Robert Curtius's famous excursus "Jest and Earnest in Medieval Literature" is of this sort (though some, including that in his tenth excursus, is concerned more purely with jest);[3] and there are many studies that deal with theories and texts involving the combination of the humorous and the serious—it is almost impossible to avoid wrestling with the pleasure-profit question when considering such subjects as the *Libro de buen amor*, the cycle drama, and the *Canterbury Tales*. Though I do discuss the latter briefly in Chapter 4, I have tried to confine myself to cases in which the recreational and medical arguments dominate rather than merely accompany.

Although I think this book breaks new ground, it is certainly not the first to notice the idea of recreation as a literary defense nor to suggest the medical values of entertainment. Some earlier criticism alluded to these ideas more or less in passing. Of the more extended work, Joachim Suchomski's *"Delectatio" und "Utilitas"* is a thorough investigation of Christian attitudes to-

[2]Chambers, *The Mediaeval Stage*, 2 vols. (1903; rpt. London: Oxford University Press, 1967). Faral, *Les jongleurs en France au Moyen Age* (1910; rpt. New York: Burt Franklin, 1970). Waddell, *The Wandering Scholars*, 6th ed. (rpt. Garden City, N.Y.: Doubleday, 1955).
[3]*European Literature and the Latin Middle Ages*, trans. Willard R. Trask (New York: Harper & Row, 1963), pp. 417–35, 478–79.

ward literary entertainment from the Bible through Aquinas, which the author then applies to Latin and German literature, principally the twelfth-century Latin comedies.[4] Though I duplicate some of his theoretical evidence in Chapters 1 and 3, my focus is generally on the later Middle Ages, beginning rather than ending with Aquinas, and my literary examples are almost entirely different, drawing on vernacular works in French, English, and Italian. Three recent full-length studies also consider in part the medical ideas of solace and therapy, principally in Renaissance texts, material that parallels in varying degrees my independent investigations of these theories in the later Middle Ages.[5] And I have found stimulating a chapter in Thomas Reed's dissertation, which attempts to delineate some nondidactic aesthetic ideas that he finds relevant to certain medieval debate poems.[6]

I am aware of the ironies inherent in a scholarly study, fully documented, on the subject of entertainment and recreation. At times it is like trying to explain a joke. But if the history of medieval literary thought is to be complete, it will have to acknowledge not just that light verse and amusing stories existed but that people in the Middle Ages had coherent ideas about the acceptability and value of that kind of discourse. This book is an exploratory step in defining some of those ideas, especially as they attained greater prominence in the later Middle Ages than they had enjoyed before, as a part of the many changes in medieval culture from the twelfth century on. It is too large a task here to relate the theories to every aspect of that culture and the literature they illuminate; my principal

---

[4]*"Delectatio" und "Utilitas": Ein Beitrag zum Verständnis mittelalterlicher komischer Literatur* (Bern: Franke, 1975). For additional work on aspects of the recreational idea in some medieval German literature, an area with which I am unfamiliar, see William C. McDonald, "Die Deutung von Hartmanns Wendung *swaere stunde senfter machen:* Befreiung von 'Betrubnis' oder 'Langeweile'?" *Studia Neophilologica*, 46 (1974), 281–94.

[5]Glenda Pritchett, "Humor and the Comic in Middle Scots Poetry: A Study of the 'Ballettis Mirry' of the Bannatyne MS" (Diss. University of Chicago, 1979), pp. 62–97. Robert J. Clements and Joseph Gibaldi, *Anatomy of the Novella: The European Tale Collection from Boccaccio and Chaucer to Cervantes* (New York: New York University Press, 1977), pp. 8–12, 36–51. Heinz-Günter Schmitz, *Physiologie des Scherzes: Bedeutung und Rechtfertigung der Ars Iocandi im 16. Jahrhundert* (Hildesheim: Georg Olms, 1972), pp. 91–183.

[6]"Middle English Debate Poetry: A Study in Form and Function" (Diss. University of Virginia, 1978).

concern is simply to explicate the theories and show where literary texts rely on them, not to offer full analyses of those texts and their values. I hope essentially to redress an imbalance in modern scholarship that fosters, intentionally or not, the notion that medieval literary thought had nothing but indifference to or contempt for the purely pleasurable. To do that may help enlarge our appreciation of the breadth and tolerance of the understanding of literature in the Middle Ages.

Throughout the book, in quotations from manuscripts and early printed editions, I have silently expanded abbreviations and modernized punctuation. Translations whose source is not specified are my own. In the absence of a bibliography, the Index of Sources will lead readers to the first and full citation of references subsequently abbreviated.

Portions of Chapters 1, 3, and 4 originally appeared, in quite different form, as "The Medieval Theory of Literature for Refreshment and Its Use in the Fabliau Tradition," *Studies in Philology*, 71 (1974), 291–313. Part of Chapter 6 first appeared as "Petrarch's View of the *Decameron*," *MLN*, 91 (1976), 69–79. I thank the University of North Carolina Press and the Johns Hopkins University Press, respectively, for permission to use that material. Passages from G. H. McWilliam's translation of the *Decameron* are reprinted by permission of Penguin Books Ltd.

A grant-in-aid from the American Council of Learned Societies enabled me to do research in England at the British Library, the Wellcome Institute for the History of Medicine, the Bodleian Library, and the John Rylands University Library of Manchester. I am grateful to these institutions and their staffs for courtesies extended, and to the British Library and the Bibliothèque Nationale for permission to print selections from manuscripts in their possession. Among the many other libraries I have used for research on this project, over a period of years, the Newberry Library in Chicago and the Allen Memorial Medical Library in Cleveland offered significant facilities.

Cleveland State University has aided my work in a variety of ways—through its professional-leave program, a helpful interlibrary loan department, a grant from the Research and Creative Activities Committee for research expenses, and the expert services of the Word Processing Center.

Many people have given me many kinds of support. My ventures into the history of medicine have profited from a conversation with C. H. Talbot and from L. J. Rather's careful reading of Chapter 2. I have received scholarly help and impetus from Judson Allen, Susan Noakes, Glenda Pritchett, A. G. Rigg, and Siegfried Wenzel. Sherron Knopp read the entire manuscript and made many suggestions that improved it substantially, as did the anonymous readers for Cornell University Press. The Press itself has been a pleasure to work with; I am particularly grateful to Bernhard Kendler and Carol Betsch. Kathleen Webber was a fine research assistant. My wife, Hester Lewellen, has helped abundantly.

To three people I owe special academic debts. I first studied the history of literary theory with Wesley Trimpi; his work has remained important to me, as has his continued interest. The learning and generosity of my colleague Phillips Salman has aided me immeasurably during the years we have talked, traded notes, and read each other's work on medieval literary thought. And V. A. Kolve, since he first saw some of these ideas take shape in a chapter of a dissertation, has always given me the insight and inspiration that make him so valuable a teacher and a friend.

GLENDING OLSON

Cleveland Heights, Ohio

Abbreviations

Archiv	*Archiv für Geschichte der Medizin*
BHM	*Bulletin of the History of Medicine*
CFMA	Les Classiques Français du Moyen Age
EETS e.s.	Early English Text Society, extra series
EETS o.s.	Early English Text Society, original series
SATF	Société des Anciens Textes Français
SP	*Studies in Philology*
ST	St. Thomas Aquinas, *Summa Theologiae*, Blackfriars text and trans., 60 vols. New York: McGraw-Hill, 1964–.

Literature as Recreation
in the Later Middle Ages

1

Medieval Attitudes toward Literary Pleasure

Literature gives pleasure. From Plato's recognition of Homer's power to charm and enthrall to Roland Barthes's *The Pleasure of the Text,* critics and theorists of literature have always acknowledged its capacity to give delight. There is even more persuasive evidence from a larger audience, the people who in the Middle Ages listened to minstrels tell stories, who in the Renaissance made Shakespeare a commercial success, who in the nineteenth century waited for the next installment of Dickens, and who today buy paperback editions of Harold Robbins or Joseph Heller. Although to some extent literary enjoyment remains suspect even now,[1] we have a fully institutionalized, philosophical rationale for it: a separate intellectual category of "aesthetic pleasure" that makes the experience of works of art a valid mode of knowledge in itself. And if such academic approaches usually restrict themselves to only the "best" literature, we have another category, popular culture, for explaining the psychological, sociological, and even artistic satisfactions that obtain from movies, television, and formula fiction. In general, gaining pleasure from works of art seems a decent, even laudable, activity.

In the Middle Ages, according to the conventional wisdom, such was not the case. The early Christian hostility to pagan

[1]Cf. *The Pleasure of the Text,* trans. Richard Miller (New York: Hill & Wang, 1975), p. 57: "No sooner has a word been said, somewhere, about the pleasure of the text, than two policemen are ready to jump on you: the political policeman and the psychoanalytical policeman: futility and/or guilt, pleasure is either idle or vain, a class notion or an illusion."

culture, and hence to classical poetry, resulted in the most cautious and restricted acceptance of literature. Throughout the period the emphasis in literary theory and in the justifications put forward by the works themselves is not on the pleasure poetry provides but on the moral benefit it bestows. This exemplum is worth hearing because it teaches you about the dangers of avarice. This ancient story is worth reading because it depicts virtuous actions you should imitate. This pagan fable, which if taken literally involves immoral acts by gods, has an allegorical meaning that is consistent with natural or religious truth. Literature becomes the servant of Christian morality and faith. To respond to a text only for the pleasure it gives is to misspend one's time; the pleasure, rather, should lie in the satisfactions of using literature to further one's understanding of right action or right belief.

No one should deny that such attitudes existed, and dominated, in the Middle Ages and that many important artists and thinkers held them, as we will see shortly. But I want to begin this survey of medieval views of literary pleasure not with statements about what literature should do but with a very broad generalization about what in fact it does. Medieval understanding of the function of poetry depended to a large extent on these lines from Horace's *Ars poetica*:

> Aut prodesse volunt aut delectare poetae   333
> aut simul et iucunda et idonea dicere vitae.
> quidquid praecipies, esto brevis, ut cito dicta
> percipiant animi dociles teneantque fideles:
> omne supervacuum pleno de pectore manat.
> ficta voluptatis causa sint proxima veris,
> ne quodcumque velit poscat sibi fabula credi,
> neu pransae Lamiae vivum puerum extrahat alvo.
> centuriae seniorum agitant expertia frugis,
> celsi praetereunt austera poemata Ramnes:
> omne tulit punctum qui miscuit utile dulci,
> lectorem delectando pariterque monendo.   344

Poets aim either to benefit, or to amuse, or to utter words at once both pleasing and helpful to life. Whenever you instruct, be brief, so that what is quickly said the mind may readily grasp and faithfully hold: every word in excess flows away from the full mind. Fictions meant to please should be close to the real, so that your story must not ask for belief in anything it chooses, nor from the Ogress's belly, after dinner, draw forth a living child. The centuries of the elders chase from the stage what is profitless; the proud Ramnes disdain poems devoid of charms. He has won every vote who has blended profit and pleasure, at once delighting and instructing the reader.[2]

The first two lines are probably the most familiar literary commonplace in the Middle Ages, and line 343 often accompanies them. I have cited the entire passage so that we can see what Horace means when he talks about the different poetic goals. Having posed three literary intentions—profit, pleasure, and the combination of the two—he first takes up the matter of instruction. That which profits in poetry should be briefly but clearly stated; Horace seems to be thinking in terms of straightforward moralizing here, points stated rather than dramatized, what Brink calls "the teaching of lessons" (*Prolegomena*, p. 263). Lines 338–40 give advice on the second goal: literary pleasure comes from a verisimilar fiction, not from fairy-tale exotica. The rest of the passage points to the superiority of the third kind of poetic work, that which combines pleasure and profit: it will appeal to both old and young, bringing, as Horace goes on to point out, fame to its author.

Certainly the *Ars poetica* intends the third kind of poetry to be valued most. But the firm categorizing of lines 333–34, emphasized by the three "aut"s, and the repeated use of words that denote one or the other poetic goal ("delectare," "iucunda," "voluptatis causa," "dulci," "delectando" versus "prodesse," "idonea . . . vitae," "praecipies," "utile," "monendo") contribute to the likelihood of the passage's being taken more descriptively than prescriptively. Quoting line 333 by itself, as medieval texts

---

[2]Lines 333–44. *Satires, Epistles and* Ars poetica, ed. and trans. H. Rushton Fairclough, Loeb Classical Library (Cambridge, Mass.: Harvard University Press, rpt. 1966), pp. 478–79. I have changed Fairclough's translation of "fabula" in line 339. See the notes to these lines in C. O. Brink, *Horace on Poetry: The* Ars poetica (Cambridge: Cambridge University Press, 1971), pp. 352–58, and for more on the evolution of the ideas of pleasure and profit from Aristotle through Neoptolemus to Horace, Brink's *Horace on Poetry: Prolegomena to the Literary Epistles* (Cambridge: Cambridge University Press, 1963), pp. 57, 128–29.

sometimes did, would lead further in that direction, especially to the frequent habit of taking the *prodesse-delectare* distinction to indicate the difference between serious and frivolous work. But the medieval understanding of Horace's lines involves more than just the reading or misreading of this passage. The evolution of a conception of fiction in the classical period which is more rhetorically based than Aristotle's in the *Poetics*, which tends to separate content (ideas, truth) and form (story, style) rather than fuse them in the way that Aristotelian mimesis does, lies behind both Horace's terminology of profit and pleasure and the even more extreme separations of content and form in medieval Christian literary thought.[3] The very fact that Horace's literary ideal combines the two functions suggests an understanding of fiction that is inherently dualistic; it is one that does not substantially change until the emergence in recent centuries of a conception of aesthetic experience more Aristotelian than Platonic or Christian in its willingness to accord works of art an independent status as a form of human understanding.

Accordingly, one strain of medieval literary thought developed by taking the distinction between pleasure and profit as a means of justifying fiction by its conformity to moral and religious truth. *Delectare* became the function of the narrative surface, *prodesse* the function of the spiritual truth embodied in the fiction. A medieval commentary on Statius known as *On the Thebiad*, attributed to Fulgentius the Mythographer but probably written some centuries later, makes explicit the allegorical use of Horace:

> I take up again, with great respect, that knowledge deserving of scrutiny and that inexhaustible vein of intellect found in those poets who, under the alluring cover of a poetic fiction, have inserted a set of moral precepts for practical use. For when Horace testifies that "poets seek to instruct or delight,

---

[3]See Wesley Trimpi, "The Ancient Hypothesis of Fiction: An Essay on the Origins of Literary Theory," *Traditio*, 27 (1971), esp. 63–65, and "The Quality of Fiction: The Rhetorical Transmission of Literary Theory," *Traditio*, 30 (1974), esp. 46–51. Also Richard McKeon, "Literary Criticism and the Concept of Imitation in Antiquity," in *Critics and Criticism*, ed. R. S. Crane (Chicago: University of Chicago Press, 1952), pp. 147–75. For twelfth-century discussions along these lines, see Edgar de Bruyne, *Etudes d'esthétique médiévale*, 3 vols. (Bruges: de Tempel, 1946), II: 146–72.

or say what is both pleasing and useful in life," they are found to be no more delightful and entertaining through their literal meaning and narrative skill than they are instructive and serviceable, for the building of habits of life, through the hidden revealing of their allegories.[4]

The commentary goes on to compare a poem to a nut, its literal meaning like a shell one needs to break in order to get to the desirable kernel of allegorical truth. "A child is happy to play with the whole nut, but a wise adult breaks it open to get the taste." The analogy not only delineates the sources of pleasure and profit but ranks the two poetic functions: being content with surface delight alone is childish play, seeking the inner wisdom is properly mature activity.

D. W. Robertson, Jr., has firmly established that such a conception of poetry was pervasive in the Middle Ages.[5] The critical approach of Robertson and those who adopt his theories, an exceptionally important influence on modern medieval studies, has occasioned so much discussion that a full-scale presentation of it here is unnecessary. But I do need to comment on it briefly from the standpoint of literary thought and as it relates to this book. Roughly, Robertson believes that the theory of poetry enunciated in the Statius commentary was virtually the only respectable one in the Middle Ages, that therefore medieval writers wrote in accord with it, and that consequently modern critics must adopt it in order to approach medieval literature in a valid historical way. Many of the critical readings that have emerged from these principles have occasioned sometimes reasonable, sometimes irrational, disagreement. I do not think specific quarrels with Robertsonian interpretations deal very effectively with the approach. A more important general question is whether Robertson is correct in imputing the views of *On the Thebiad* to all writers of medieval literature, and one (certainly not the only) means of answering that question is to see exactly what other ideas about literature were current. That there were

---

[4]Trans. Leslie George Whitbread, *Fulgentius the Mythographer* (n.p.: Ohio State University Press, 1971), p. 239.

[5]See especially "Some Medieval Literary Terminology, with Special Reference to Chrétien de Troyes," *SP*, 48 (1951), 669–92, and *A Preface to Chaucer* (Princeton: Princeton University Press, 1962).

other ideas seems to me undeniable, and this book is about a few of them. It is meant not to refute Robertson's assertions of a medieval theory of allegory but to suggest that there are limits to its applicability, that the belief in a single "medieval" way of responding to literature is unwarranted, and that accordingly the judicious use of medieval literary thought in the interpretation of any individual work entails first establishing rather than assuming what critical ideas are most relevant to it.

So let us return to the Horatian distinctions and to some references that use them not to justify allegorical readings but to indicate, frequently with some objectivity, the varying functions poetry may serve. A fourteenth-century commentator handily summarizes the three goals of fiction as he explains Ovid's purpose in composing the *Metamorphoses:* "His intention is to write down fables so that he may please and profit by means of their presentation, as Horace says: 'Poets wish either to profit or to please.' Some profit but do not please, as when they produce unpolished sermons; some deal with buffoonery that pleases but does not profit; some do both, and they are complete. Ovid is one of these."[6] That a tale from the *Metamorphoses* offers both pleasure and profit is understandable enough when one considers medieval allegorizations of that book. But what is the commentator thinking of when he speaks of "sermones scabros" that only profit and "scurrilia" that only please? "Sermo" has a variety of meanings in the Middle Ages; here it perhaps suggests something of the classical conversational *sermo*, something of its Christian adaptation into *sermo humilis*. Seneca in one of his letters contrasts a plain style meant to profit the soul with a more ornate style meant to please, and this seems to be much the sense here, in which the purely profitable is linked with both a stylistic level and a nonfictional genre.[7] "Scurrilia" also suggests both content and style. What

[6]"Intentio sua est describere fabulas ut per harum descriptionem delectet et prosit, ut ait Flaccus: 'aut prodesse volunt aut delectare poete.' Quidam prosunt et non delectant cum habeant sermones scabros; quidam scurrilia tractant que delectant et non prosunt; quidam faciunt utrumque, et isti sunt perfecti: de his est Ovidius." Ed. Fausto Ghisalberti, "Mediaeval Biographies of Ovid," *Journal of the Warburg and Courtauld Institutes*, 9 (1946), 58.

[7]For the classical background see Wesley Trimpi, *Ben Jonson's Poems: A Study of the Plain Style* (Stanford: Stanford University Press, 1962), pp. 5–19; the passage from Seneca is on p. 11. For the Christian, see Erich Auerbach,

pleases is the buffoonery of jests and funny stories, doubtless with some implication of vulgarity in language or action, though it is not always appropriate to read modern senses of "scurrilous" into the Latin, which on occasion may simply refer to improper levity.[8] In any case, this passage acknowledges that although the best poetry fulfills both Horatian precepts, there are recognized types of literature that aim at only one.

Other testimony throughout the Middle Ages confirms the polarization of pleasure and profit as indications of literary purpose. Augustine defines *fabula* as "a lie composed for profit or delight (compositum ad utilitatem delectationemve mendacium)," the disjunction indicating that he does not consider all fictions to be profitable. This definition occurs in the *Soliloquia*, following a discussion of falsity, in which Reason distinguishes between two types, the deceptive and the feigned, saying that only the former intends duplicity: "What I call feigned is created by fabricators, who differ thus from deceivers: every

---

"Sermo Humilis," in his *Literary Language and its Public in Late Latin Antiquity and in the Middle Ages*, trans. Ralph Manheim (London: Routledge & Kegan Paul, 1965), pp. 27–66. Perhaps a good example of a *sermo scaber* is John Gower's *Vox clamantis;* at least in the Prologue to Book II he points up his use of plain speech for moral ends. That Gower thought of his Latin poem as meant for profit rather than pleasure is implied in the later *Confessio amantis*, where he explicitly tries to write "somwhat of lust, somwhat of lore," i.e., to combine pleasure and profit. He observes, with what I take to be a rueful allusion to his two earlier, lengthy, nonfictional, moral poems: "who that al of wisdom writ / It dulleth ofte a mannes wit / To him that schal it aldai rede." Prologue, lines 13–21, ed. G. C. Macaulay, *The English Works of John Gower*, I, EETS e.s. 81 (1900; rpt. London: Oxford University Press, 1969), p. 2.

[8]In 1300 Bishop Ralph of Walpole drew up statutes for the Benedictine priory of Ely. One of them, alluding to the Rule of St. Benedict's prohibition against "scurilitas" and idle speech provoking laughter, defines *verba'scurilia* as speech that is "unreasonable and destructive to mature behavior," a definition that seems to refer to most any kind of verbal frivolity, not just the coarse and insulting. *Ely Chapter Ordinances and Visitation Records 1241–1515*, ed. S. J. A. Evans, Camden Third Series, LXIV, Camden Miscellany 17 (London: Royal Historical Society, 1940), p. 13. Cf. Bernard of Clairvaux on the third step of pride, "foolish mirth (inepta laetitia)," in *The Steps of Humility*, trans. George B. Burch (Cambridge, Mass.: Harvard University Press, 1950), pp. 200–3. The fifteenth-century *Summa theologica* of Antoninus of Florence, following Aquinas who followed Gregory, lists "scurrilitas" as one of the daughters of gluttony and gives a wide range of meanings for it, from the fairly innocuous "enjoyment that stirs laughter (jucunditas, quae risum movere solet)" to much more pejorative descriptions involving insults and sexual provocation. Pars I, tit. VI, c. 4, § v (Verona, 1740), col. 779.

deceiver tries to trick, but not everyone who fabricates wishes to trick. For mimes, comedies, and many poems are full of lies in the desire to please rather than to trick (delectandi potius quam fallendi voluntate), and almost everyone who makes jokes (jocantur) fabricates."[9] Here is an inventory of a range of verbal expression, from jokes to stage performance to "poemata," that is apparently concerned only with pleasing. Although fiction is a kind of lying and thus never rises very high in Augustine's estimation, he recognizes at least that it need not be created from evil intent, and that while some of it has usefulness, some seems to be purely entertaining.

Augustine's reference to jokes leads us to another treatise defending their use, Macrobius's *Saturnalia*. In the *Commentary on the* Dream of Scipio, he acknowledges that one type of *fabula* has no moral purpose, and he separates fictions that simply "gratify the ear" from those with serious moral aims, admitting into a philosophical work only a fraction of the latter.[10] But in the context of the *Saturnalia* he is more tolerant of discourse meant principally to entertain. There the speakers deal not only with philosophic concerns but with more trivial subjects; in fact, Macrobius describes Saturnalia as a festivity in which distinguished men speak during the day on serious matters relating to the liberal arts and then after dinner turn to "merrier talk, meant more for pleasure than for seriousness (sermo iucundior, ut habeat voluptatis amplius, severitatis minus)."[11] Book II begins as the first day's dinner is over; the participants, wishing neither to reject pleasure nor to place too high a value on it, decide to amuse themselves by rehearsing some witticisms

---

[9]*Soliloquia*, II, 9, 16; ed. J.-P. Migne, *Patrologia Latina*, vol. 32, col. 892. The definition is from II, 11, 19; *PL*, 32, col. 894.

[10]*Macrobius*, ed. J. Willis, 2 vols. (Leipzig: Teubner, 1970), II: 5–8. Trans. W. H. Stahl, *Commentary on the* Dream of Scipio (New York: Columbia University Press, 1952), pp. 83–87. See below, n. 18. Macrobius's chapter on poetry was well known in the later Middle Ages and used by humanists to defend morally useful literature while rejecting worthless tales. It certainly seems to have contributed to Boccaccio's classification of fictions in the *Genealogy of the Gods*, XIV, 9. The early fifteenth-century encyclopedia of Jacques Legrand cites its distinction between stories for pleasure ("fabule voluptatis gratia") and those for exhortation in order to separate useless from useful fictions. *Sophilogium*, II, 5 (Lyons, 1495), f. 24v.

[11]*Saturnalia*, I, 1; Willis, I: 4.

of the ancients, citing Plautus and Cicero as frequent tellers of such *joca*. This literate enjoyment is more dignified than the cruder pleasures usually introduced at such banquets; it pleases the speakers, who all laugh at the tales related.[12] These *joca* cannot be equated with any category in the classification of *fabulae* in the *Commentary*, for they are so short as to be more like puns or quips than narratives, and Macrobius calls them "dicta." Many, too, are jests with a distinct purpose and usefulness, and in this sense can claim satiric or moral relevance. Still, it is clear that the author thinks of them essentially as entertainments. Like Augustine, he appears to include *joca* as part of that kind of discourse which is meant to please, and their presence in the *Saturnalia* as an after-dinner pastime, along with the discussions of moral and scientific matters, suggests the legitimacy of entertainment as long as it observes due place and time.

Isidore of Seville is less judgmental in his classification of fictions than the Macrobius of the *Commentary*. In the *Etymologiae* he devotes a chapter to *fabula*, defining its functions: "Poets have created some fictions for the purpose of delighting, some in regard to the nature of things, and have put forth many dealing with human behavior."[13] He then gives examples of each type. Fictions for the purpose of delight include stories for the multitude and the plays of Plautus and Terence. One instance of a fiction "ad naturam rerum" is the story of limping Vulcan, which shows that fire never moves straight upward. Of fictions "ad mores" Isidore gives three examples: Horace's use of animal stories in his satires, Aesop's fables, and the parable in the Book of Judges of the trees choosing a king. He emphasizes that this last kind of *fabula* is made for the purpose of morality, that even though it is fictitious it has a true meaning. Opposed to it implicitly are those stories made "delectandi causa," where Isidore puts, without comment, Roman comedy and popular tales.

This classification was highly influential, and one can find it

---

[12]*Saturnalia*, II, 1; Willis, I: 134–35.

[13]"Fabulas poetae quasdam delectandi causa finxerunt, quasdam ad naturam rerum, nonnullas ad mores hominum interpretati sunt." *Etymologiae*, I, 40, ed. W. M. Lindsay (Oxford, 1911). Isidore's other comments on poetry are in VIII, 7, as part of a series of chapters on aspects of the pagan world.

repeated throughout the Middle Ages.[14] It appears in conjunction with Horace in the twelfth-century treatise of Dominicus
Gundissalinus, *De divisione philosophiae*. He says that poetry "delights or instructs in knowledge or behavior (delectat uel edifi-
cat in sciencia uel in moribus)." Discussing *fabula*, he repeats
Isidore almost verbatim, noting that some fictions are written
to delight, some to edify. About the purpose of poetry he says:
"Its goal is to delight through playful material or instruct
through serious material (Finis eius est aut ludicris delectare
aut seriis edificare)," and he quotes lines 333 and 343 of the *Ars
poetica* as authority. But although he cites Horace's ideal that
pleasure and profit be combined, his own definitions (based
more on Isidore's classification, apparently) always separate the
two functions: a poem is composed either for delight or usefulness ("causa delectacionis uel utilitatis").[15] He also alters, in
characteristically medieval ways, the Horatian understanding of
the causes of pleasure and profit. Delight is the result of *ludicra*, of sportive and trifling matters, edification of *seria*, of serious thought; the distinction between pleasure and profit becomes that between game and earnest, between the frivolous
and the substantial. The tendency to equate literary delight
with sport or play is also observable in less objective discussions.
John of Capua, changing the Horatian terms, says that his collection of fables is intended for knowledge and play ("scientiam
et ludum"), the wise man finding the wisdom in it, the fool
finding "ludum et solacium."[16] We have seen *On the Thebiad*
describe taking pleasure in fictional surfaces as like a child's
play. When there is a truth underneath the covering, then it

[14]For verbatim borrowings, see Vincent of Beauvais, *Speculum doctrinale*, III,
c. 113 (Douay, 1624), cols. 289–90, and the epilogue to a collection of fables of
Romulus, ed. Léopold Hervieux, *Les fabulistes latins*, 5 vols. (Paris, 1893–99;
rpt. New York: Burt Franklin, n.d.), II: 454. Conrad of Hirsau uses it as the
basis for his discussion of *fabula* in the section on Aesop in the *Dialogus super
auctores*, ed. R. B. C. Huygens, Collection Latomus 17 (Brussels, 1955), pp. 24–
25.

[15]Ed. Ludwig Baur (Münster, 1903), pp. 54–56; see also p. 68.

[16]Hervieux, V: 80. For this and other medieval references to pleasure and
profit I owe a debt to Stephen Manning, "The Nun's Priest's Morality and the
Medieval Attitude toward Fables," *JEGP*, 59 (1960), 403–16. For a variety of
ways in which the Horatian distinction appears in French literature, see Tony
Hunt, " 'Prodesse et Delectare': Metaphors of Pleasure and Instruction in Old
French," *Neuphilologische Mitteilungen*, 80 (1979), 17–35.

is immature to enjoy the fiction alone. But in regard to that type of literature which has no kernel, which exists solely "causa delectandi," it would seem that there is nothing to do but enjoy the sport.

Distinctions between *fabula* and *apologus* also rest on Isidore's classification, or at least on its principle. Pietro Alighieri alludes to it when discussing his father's use of the apologue, a fictitious "oratio" meant for edification, in the *Divine Comedy:* "[Apologues] differ from the usual tale (fabula), a word deriving from the word *hearsay,* which contains no ideas but only words. Moreover, the poet employs these tales either to delight, or to expose to view the nature of things, or to shape morals, as Isidore says in his *Etymologies:* concerning whose views see the *Dream of Scipio,* by Macrobius, near the beginning."[17] The linking of Isidore's categories with Macrobius's is intriguing, especially since the *Commentary* does not cite Isidore and offers a different, though reconcilable, schema of *fabulae.*[18] Pietro must have been most struck by the resemblance between Isidore's fictions "delectationis causa" and those which Macrobius says merely gratify the ear, both of which point to a strain of nondidactic literature. There may be some echo of Isidore in John of Garland's observation that every apologue is a *fabula,* "but not vice versa." He defines apologues as narratives in which "dumb animals are made to speak for our edification, as in Avianus and Aesop."[19] Although the context involves a distinction between the beast fable and other types of fiction which convey truth, it is reasonable to infer that John would not claim that all *fabulae* operate allegorically for the purpose of instruction.

[17]Trans. Robert Hollander, *Allegory in Dante's* Commedia (Princeton: Princeton University Press, 1969), p. 281; text p. 278.

[18]Isidore's distinctions are based wholly on function: (I) fictions that please; (II) fictions that explain the natural world; (III) fictions that treat human behavior. Macrobius first makes a functional distinction between (I) fictions that merely please the ear and (II) fictions that "encourage the reader to good works" (Stahl, p. 84). Within this second category tales are divided according to content: (A) wholly fictitious stories, such as Aesop's; (B) stories based on truth, such as legends of the gods. Macrobius further divides (B) into unworthy and respectable stories. Macrobius's II.A certainly encompasses Isidore's III and probably II as well, assuming the kind of encyclopedic knowledge it offers is taken as conducive to useful action.

[19]Ed. and trans. Traugott Lawler, *The Parisiana Poetria of John of Garland* (New Haven: Yale University Press, 1974), pp. 104–5; see p. 331 for John's source.

Even Ovid, though we have seen him praised for combining pleasure and profit, might be explained in terms of pleasure alone, and not only by way of censuring the *Ars amatoria*. One thirteenth-century *accessus* to the *Amores* takes up the traditional introductory questions, including *materia, intentio, utilitas,* and the *pars philosophiae* to which the work belongs:

> The author's subject is his own love. The work differs from the *Art of Love* in that there Ovid puts forth rules of love and here he deals with frivolous and amusing episodes. His intention is to describe humorously some aspects of his love affairs. There are two motives behind this intention, one to delight (for, as Horace says, "Poets wish either to profit or to please"), one to recommend himself to his lover, whom he calls by the fictitious name Corinna. The work's usefulness is delight, or commendation from Corinna. It pertains to ethics, because in speaking about his behavior he reveals the characters of bawds and of certain concubines who are rivals of his mistress.[20]

Although the last sentence, doubtless prompted in great part by the section in the *Amores* on Dipsas (I, 8), may seem typical of the medieval effort to moralize Ovid into acceptability, the passage as a whole is remarkably sympathetic to the poem, alert particularly to its wit and humor. The double motive and double *utilitas* is based on a distinction explicit in other commentaries between public and private values (see Ghisalberti, 52, 58). For Ovid personally the work is useful in that his poetry is his means of attracting Corinna (for the rival claims of poetry and wealth on Corinna's affections, see I, 8, 10; III, 8). For the larger audience, the result is the *delectatio* of amusing literature—we will consider later the implications of delight

---

[20]"Actoris siquidem materia est de amore suo. Distat autem hoc opus ab opere Artis Amatorie, quia in Arte Amatoria dat precepta de amore, in hoc opere ludicra tractat et iocosa. Intentio sua est quedam de amoribus suis iocose exponere. Causa intentionis duplex: vel ut ille delectet quia ut ait Horatius: 'aut prodesse volunt aut delectare poete' etc., vel amice sue quam falso nomine Corinnam appellat se commendet. Utilitas est delectatio, vel apud Corinnam suam commendatio. Ad eticam spectat quia de suis moribus loquendo quarumlibet succubarum pelicis rivalium et lenarum mores insinuat." Ghisalberti, 46. For similar evaluations of the *Amores* see 39 n. 1. Rand obviously saw a manuscript in this tradition. On the history and organization of the medieval accessus, see Edwin A. Quain, S.J., "The Medieval Accessus ad Auctores," *Traditio,* 3 (1945), 215–64.

being perceived as *utilitas*. The work belongs to the philosophical category of ethics, as almost all poetry does, because it deals with human behavior and one can make judgments about character; but the author of this commentary does not suggest that moral evaluation is part of either Ovid's *intentio* or the principal *utilitas* of the poem.[21] To be sure, such nondidactic readings of Ovid are rare in the Middle Ages, but that they exist at all should remind us that when Robertson, by way of arguing a monolithic approach to fiction in the period, asks, "Had not medieval men been making 'ernest of game' for centuries in Ovid's stories?" (*Preface to Chaucer*, p. 367), the answer is "not always." Even one of the classical *auctores* could be accepted as writing to delight rather than to instruct.

The evidence thus far reveals that literature for pleasure rather than profit was acknowledged, if not venerated, in the Middle Ages. Some classical compositions were thought by at least some critics to be for enjoyment rather than edification, and it would follow that medieval works might make the same appeal. At this point we need to look more closely at what constitutes literary pleasure, and for that we do not need to restrict ourselves to the criticism of works meant for delight alone, since those that offer both pleasure and profit would obviously meet criteria for entertainment as well as instruction.

Basically, medieval generalizations about what gives literary pleasure fall into two groups (I except for now theories in which profit is also referred to as a source of delight). The first has to do with formal considerations. A pleasing style delights the ear. "Style" here involves all verbal resources, the rhetorical devices so familiar from the arts of discourse, and in the case of poetry, meter and rhyme as well. As one example of this familiar medieval idea we may consider a letter from Petrarch to his brother Gherardo, a monk, which contains an allegorical eclogue. In it he defends poetry by appealing not only to the values of allegory but also to those of heightened language. He

[21]The fact that poets treat human activity and that therefore their works are classified as a part of ethics does not necessarily mean that every poem is didactic in intent or usefulness. Conrad of Hirsau specifies only three categories of philosophy within which a work may fit: logic, physics, and ethics (Quain, 217; cf. 239 n. 56). Any text dealing with human behavior thus belongs to ethics regardless of its specific purpose. As Quain points out, 251–52, the categorization was often applied quite mechanically.

explains that poetry originated in praise of God, "sacred hymns remote from all the forms of speech that pertain to common usage and to the affairs of state, and embellished moreover by numbers, which add a charm and drive tedium away." He anticipates his brother's objection to such "sweetness" and points out the biblical use of meter and the Church fathers' employment of "poetic forms and rhythms." He asks Gherardo to "consider the underlying meaning alone, and if that is sound and true accept it gladly, no matter what the outward form may be."[22] But if poetic charm is an impediment to the austere Gherardo, it certainly is not to Petrarch. Allegory is central to poetry, but there is also pleasure—a natural pleasure fully demonstrated throughout history—in the response to verbal beauty. Petrarch would have us break the shell to get the kernel, but not until we appreciate how attractive the shell is.

Pleasure also comes from narrative itself, from what it is that a poem or story presents to its audience at the literal level of detail or plot. An accessus to the Latin bestiary *Physiologus* explains the work's intention as "delectare in animalibus et prodesse in figuris."[23] The profit is in the allegorizations, but the pleasure is simply in finding out about the animals. The Middle Ages did not need Aristotle's *Poetics* to tell them that people naturally delight in representations, though by the later thirteenth century Aquinas had cited him on that score.[24] If allegorical poetics turned Horace's delight into the attractions of a distinctly fictitious surface, other approaches, such the Averroistic Aristotle, which tend to be exemplary rather than allegorical, maintained the association of pleasure with the verisimilar,

---

[22]*Familiares*, X, 4. Robinson and Rolfe's translation, in *Petrarch*, ed. David Thompson (New York: Harper & Row, 1971), pp. 90–93.

[23]*Accessus ad auctores*, ed. R. B. C. Huygens, Collection Latomus 15 (Brussels, 1954), p. 21.

[24]Using the Hermannus Alemannus translation of Averroes's *Middle Commentary on the Poetics*. For the references in the *Summa theologica* to this principle, see William F. Boggess, "Aristotle's *Poetics* in the Fourteenth Century," *SP*, 67 (1970), 284. According to Hermannus, man naturally delights both in representation and in "meter and melody." Poetic delight, however, is distinctly moral: "The art of poetry does not seek any sort of pleasure (delectatio) but seeks the level of pleasure which moves to virtue through imagination." Trans. Hardison in *Classical and Medieval Literary Criticism*, ed. Alex Preminger, O. B. Hardison, Jr., and Kevin Kerrane (New York: Ungar, 1974), pp. 352–53, 363. Text in Boggess, ed., "Averrois Cordubensis Commentarium Medium in Aristotelis Poetriam" (Diss. University of North Carolina, 1965), pp. 11–12, 43.

with fidelity to real life. Hence the truth-claims of a variety of medieval tales, even some preposterous ones—not only, I suspect, for the sake of authentication, but also for the pleasure induced by the contemplation of an event that could have or might really have happened.[25] John Barbour's *Bruce* begins by claiming a "doubill plesance" for itself: one in the "carpyng," the stylistic delight that obtains even in tales that are "nocht bot fabill"; the other in "the suthfastnes, / That schawys the thing rycht as it wes; / And suth thyngis that ar likand / Tyll mannys heryng, ar plesand."[26]

These and other medieval texts explain what aspects of literature cause delight, but they do not analyze the process of literary response that engenders it. Is it possible to be any more precise about the nature of literary pleasure? Phillips Salman has explored this question in important ways, relating literary *delectatio* to the faculty psychology of the Middle Ages and Renaissance, which was influenced in great part by such Aristotelian texts as the *De anima* and the *Nicomachean Ethics*.[27] I can do no better than summarize certain of his arguments here. His central insight is to see literary response as one species of human perception generally. "A response to a text is essentially the same as a response to any sense datum except that an artist causes a text to mediate between the reader and the created world. A response to a text is therefore part of one's general movement toward his last end, and a text must therefore be used the way any perception is" (315–16). That way involves the activation of the faculties receiving the data, abstraction and judgment by the intellect, the movement of the soul to-

[25]See, on this complicated matter, William Nelson, *Fact or Fiction: The Dilemma of the Renaissance Storyteller* (Cambridge, Mass.: Harvard University Press, 1973), pp. 1–37, esp. 22–28. We may be better able to understand the habit and the appeal of stories claiming factual status in light of such recent forms of discourse as nonfiction novels and television docudramas. Paul Theiner applies Morton Bloomfield's idea of authentication to fabliau truth-claims in "Fabliau Settings," in *The Humor of the Fabliaux: A Collection of Critical Essays*, ed. Thomas D. Cooke and Benjamin L. Honeycutt (Columbia: University of Missouri Press, 1974), pp. 120–23.
[26]Ed. W. W. Skeat, I, EETS e.s. 11 (1870; rpt. London: Oxford University Press, 1968), pp. 1–2.
[27]"Instruction and Delight in Medieval and Renaissance Literary Criticism," *Renaissance Quarterly*, 32 (1979), 303–32. Salman has completed a book that deals with ideas of literary delight from Plato through the Renaissance.

ward the desired object, and the delight attendant upon its possession. There are a variety of delights in literature as there are in life—delights of the sensitive soul, delights of the rational soul. Salman shows the varying attitudes of Augustine, Aquinas, and some Renaissance critics toward these delights, from Augustine's firm insistence that any sensual delight is valid only insofar as it conduces to spiritual pleasure, to a Renaissance willingness to accept "that a faculty may be activated and pleasured without either that activity or that pleasure being related directly to one's last end" (317).

Delight is possession, rest. We desire something that we perceive as good, and upon attaining it we are satisfied, resting in it. Delight is thus necessarily attendant on happiness, Aquinas says, whether it be the perfect happiness of achieving man's last end or the imperfect happiness of man in this life. The supreme delight is, of course, enjoyment of union with God; sensual delights can hinder the attainment of perfect happiness because they distract one from the higher delights of the intellect (*ST*, I–II, q. 4, a. 1; for background see all of questions 2–5). Hence the innumerable medieval criticisms of those works of art which offer only sensory delight by merely pleasing the ear or which encourage sensual indulgence. Even less frankly pejorative views of surface pleasure acknowledge a hierarchy of delights, such as this well-known passage from Dante's *Convivio:* "the goodness and the beauty of any discourse are separate and distinct from each other, because the goodness lies in the meaning while the beauty lies in the adornment of the language; and while both the one and the other are accompanied by delight, it is the goodness which is to the greatest degree delightful."[28] Both pleasure and profit are "con diletto." In one case the ear, in the other the intellect, moves to possess that which is desired. Both possessions produce delight, but intellectual satisfaction is superior to that which gives rest to the senses.

Salman presents a medieval psychology of *delectatio*. We will see it echoed in Chapter 3, in discussions of recreation which equate the delights of entertainment with rest, *quies*. But there

[28]*Convivio*, II, 11, 4, trans. Robert S. Haller, *Literary Criticism of Dante Alighieri* (Lincoln: University of Nebraska Press, 1973), p. 71. Cf. *De vulgari eloquentia*, II, 1, in Haller, p. 33.

the context is earthly living rather than final goals, and lesser pleasures are not as deprecated as in some of Salman's evidence. His study is important for understanding the role of pleasure in all literary works, especially as it accompanies the acquisition of profit. I am more concerned with pleasure per se, within the framework of the Horatian dichotomy, which Salman's article tends to resolve in basically Aristotelian ways. He shows what literary pleasure is. The Middle Ages was often more concerned with what it does, and it is the justification of pleasure in terms of its effect on an audience that is the principal concern of this book. That fascinating line from the commentary on the *Amores*—*utilitas est delectatio*—still needs explication. How can pleasure be profitable?

Some of the medieval answers to that question are reasonably familiar. They find in *delectatio* some further educational or literary usefulness. One approach, treating delight as a result of stylistic elegance, justifies it by making it a means of improving one's skill in writing. Ruotger's tenth-century biography of Bruno of Cologne, discussing his learning, notes that his Latin was excellent and suggests a reason: "Jests and buffoonery which make everybody shake with laughter when put in the mouths of various persons in tragedy and comedy, he read through gravely and seriously. He thought their meaning was worthless; he estimated the style as the main thing."[29] In the *Philobiblon*, Richard de Bury argues that "even in an unseemly subject-matter we may learn a charming fashion of speech." But he spends most of his time on another defense of pleasure, its role in leading the reader of more substantial fictions into their allegorical meaning. Not all people, he says, "take the same pleasure in learning," and in fact some "fling away the nut, before they have broken the shell and reached the kernel." The ancients realized that they could "entice" men to learning by concealing it beneath "the mask of pleasure." He cites lines 333 and 343 of the *Ars poetica* by way of further explanation, transferring Horace's ideas, as *On the Thebiad* did, to the argument of allegorical poetics. This notion of a pleasing fiction as sugarcoating over the pill of moral truth is well known in the

[29]Trans. James Harvey Robinson, *Readings in European History,* I (Boston: Ginn, 1904), p. 260. Text in Suchomski, p. 83. On Bruno, see Auerbach, pp. 159–63.

Middle Ages and Renaissance. Related to it is the idea that the process of moving from surface to depths, by virtue of one's having to think through the allegorical implications, makes the final discovery of meaning all the more pleasurable.[30]

The educational benefits of both style and content appear in a passage from the preface to Bernardus Silvestris's commentary on the *Aeneid,* which sums up a number of the concerns of this chapter:

> Some poets (such as the satirists) write for instruction; some (such as the comic playwrights) write for delight; and some (such as the historians) write for both. Horace speaks about this: "Poets aim either to benefit or to amuse or to utter words at once both pleasing and helpful to life".... The *Aeneid* gives pleasure because of verbal ornament, the figures of speech, and the diverse adventures and works of men which it describes. Indeed, anyone who imitates these matters diligently will attain the greatest skill in the art of writing, and he will also find in the narrative the greatest examples of and inspiration for pursuing virtue and avoiding vice. Thus, there is a double gain for the reader: the first is skill in composition which comes from imitation, and the second is the good sense to act properly which comes from the stimulus of examples.[31]

First comes the division of poetry by Horatian functions; like Isidore, Bernardus views comedy as meant to delight. Then comes a more detailed consideration of the *Aeneid:* it meets the goal of *delectatio* through both its pleasing language and its representation of human events, its story line. These sources of delight, when probed further, yield profit. From the style one learns to write better, and, more important, from the actions one learns virtuous behavior. Bernardus goes on to give examples of the latter: Aeneas's labors reveal patience, his piety promotes religious devotion. (As Schreiber and Maresca note, p. xxi, all these benefits accrue through a literal reading of the epic, a response to Virgil the historical poet. The allegorical

---

[30]*Philobiblon,* c. 13, ed. and trans. E. C. Thomas (New York: Barnes & Noble, 1970), pp. 124–27. On the relative pleasures of *cortex* and *nucleus,* and of getting from one to the other, see *Preface to Chaucer,* pp. 53–54, 60–64.

[31]*Commentary on the First Six Books of Virgil's* Aeneid, trans. Earl G. Schreiber and Thomas E. Maresca (Lincoln: University of Nebraska Press, 1979), p. 4.

meanings of the *Aeneid,* the work of Virgil the philosopher, lie hidden in its *involucrum.*) This succinct analysis of the values of even a literal reading of the poem recognizes delight as a part of literary response and then refers that delight to what it perceives as higher kinds of *utilitas,* the acquisition of intellectual and moral knowledge. And surely, as Dante would say, there is even greater delight in these possessions than in the immediate pleasures of Virgil's eloquent Latin and compelling story.

So much for that perfect poetry which combines pleasure and profit. But what of that imperfect poetry which exists only (or principally—surely pleasure and profit may coexist in varying proportions) to provide *delectatio?* Are the Ovidian commentator's *scurrilia,* Gundissalinus's *ludicra,* Ovid's *Amores,* Bernardus's *commediae* defensible only on the grounds that they help people write more elegantly? And what even of the role of pleasure in the best poetry—is it always and only to be referred to a didactic end? *Utilitas est delectatio.* Delight does not lead to usefulness, it is itself useful. Or as a modern critic said of Cervantes's view of fiction, " 'delectare' *is* 'prodesse.' "[32] The phrase certainly implies values in literary pleasure different from those emphasized in moral theories of poetry, ones seemingly unrelated to whatever, if any, rational profit a work might offer. What are those values? How can pleasure per se be profitable?

The following two chapters attempt to define medieval theories that justify pleasure, and consequently literary pleasure, on medical and psychological grounds, and to show that these justifications tend to become ethical as well. On the one hand, the evidence that will be presented works to challenge severely the idea that medieval literary thought ignored or denigrated pleasure without profit, for as we will see there are some spirited defenses of the value of taking delight in fictions. On the other hand, the theories discussed are certainly not modern in any sense, not efforts to create a category of aesthetic delight or to define literary pleasure as an end in itself. Indeed, the justifications of pleasure to be investigated remain distinctively medieval in their "pragmatic" concern, to use M. H. Abrams's helpful

[32]Quoted in Clements and Gibaldi, p. 12.

schema of critical orientations.[33] They look principally at what value the work has for an audience, what effects it produces in the reader or listener, what we have seen the medieval accessus refer to as *utilitas*. Hence the defenses of pleasure, though based on medical and psychological principles, almost always have a moral dimension. Taking pleasure in a fiction, even one that may not instruct the intellect, is a response that, in the proper circumstances, contributes to physical or mental well-being and hence to one's capacity for activities more directly related to one's final end.

Of course, a work that combines pleasure and profit would thus be doubly useful. In that sense justifications of literary pleasure in no way contradict what more didactic theories may argue about the value of fiction. But since profit was always more respectable than pleasure in the Middle Ages, a work that could lay claim to moral purpose would naturally do so, perhaps to the neglect of claims to please. Hence most of the evidence dealing with the values of pleasure comes in the context of more trivial literature, and in order to keep the arguments as clean as possible I will generally treat them as they apply to nondidactic material. But I do not consider the theories defined here applicable only, say, to the fabliaux, and I hope that in the long run they will find their due place, much as Augustine has found his, in the modern understanding of medieval literary thought and of the light it can shed on the status of poetry in the Middle Ages.

[33]*The Mirror and the Lamp* (New York: Norton, 1953), pp. 14–21.

2

The Hygienic
Justification

If literature gives pleasure, one possible means of justifying that pleasure is to show that it has beneficial effects. The argument can be put very simply: entertainment is good for you. The most common expression of that idea in the Middle Ages appears in discussions of recreation, which I treat in Chapter 3. Here I want to focus on a somewhat more technical medical argument, implicit in the idea of recreation but usually not fully articulated there. I refer to the theory as "hygienic" because that is the medical area in which it lies, the science of maintaining health. I will also call it "therapeutic," since the theory applies as well to recovery from illness or disability and since "therapy" has both mental and physical meanings appropriate to medieval medical views of literature. If these terms initially seem jarring, it is because we no longer categorize some things as the Middle Ages did. I hope that by the end of this chapter the inclusion of literary pleasure within a conceptual context that also encompasses regularity and proper diet will seem thoroughly justifiable. To understand the hygienic argument fully we must understand that medieval context, and to do that we must begin with the medical theory of the nonnaturals. I treat it at some length because it is not well known outside the history of medicine and because it is fundamental to an understanding of medieval views of the emotional effects of literature.

The Nonnaturals and the Accidents of the Soul

The history of medieval medicine has been written many times, and in broad outline it is well known. I am concerned only with that period from the twelfth century on, when the translation of Arabic works gave the Latin West abundant medical material derived in great part from Hippocratic and Galenic writings. One of the most important texts throughout these centuries was the *Isagoge* of Johannitius. It was available in Latin translation by 1100, and as an introduction to Galen's *Ars medica* (or *Tegni*, as it was often called), it became the first book in the corpus of treatises known as the *Articella*, the standard medieval medical textbook anthology. It was the subject of many commentaries and was widely known; later in this chapter we will see Hugh of St. Victor citing it extensively.[1] The *Isagoge*'s categorization of the parts of medicine, which had great influence on medical thinking in the Middle Ages, begins with a separation of theoretical and practical spheres. Theoretical medicine consists of three divisions: *res naturales* (those things which constitute the body, such as elements, humors, faculties, spirits); *res non naturales* (those things which affect bodily health, such as air, food and drink, exercise); and *res contra naturam* (diseases, the causes of disease, the sequels of disease). Practical medicine also has three parts: the correct use of the nonnaturals (that is, a regimen of health), the use of drugs, and surgery. As L. J. Rather has pointed out, the classification parallels that in Avicenna's most influential works, and one finds these basic divisions throughout medieval medicine.[2]

The conception least familiar to a modern audience and most

---

[1] On the *Isagoge* and its place in the *Articella* see Oswei Temkin, *Galenism: Rise and Decline of a Medical Philosophy* (Ithaca: Cornell University Press, 1973), pp. 100–8; Paul O. Kristeller, "Bartholomaeus, Musandinus, and Maurus of Salerno and Other Early Commentators of the 'Articella,' with a Tentative List of Texts and Manuscripts," *Italia medioevale e umanistica*, 19 (1976), 57–87; and the introduction by Diego Gracia and José-Luis Vidal to their edition (based on Renaissance texts) and Spanish translation of the *Isagoge* in *Asclepio*, 26–27 (1974–75), 267–382. H. P. Cholmeley has translated the *Isagoge* into English as an appendix to his *John of Gaddesden and the Rosa Medicinae* (Oxford: Clarendon Press, 1912), pp. 136–66. There is a Middle English translation in a fifteenth-century manuscript, British Library MS Sloane 6, ff. 1–9.

[2] "Systematic Medical Treatises From the Ninth to the Nineteenth Century: The Unchanging Scope and Structure of Academic Medicine in the West," *Clio Medica*, 11 (1976), 289–305.

relevant to this chapter is that of the nonnaturals. The idea, which Temkin calls "one of the most enduring contributions of Galenism to medical thought," has a complex history that only recently has been brought to light and still awaits a full-scale investigation.[3] Briefly, the term "nonnaturals" refers to a set of factors external to the body itself but which affect bodily health depending on how they are used. "Nonnatural" does not mean "unnatural" but indicates rather a special category of things that are separate from one's own constitution (hence not natural) and causative of either health or sickness (hence not inherently contranatural, though a misused nonnatural would become a contranatural in effect). The terminology and logic go back to Galen, though not in any simple way. In the *Ars medica* Galen discusses six necessary causes, "constantly and inevitably acting on the human body in such a way as to alter the balance of the primary qualities (the hot, cold, moist and dry) and thus to affect the character of the humours and the state of humoral balance. Acting in due order and magnitude they promote health. Otherwise they promote disease."[4] Galen does not here use the term "nonnatural," though he does elsewhere; nevertheless, in the Middle Ages his six necessary causes become the standard list of nonnaturals, perhaps due in great part, as Niebyl suggests, to Haly Abbas, who explicitly equates the idea of the nonnaturals in the *Isagoge* with Galen's six necessary causes. One can see the same assimilation at work in the Middle English translation of the *Isagoge*. The original, discussing the causes (*occasiones*) of illness or health, mentions Galen's six but does not call them nonnaturals; the rubric at the side of the translation of this section, though, does: it reads (with the help of ultraviolet light) "6 maners of occasions, þat is 6 þings noȝt naturel" (f. 5v).

[3]Temkin, p. 180. Rather, "The 'Six Things Non-Natural': A Note on the Origins and Fate of a Doctrine and a Phrase," *Clio Medica*, 3 (1968), 337–47; Saul Jarcho, "Galen's Six Non-Naturals: A Bibliographic Note and Translation," *BHM*, 44 (1970), 372–77; Jerome J. Bylebyl, "Galen on the Non-Natural Causes of Variation in the Pulse," *BHM*, 45 (1971), 482–85; Peter H. Niebyl, "The Non-Naturals," *BHM*, 45 (1971), 486–92; Chester R. Burns, "The Nonnaturals: A Paradox in the Western Concept of Health," *Journal of Medicine and Philosophy*, 1 (1976), 202–11. Students of English literature may know of the concept from Robert Burton's *Anatomy of Melancholy*, where it plays an important organizational role.

[4]Rather, "The 'Six Things Non-Natural,' " 339; Galen's text is on 344–45.

What are the six nonnaturals? The usual list follows the order of *occasiones* in the *Isagoge:* air, food and drink, motion and rest, sleep and waking, repletion and evacuation, and the accidents of the soul. Some of these are self-explanatory; it is obvious that eating and drinking the right foods and beverages, getting the proper amount of sleep, and avoiding constipation all contribute to health. Others require some comment. The category of air includes not only questions of its cleanliness but also such matters as climate and seasonal variations; and since medieval medicine generally viewed infectious disease not as contagious but as spread by corrupted air, this subdivision often deals with avoidance of miasmic places and means of purifying the air. Motion and rest is often called "exercise and rest" and entails medieval principles of proper exercise. Finally, and most interesting, is the sixth nonnatural, the *accidentia animae,* what today we would call the emotions. I will return to this category shortly.

In the *Isagoge,* these six factors are listed as *occasiones* of health or sickness. The list of *res non naturales* earlier in the treatise is different: air, exercise, baths, food and drink, sleep and waking, coitus, and the accidents of the soul. The fact that the *Isagoge* has two lists helps create some diversity in subsequent discussions. Bathing and coitus may or may not appear, and when they do may or may not be treated as one of the standard six. Depending on the treatise, coitus may appear as a separate category, as a part of motion and rest (since it involves bodily movement), as a part of repletion and evacuation (since it involves the discharge of semen), or as a part of the accidents of the soul (since it involves so much delight). Arnold of Villanova, in his *Introductionum medicinalium,* offers the most elaborate categorization of the nonnaturals I have encountered: he accepts the standard six as "principales" and argues that an additional seven are secondary nonnaturals that also affect the body.[5]

It is enough for our purposes to think only of the standard

---

[5]Chaps. 13, 81–87, in *Opera medica* (Lyons, 1504), ff. 5v, 31–32v. Arnold's additional seven are the seasons, locale, sex, occupation, play, bathing, and habit. Together with the first six, these secondary factors, which theoretically include all personal dispositions and activities, suggest a holistic view of health in which all one's actions and attitudes have medical relevance.

six nonnaturals and to focus more intently on the last, the *accidentia animae*. It may seem surprising at first to find a psychological factor listed along with environmental and physical concerns, but the strangeness of this conjunction is perhaps due as much to a conceptual limitation fostered by the medical history of the last century as to any lack of sophistication in medieval thinking. For like the other nonnaturals, the passions of the mind are forces that one must live with, that one can—at least according to medieval theory—exercise control over, and that do affect the body. An emotion is an *accidens* not only in the philosophic sense of being something that inheres in a substance but also in the medical sense of being an unintentioned external cause of physical change—external to the body, that is, since emotions are movements of the soul.[6]

The *Isagoge*'s summary of the accidents of the soul is as good an introduction as any to a médieval attitude that can only be called psychosomatic:

> Sundry affections of the mind produce an effect within the body, such as those which bring the natural heat from the interior of the body to the outer parts or the surface of the skin. Sometimes this happens suddenly, as with anger; sometimes gently and slowly, as with delight and joy. Some affections, again, withdraw the natural heat and conceal it either suddenly, as with fear and terror, or again gradually, as distress. And again some affections disturb the natural energy both internal and external, as, for instance, grief.[7]

---

[6]The fourteenth-century physician Dino del Garbo, in his commentary on Guido Cavalcanti's poem "Donna me prega," lists three reasons why love is an *accidens:* it is an appetite of the soul, as are the other passions, rather than a substance; it may come or go; it arrives from outside the body, even though different people may have different intrinsic susceptibility to it. For text, translation, and commentary on this passage, see Otto Bird, "The Canzone d'Amore of Cavalcanti According to the Commentary of Dino del Garbo," *Mediaeval Studies*, 2 (1940), 161, 178–79. Dino believes that all accidents of the soul alter the body, love only more so (161). Robert Hollander has recently argued the relevance of Dino's commentary to Boccaccio, in *Boccaccio's Two Venuses* (New York: Columbia University Press, 1977).

[7]Cholmeley, pp. 146–47, with one change in translation. Text in Gracia and Vidal, 335. For similar views in Hippocratic medicine, see Pedro Laín Entralgo, *The Therapy of the Word in Classical Antiquity*, ed. and trans. L. J. Rather and John M. Sharp (New Haven: Yale University Press, 1970), pp. 160–63.

The basic principle is relatively simple. Emotions affect the body by causing its natural heat (and, according to most texts, the body's *spiritus*, those ethereal substances that enable bodily functions to operate) to move either outward or inward or in both directions. Insofar as these movements of heat and spirit are extreme and violent, they produce severe bodily imbalances. An overabundance of heat at the exterior of the body leaves the heart in a weakened condition; as many discussions note, both extreme anger and extreme joy can cause death in this way. Excessive fear or sorrow, driving all the body's heat and *spiritus* to the interior, leaves one torpid, even insensate. The woeful knight in Chaucer's *Book of the Duchess* is a famous, almost clinically depicted, case of a man whose sorrow has wrought marked physical disability. In some cases a passion causes varied movement, at times inward and at times outward; the *Isagoge* gives *tristitia* as an example, but later treatises tend to see sadness as an interior movement only and cite, among others, the *passio* of love as causing the double motion.[8]

Other treatises offer more extensive discussions. Avicenna's *Canon*, for instance, has a somewhat longer analysis that often appears in later texts. Like the *Isagoge*, the *Canon* associates specific emotions with specific internal movements, but it includes the movement of *spiritus* as well as that of the body's natural heat, and it goes on to argue that the imagination as well as the emotions may have corporeal effects, citing as evidence the belief that the parents' thoughts at the moment of conception have an influence on the physical characteristics of their child. His treatise known in the West as *De viribus cordis* discusses extensively the interrelationship between emotions and the *spiritus* of the heart. Avicenna believes that an abundant and well-balanced *spiritus* promotes joy (*gaudium*) and that reciprocally the emotions affect the characteristics of the spirit and hence one's bodily condition.[9]

[8]For the medical theory of love, see Bird, *Mediaeval Studies*, 2 (1940), 150–203; 3 (1941), 117–60, esp. 123–33 on the physical effects of love. And, of course, John Livingston Lowes, "The Loveres Maladye of Hereos," *Modern Philology*, 11 (1913–14), 491–546.

[9]*Liber canonis*, Lib. I, Fen II, Doct. II, Sum. I, c. xiv (1507; rpt. Hildesheim: Georg Olms, 1964), ff. 33–33v. English version by O. Cameron Gruner, *A Treatise on the Canon of Medicine of Avicenna Incorporating a Translation of the First*

A late Middle English treatise on medicine, in dialogue form, does not use the term "nonnaturals" but treats the idea nevertheless, discussing their bodily effects as resultant qualities rather than as movements of heat and spirit. It distinguishes between a person's natural complexion (that balance of humors basic to the individual which does not vary) and his accidental complexion (that part of his humoral makeup which can be changed). One's accidental complexion alters in two ways: either "kyndelich," naturally, through aging, in the course of which the changing complexion "dryeth till a man be ded" but causes no specific illness; or "vnkyndelich," which causes sickness. The approach is predicated on the *Isagoge*'s distinction between *res naturales,* which include not only the humors and the qualities (hot, dry, and so forth) but also the four ages of man and their corresponding humoral emphases, and the *res contra naturam,* the "vnkyndelich" causes of disease. Here, as in some other medieval discussions, the nonnaturals disappear as a separate category but surface in their role as contranatural factors when misused. Accordingly, the treatise offers a list of contranatural changes that make people ill, all of which are part of the tradition of the nonnaturals:

> . . . such changyng cometh in many maner wyse, as in chaungyng of metis other of drynkes. Also in takyng to moche outher to lytol of mete and drynk, in slepyng to moche other wakyng to moche, outher travaylyng to moche, bathyng to moche, or jestyng to moche, thynkyng to moche, gret joye, gret sorowe, gret angir, gret hete other of cold outher of drynesse outher of moystenes of the place and of the eyre that a man is in.

The treatise goes on to specify the humoral and qualitative imbalances that result from such excesses. Too much wakefulness, working, bathing, or anger makes people choleric. "Moche joye maketh a man moist and hote for the tyme of his joye and aftirward. And sorowe maketh a man cold and drie in complexion." From the *Isagoge* and the *Canon* one would know that these imbalances are due to internal movements of heat and *spiritus.*

Book (London: Luzac, 1930), pp. 212–14, and 535–47 for a translation of the relevant chapters of *De viribus cordis.*

Implicit in this discussion is a principle of therapy made explicit in the following chapter, which states the standard medieval view of allopathic medicine: one should use cold medicines
to cure hot sicknesses, dry medicines for moist sicknesses, and
so on (though in some cases the treatise advises homeopathic
rather than "contrarie" remedies). What is most revealing for
our purposes is that the treatise acknowledges here a curative
role for the *accidentia animae* as well: "And syknes that cometh
of angir and of sorow ben heled with joy and murth." The
regulation of the emotions, then, has value not only in hygiene,
in preventive medicine, but may play a role in therapeutics as
well.[10]

In order to see the impact of the doctrine of the nonnaturals
beyond the realm of academic medicine, we may turn to texts
more specifically concerned with hygiene and more prescriptive in intent than purely theoretical tracts. As we know from
the *Isagoge*, practical medicine consists of regimen, drugs, and
surgery, and regimen is the proper use of the nonnaturals.
Medieval theory and medieval practice meet in those texts
where physicians make specific recommendations to laymen

[10]British Library MS Sloane 3489, ff. 31–31v. Two examples may serve to
indicate how seriously the Middle Ages could take the idea of the emotions as a
factor in therapy. The Middle English translation of Lanfranc's *Chirurgia
magna*, a highly respected surgical text written in 1296, argues that a good
surgeon must know every aspect of medicine, including "thynges þat beþ noȝt
natureles." It then explains how each of the nonnaturals is applicable to the
treatment of wounds; the *accidentia animae* are relevant because the surgeon
should "entempre . . . þe hert of hym þat ys seke, ffor to gret wratthe makyþ þe
spirites renne to myche to þe wounde, & þat ys cause of swellynge; to grete
drede, oþere vntryst of helpe of hys wounde holdiþ spyrites withynne hys body,
þat mater may nouȝt come to hele þe wounde." *Lanfrank's "Science of Cirurgie."
Part I*, ed. Robert von Fleischhacker, EETS o.s. 102 (1894; rpt. Millwood, N.Y.:
Kraus Reprint, 1973), pp. 15–17. A work on poisons by William de Marra says
that music relieves the effect of tarantula bite, since the poison produces melancholy and music produces joy, the most effective antidote; he thinks that by
moving the *spiritus* outward joy prevents the poison from destroying the vital
organs. See Lynn Thorndike, *A History of Magic and Experimental Science*, 8 vols.
(New York: Columbia University Press, 1923–58), III: 534. In Chap. 5 we will
see evidence of the hygienic belief that cheerfulness could ward off plague.
Scientific views of the power of the emotions over the body enter into some
thirteenth-century biblical commentaries on the fast of the Hebrew children
described in Dan. 1. The medical attitude is consistent with such scriptural
passages as Prov. 17:22 and 15:13. See Beryl Smalley, *The Study of the Bible in the
Middle Ages* (1952; rpt. Notre Dame, Ind.: University of Notre Dame Press,
1964), pp. 314–16.

about how to conduct themselves: in the many regimens of health and in those *consilia* that have survived from a few doctors of the later Middle Ages.

The idea of a regimen of health, a set of rules for maintaining the soundness of the body, is as old as Hippocratic medicine and as new as the latest paperbacks on what to eat and how to jog. Galen's *De sanitate tuenda* is one of the major efforts of its kind and is available in a modern English translation. One medieval regimen is very well known, the *Regimen sanitatis salernitanum,* which we will consider later; but it is only one of a slew of hygienic treatises that appeared in the later Middle Ages. Almost all of these must be read in manuscript or in Renaissance editions, and even historians of medicine do not seem to have devoted extensive study to them. Only recently, for example, was it shown that the regimen attributed to Ugo Benzi (Hugh of Siena) is in fact an Italian translation of a fifteenth-century regimen by Benedetto Reguardati of Nursia, which in turn is based in great part on two fourteenth-century works.[11] Much in the medieval regimens has been borrowed and reborrowed, and there is no full-scale study that has disentangled the lines of filiation. What I cite from these sources, then, should probably be taken more as conventional wisdom than as independent medical thinking, though, as we can see in Hill Cotton's analysis of Benedetto's distinctly Neapolitan touches in his remarks on diet, individuality does at times intrude into the otherwise routine and usually unacknowledged copying of earlier authorities. It should also be clear that my own survey of the regimens has been quite limited and that I do not attempt to deal with questions of sources and influence, merely with a few hygienic ideas that we can say are at least present, most likely quite widespread, in the fourteenth and fifteenth centuries.[12]

[11]Juliana Hill Cotton, "Benedetto Reguardati: Author of Ugo Benzi's *Tractato de la conservatione de la sanitade,*" *Medical History,* 12 (1968), 76–83.

[12]My primary reference sources have been these classics of medieval scientific scholarship: George Sarton, *Introduction to the History of Science,* 3 vols. in 5 (Baltimore: Williams and Wilkins, 1927–48); Thorndike's *History;* Thorndike and Pearl Kibre, *A Catalogue of Incipits of Mediaeval Scientific Writings in Latin,* rev. ed. (Cambridge, Mass.: Mediaeval Academy of America, 1963)—hereafter "TK"; and Dorothea Waley Singer, *Hand-List of Western Scientific Manuscripts in Great Britain and Ireland,* available in MS at the British Library.

The regimens vary greatly in length, but most are organized according to the nonnaturals. That schema was so pervasive in the Middle Ages and Renaissance that when in 1584 Thomas Cogan published his *Haven of Health,* a regimen based on a five-point Hippocratic outline (exercise, food, drink, sleep, sex), he felt the need to preface his text with the acknowledgment that "such as haue written of the preseruation of health before me, for the most part haue followed the diuision of *Galen* of things not naturall which be sixe in number." He argues, somewhat desperately, that his own conceptual choice "is more conuenient for the diet of our English Nation" in that no one is "so dull of vnderstanding" that he cannot keep the five single terms in mind. He also explains that one category ostensibly omitted in his formula, the accidents of the soul, is in fact included in the five, since "affections of the minde doe commonlie folowe the temperature of the bodie which is chiefely preserued by the moderate vse of those fiue thinges."[13] Mind-body interaction remains an assumption, though here the sixth nonnatural is viewed only as a consequence of a purely somatic regimen.

What do the regimens recommend in regard to the *accidentia animae?* The briefer ones tend just to warn against extreme emotions. Fuller treatments go into the same kind of technical explanations we have seen in the *Isagoge* and the *Canon,* spell out the dangers of excessive joy or anger, and usually advise not simply a Stoic rejection of all emotion but adoption of a moderate cheerfulness. Bernard Gordon, whose *Regimen sanitatis* is the final book of a longer work, *De conservatione vitae humanae* (1308), but circulated in manuscript as a separate hygienic treatise, cites the hazards of inordinate passions but then adds: "Nevertheless, you should know that a moderate cheerfulness is fitting for every age, every temperament, and every person, except for those who do not want to gain weight, for according to Avicenna a moderate cheerfulness is fattening."[14]

[13]*The Haven of Health* (London, 1584), ff. 4–4v.
[14]"Intelligendum tamen, quod gaudium temperatum competit omni aetati, et omni complexioni et omni homini, nisi quando non vult impinguari, quoniam gaudium temperatum impinguat, secundum Auicen." *De conservatione vitae humanae,* c. 15 (Leipzig, 1570), p. 79. On the circulation of this text see Ynez Violé O'Neill, "The History of the Publication of Bernard of Gordon's Liber de Conservatione Vitae Humanae," *Sudhoffs Archiv,* 49 (1965), 269–79. Bernard

His concern about weight gain is not an issue for other physicians. Maino de' Maineri, author of a fourteenth-century regimen often attributed to Arnold of Villanova, thinks of temperate joy as an important element of hygiene:

> In regard to *gaudium* and tranquillity of mind, you should know that a moderate cheerfulness belongs to a regimen of health because it is one of the means of strengthening bodily energy. Energy is promoted by tranquillity and cheerfulness, though the cheerfulness ought not be excessive, since that leads to syncope and death. Cheerfulness is especially appropriate for those who worry a lot and are worn down with troubles and are frequently harrassed. Similarly, it is appropriate for those who are continually and excessively cheerful to be saddened at times.[15]

The use of emotions as a part of allopathic medicine is clear. Cheerfulness (*gaudium*) is not only helpful to the body per se but is also a remedy for anxiety and depression. To anticipate later arguments: anything that produces temperate cheerfulness, such as reading a fiction, is thus functioning to preserve health; cheerfulness induced by storytelling, for example, would be particularly useful to people burdened with cares, such as the horrors of the Black Death.

---

may be misrepresenting Avicenna's *Cantica*, which states: "A great joy makes the body prosperous. There are some noxious ones which generate too much obesity." Trans. Haven C. Krueger, *Avicenna's Poem on Medicine* (Springfield, Ill.: Charles C. Thomas, 1963), pp. 25–26.

[15]"De gaudio autem et mentis tranquillitate sciendum quod gaudium temperatum competit in regimine sanitatis ex eo quod est vnum de confortantibus virtutem. Virtus enim confortatur tranquillitate et gaudio, sed gaudium non debet esse excessiuum quia inducit sincopim et mortem; et maxime gaudium competit hiis qui multum curant et sollicitudinibus destruuntur et crebro punguntur. Et similiter hiis qui sunt in gaudio continuo et immoderato interdum tristari conuenit." Magninus Mediolanensis, *Regimen sanitatis*, pars III, c. viii (Louvain, 1486), sig. k 7. For more on Maino see Lynn Thorndike, "A Mediaeval Sauce-Book," *Speculum,* 9 (1934), 183–90. In the 1504 edition of Arnold's works, this passage, worded somewhat differently, is on f. 63. Arnold's own regimen for the King of Aragon recommends *gaudium* in similar circumstances: "People who are distracted by many cares and troubles and who are frequently harrassed should take time out for cheerfulness and for proper recreations, so that their minds may flourish anew and their spirits be reinvigorated (Qui vero multis curis et sollicitudinibus distrahuntur et crebro punguntur gaudio sepe vacare debent et honestis solatiis vt animus refloreat et spiritus recreentur)." F. 81.

The most extensive claims for the value of *gaudium temperatum* I have seen appear in the regimen of Benedetto Reguardati, which Hill Cotton dates ca. 1435–38, though it draws on material written a century earlier. Benedetto has a long chapter on the *accidentia animae,* and after discussing the dangers of excessive *tristitia* and *gaudium* (complete with anecdotes of people who dropped dead from sudden great joy), he presents the preferred emotional attitude:

> For the preservation of health we should strive most resolutely for moderate pleasures and for gladdening solaces, so that as much as possible we may live happily in temperate gaiety. That condition expands the *spiritus* and natural heat to the outer parts of the body and makes the blood purer; it sharpens one's wit and makes the understanding more capable; it promotes a healthy complexion and a pleasing appearance; it stimulates the energies throughout the whole body and makes them more vigorous in their activity.[16]

For Benedetto the proper emotional disposition has consequences not only for the body but for the mind as well. The *spiritus* and natural heat functioning at their optimum effectiveness enhance mental ability. *Gaudium* improves the whole person. And not only physicians impute mental values to a well-disposed body. Aquinas asserts that even though happiness does not consist of bodily well-being, perfection of the body is necessary for acquiring happiness in this life (*ST,* I–II, q. 4, a. 6).

At this point we have clearly transcended the more limited goal of medicine which is the maintenance of bodily health. And the implications of dealing with the passions were not lost on some of the authors of the regimens. They were aware that, as Moses Maimonides pointed out, the study and correc-

---

[16]"Pro sanitatis igitur conseruatione summopere ad temperata gaudia et solatia alacriora conari debemus, ut quam possibile sit lete uiuamus moderata cum letitia. Spiritus, naturalem calorem ad exteriora expandit membra; clariorum sanguinem facit; ingenium acuit; intellectum solertiorem efficit; et uiuidum colorem placidumque aspectum inducit, atque totius nostre corporis uirtutes excitat et in eorum operibus agiliores prestat." *Pulcherrimum et utilissimum opus ad sanitatis conseruationem* ([Bologna], 1477), ff. 124v–125.

tion of the emotions belong chiefly to moral philosophy.[17] But they staked a claim for their attention to the *accidentia animae* on the grounds that the emotions affect the body, hence affect health, hence pertain to the physician.[18] Bernard Gordon's *Regimen sanitatis* features a *quaestio* devoted to this issue: whether it is proper for the physician qua physician to deal with the accidents of the soul. Not only does he decide that it is right, he goes so far as to suggest that the physician in correcting the passions becomes a moral philosopher of sorts, and a distinctive one, since he can instruct people of all kinds and speak about both the body and the soul.[19] To what degree these arguments reflect motives beyond self-justification is unclear, but the concept of the *accidentia animae* is certainly a precise point of connection between medicine and moral philosophy.[20] The attention to proper disposition of the passions in medieval treatises thus carries an implicit and sometimes explicit ethical dimension, which doubtless helps account for what later evidence will reveal: the easy assimilation of essentially hygienic principles into moral justifications of entertainment.

The most famous medieval regimen, known by a variety of titles but most commonly as the *Regimen sanitatis salernitanum*, is not explicitly organized around the nonnaturals. But within the first few lines it gives prominence to the role of mental attitude in health in a way that clearly reveals the influence of the psychosomatic principles of the *accidentia animae:*

[17]See Ariel Bar-Sela, Hebbel E. Hoff, and Elias Faris, "Moses Maimonides' Two Treatises on the Regimen of Health," *Transactions of the American Philosophical Society*, n.s. 54, pt. 4 (1964), pp. 25–27; and his *Treatise on Asthma*, trans. Suessman Muntner (Philadelphia: Lippincott, 1963), pp. 36–38. These texts were available to the West in Latin translation by the early fourteenth century.

[18]Magninus Mediolanensis, sig. k 6: "et quia anime accidentia ex necessitate alterant corpus, et eorum correctio et moderatio ad medicum pertinet." Another regimen, the *Sermo de conservatione sanitatis* by Philippus, son of Bandini of Arezzo (TK, col. 1294), argues that depending on how they are studied the *accidentia animae* may be the province of the physician, the natural philosopher, or the moral philosopher; Bodleian Library MS Canon. Misc. 192, f. 33.

[19]*De conservatione vitae humanae*, quaestio IV, pp. 158–60.

[20]See on this subject the fascinating article of Patrick Gallacher, "Food, Laxatives, and Catharsis in Chaucer's Nun's Priest's Tale," *Speculum*, 51 (1976), 49–68. On the more general connection between physical and moral law, see John A. Alford, "Medicine in the Middle Ages: The Theory of a Profession," *Centennial Review*, 23 (1979), 377–96, esp. 385–91.

Anglorum regi scripsit scola tota Salerni:
Si vis incolumen, si vis te reddere sanum,
Curas tolle graves, irasci crede prophanum. . . .
Si tibi deficiant medici, medici tibi fiant
Hec tria: mens leta, requies, moderata dieta.

The whole School of Salerno wrote for the English king:
If you want to be healthy, if you want to remain sound,
Take away your heavy cares, and refrain from anger. . . .
Should you lack physicians, these three doctors will suffice:
A joyful mind, rest, and a moderate diet.[21]

The Salernitan regimen's three physicians make their way into
another poem of widespread popularity, John Lydgate's *Dietary:*

Ther be thre lechees consarue a mannys myht,
First a glad hert, he carith lite or nouht,
Temperat diet, holsom for every wiht,
And best of all, for no thyng take no thouht.[22]

Here in its most general form is the medical principle that a
cheerful disposition is life-conserving. The *Regimen*'s "mens
leta" becomes Lydgate's "glad hert," a joyful attitude that does
not let cares weigh on it. *Requies,* which probably implies both
physical and mental recuperation, seems to be more purely
psychological in Lydgate: avoiding "thouht" in one of the standard medieval meanings of that word, troublesome thoughts,
vexation. Lydgate's three doctors seem more like two.

The *Dietary* is interesting, also, for the way in which it mixes
physical and moral recommendations. The ethical implications
of the regimens become more explicit in the hands of someone

---

[21]Lines 1–3, 8–9. Ed. and trans. Patricia W. Cummins, "A Salernitan Regi-
men of Health," *Allegorica,* 1, no. 2 (1976), pp. 82–83. The poem exists in many
versions. Of the several English translations, perhaps the best known is Sir
John Harrington's (1607). On the influence of the Salernitan regimen in the
Renaissance, see Pritchett, pp. 79–81. On its origins, see Paul Oskar Kristeller,
"The School of Salerno," *BHM,* 17 (1945), 169–70.

[22]*The Minor Poems of John Lydgate,* ed. Henry Noble MacCracken, 2 vols.,
EETS e.s. 107, o.s. 192 (1911, 1934; rpt. London: Oxford University Press,
1961–62), II: 704. The Robbins-Cutler *Supplement to the Index of Middle English
Verse* (Lexington: University of Kentucky Press, 1965), p. 521, puts the *Dietary,*
with its 55 MSS, third among all Middle English verse in terms of number of
texts preserved.

writing not as a physician but as a wise and learned counselor. The same phenomenon can be seen in the development of the various versions of the *Secretum secretorum,* which along with the *Regimen sanitatis salernitanum* is (in part) the Middle Ages' best-known treatise on health. The *Secretum,* supposedly a letter of advice from Aristotle to Alexander, came into Latin from Arabic; it has both short and long versions, some five hundred manuscripts in Latin alone, and an immensely complex textual history. The short Latin version of Johannes Hispaniensis, which I will quote in a Middle English translation, is essentially a manual of hygiene. Like the Salernitan regimen, it does not use the nonnaturals structurally but reveals their principles at work. The second precept for Alexander, and by implication for any prince interested in his own well-being, has to do with clothing:

> Se that thi clothis be precious and riȝt feire to the eye, for beauté and preciousenes of þe clothis liȝtenith and gladdith the spiritte of man, which gladnes of spiritte is cause of a continuaunce in helth like as heuynes of spiritte and sorow inducith sikenes. Hit causith also a man to be more quick in all his deedis, and þe bettir to execute all that perteynith to his office.

Similarly, perfuming the body "refresshith" the spirit "like as holsum mete confortith þe body," and such refreshment helps the heart and promotes the movement of blood. At the end of the treatise comes a reassertion of the value of these and other secular pleasures:

> And þe bettir for helth and digestion if þe man haue ioy and gladnes, and with þat goode fortune, as glory, worship, fame and worship of þe peple, victory of his ennemyis. Also if he may beholde beauteuous parsonis, and delectabil bookis, and here pleasaunt songis, and be in cumpany of such as a man louith, and to were goode clothis, and to be anoyntid with swete oynementis.

This list is followed by one of dangers to the body, including excessive drink, work, and sex, bad choices in food and drink, and "ofte to be in drede and to haue grete sorow."[23]

[23]Ed. M. A. Manzalaoui, Secretum secretorum: *Nine English Versions,* EETS o.s. 276 (Oxford: Oxford University Press, 1977), pp. 4, 8–9. For textual his-

In translations of the long version of the *Secretum*, the *regimen sanitatis* becomes part of a *regimen principum*. Health becomes but one aspect of the responsibilities of a ruler, and these texts include a great deal of ethical and political advice, as well as encyclopedic additions to the material on health; there may be sections on physiognomy, parts of the body, natural history, and so on. The summary statement just cited remains intact, at least in the Middle English translations I have seen, with varying degrees of expansion.[24] The long version of the *Secretum* thus occupies a kind of middle ground between the medical regimens and the purely ethical manuals for princes that had substantial currency in the later Middle Ages. At that end of the spectrum we have works like Thomas Hoccleve's *Regement of Princes*, which borrowed in part from the *Secretum* and from Giles of Rome's *De regimine principum;* the only attention to matters of hygiene comes in some general remarks on diet, significantly, in the context of a section on chastity: abstinence is necessary to put down lust, so one's diet must be restrained in order to avoid gluttony and the consequent arousal of carnal desire and other debilitating vices.[25]

The fusion of medical and ethical precepts in the long *Secretum* is perfectly natural. As the prince rules the state, so reason must rule the emotions and control the body. All such operations are examples of proper "governance." Hygiene is ethical activity, for it both reveals and reinforces a properly functioning hierarchy within the individual. The *Secretum secretorum* not only accepts the value accorded a "mens leta" by the Salernitan regimen but also suggests means of attaining such useful joy-

tory see Manzalaoui's introduction and references. The accessus to a Latin verse rendering of Hispaniensis categorizes the text as belonging principally to physics, "that is, to natural science," and incidentally to ethics, "because it instructs people in regard to behavior." Ed. R. A. Pack, "Pseudo-Aristotelis *Epistola ad Alexandrum de regimine sanitatis* a quodam Nicolao versificata," *Archives d'histoire doctrinale et littéraire du moyen âge*, 45 (1979), 313.

[24]In addition to the English translations of the long version in Manzalaoui, see *Three Prose Versions of the* Secreta secretorum, ed. Robert Steele, EETS e.s. 74 (1898; rpt. Millwood, N.Y.: Kraus Reprint, 1973), pp. 30, 75–76, and 247–48.

[25]Ed. Frederick J. Furnivall, EETS e.s. 72 (1897; rpt. Millwood, N.Y.: Kraus Reprint, 1973), pp. 137–40.

fulness. These two most popular regimens confirm what may be concluded from the others: that recommendations for cheerfulness constitute the most familiar piece of advice in medieval medicine regarding proper mental outlook, and that such advice is rooted not just in common sense but in a physiological theory of what happens to body and mind when one's emotional state is moderately joyful.

Literature as a Source of Cheerfulness

The relevance of these medical ideas to literary theory becomes clear when one asks the practical question of how to attain the *gaudium temperatum* recommended by the regimens. We have just seen the *Secretum secretorum* supply a variety of answers, including "delectabil bookis," and many of the items in its list of pleasures are repeated throughout the later Middle Ages. Our interests lie in the role of literature as a factor in hygiene and therapy. We may begin with a fifteenth-century addition to the regimen of Aldobrandino of Siena. Written in the middle of the thirteenth century for Beatrice of Savoy, countess of Provence, who was about to travel to see her four daughters (well situated as the queens of France, England, and Germany, and as the countess of Anjou), Aldobrandino's *Régime du corps* is one of the major early French medical texts, and to judge from surviving manuscripts it must have been quite popular throughout the fourteenth and fifteenth centuries.[26] It is a full-scale medical manual in four parts: general regimen (including the nonnaturals, bloodletting, and special regimens for travel, pregnancy, and the different age groups); specific maladies and their treatment; simples; and a short section on physiognomy. In the chapter on the accidents of the soul, Aldobrandino repeats the standard discussion of different emotions based on movements of heat and spirit, and he com-

---

[26]The modern edition, *Le régime du corps de Maitre Aldebrandin de Sienne*, ed. Louis Landouzy and Roger Pépin (Paris: Champion, 1911), identifies 35 MSS. But since then have appeared a number of notices of other MSS, and without much searching I have seen nine in England not mentioned by Landouzy and Pépin: British Library MSS Add. 8863, Royal 16 F. VIII, Royal 19 A. V, Royal 19 B. X, Royal 20 B. IX; Wellcome MSS 31, 32, 546; Rylands French MS 7. There are also MSS of Italian translations.

ments briefly on melancholy. Though highly destructive to the
body, it can be treated by purgation, by lectuaries such as
"Galen's Happiness," and by being joyful and cheerful ("et
avoir joie et lieche"). In much medieval thinking melancholy is
of course a more serious disability than a simple emotional
imbalance; but Aldobrandino, like others, sees it in the context
of the passions, and he recognizes as therapy not only medici-
nal but emotional remedies.[27]

How does one gain cheerfulness and happiness? There is no
specification in the original text itself, but the earliest manuscript has illuminations for each chapter, printed by Landouzy
and Pépin, and the illustration for the accidents of the soul is
that of a figure playing a stringed instrument. Another manuscript, the British Library's beautifully illuminated Sloane 2435,
which contains texts of the *Régime du corps* and the *Image du
monde*, has two antithetical figures in its illustration of this
chapter (f. 10v): an instrumentalist on top, below him a man
seated, hand on cheek, in the traditional pose of sorrow or
melancholy. In light of the long tradition of regarding music as
emotionally therapeutic and as a cure for melancholy, and of
the nature of the other illuminations in the text, the depiction
of a man playing a musical instrument to illustrate emotional
attitude probably functions not only as an icon of joy but also as
a practical indication of one way of attaining it.[28]

Some later manuscripts of the *Régime du corps* indicate another, for in a revision of Aldobrandino's text the advice for
those who are melancholy is not just to "avoir joie et lieche" but

[27]Landouzy and Pépin, p. 32, based on the oldest Aldobrandino MS. For the
contents of the lectuary known as *leticia Galieni*, see their note, p. 233. On the
complex history of views of melancholy in the Middle Ages, see Raymond
Klibansky, Erwin Panofsky, and Fritz Saxl, *Saturn and Melancholy* (New York:
Basic Books, 1964), pp. 67–123. One of the most influential medieval treatises
on melancholy, by Constantinus Africanus, recognizes the need for emotional
treatment as part of a regimen of nonnaturals. *Saturn and Melancholy*, p. 85,
misrepresents Constantinus's organizational scheme: the "sex necessaria" include the *accidentia animae;* see *De melancholia*, in *Opera medica* (Basle, 1536), pp.
291–94 (misnumbered as 391–94).
[28]The Sloane illumination is printed in *Saturn and Melancholy*, pl. 67; see pp.
286–91 for discussion of the pictorial tradition of the melancholic pose. On
music as therapy in the Middle Ages, see Madeleine Pelner Cosman, "Machaut's Medical Musical World," in *Machaut's World: Science and Art in the Fourteenth Century*, ed. Madeleine Cosman and Bruce Chandler, *Annals of the New
York Academy of Sciences*, 314 (1978), pp. 1–36.

to "be joyful and happy and associate with cheerful people and read pleasant and unusual things (prendre ioye et leesse et hanter gens ioyeux et lire ioyeuses choses et estranges)."[29] With this line we arrive at an explicit connection between literature and the *accidentia animae*. Clearly some reviser of Aldobrandino in the fifteenth century felt that the recommendation to be cheerful needed supplementing, and he added two means of removing melancholy: associating with cheerful people (one thinks of the gregarious friends of Dorigen in Chaucer's *Franklin's Tale* who try to take her mind off the grisly rocks; later we will see Boccaccio's *Decameron* storytellers becoming "gens ioyeux" in an act of self-remedy against the plague), and reading delightful and unusual works. What is the author thinking of here? What kind of writing is "ioyeuses" and "estranges"? I would imagine the passage refers to some kind of exciting or exotic narrative, perhaps a romance or something like Mandeville's travels. In any case, there is a precise connection established between the reading of enjoyable material and one's health. Writing that makes one cheerful has a role in the cure of melancholy and, for the same reasons, in hygiene as well.

For confirmation of the therapeutic value of literary entertainment, whether read or heard, we may turn to the late medieval *consilia*, reports by physicians on specific cases they have either seen or been informed of. The basic structure of the medical *consilium*, as outlined by Dean Putnam Lockwood, is tripartite: a description of the symptoms, perhaps with an attempt at diagnosis; a prescribed regimen based on the nonnaturals; and a final section on medical treatment. Not all *consilia* follow this pattern, and many shorter ones are little more than recipes for a particular malady. Moreover, not all writers of *consilia* adhere to the form as rigorously as Ugo Benzi, the subject of Lockwood's study.[30] But the attention to regimen in many *consilia* offers a chance to see medieval physicians working with the theory of the *accidentia animae* in specific practical circumstances.

[29]E.g. British Library MSS Royal 20 B. IX, f. 19v; Sloane 3152, f. 14; Rylands French MS 7, f. 17v (reading "choses plaisantes" for "ioyeux choses").
[30]*Ugo Benzi, Medieval Philosopher and Physician 1376–1439* (Chicago: University of Chicago Press, 1951); see pp. 44–78 for a discussion of the *consilia*, pp. 86–138 for what one can infer from Ugo's about medical practice.

Lockwood mentions five physicians, through the middle of the fifteenth century, whose *consilia* have survived in substantial collections. The earliest of these is Taddeo Alderotti, a distinguished thirteenth-century doctor and teacher. His *consilia*, the only collection of the five to have a modern edition, generally include brief formulaic statements about the accidents of the soul which are usually no more specific than those in the regimens. The following is typical: "The patient should avoid all sadness and worry; bring joy and happiness to him by means of all those things he finds delightful."[31] But just what are the things that produce cheerfulness? Only once does he enter into some detail, in a *consilium* dealing with a marquis's melancholy and sleeplessness: "His cheerfulness, gaiety, and solace should be promoted by taking walks at times, by seeing things that are beautiful and delightful to him, by hearing songs and instruments that he likes, by being told about and promised great yields from profitable markets, or by some other means."[32] Visual and aural delights are familiar sources of temperate joy, but the economic recommendation is unusual and may reflect some specific knowledge Taddeo had about the patient. He does not mention literary narratives, but his reference to "cantilenas" doubtless includes works that today would be treated as lyric poetry. Here we see the regimens' recommendation of *gaudium temperatum* being given specific secular application; certainly in this case Taddeo recognizes mental attitude as a factor in therapeutics and countenances a variety of means to promote the patient's cheerfulness.

Though his *consilia* are less explicitly structured than Taddeo's, and though he is more likely to omit any mention of the *accidentia animae* in regimens where apparently he does not think them relevant, Gentile da Foligno (who died of the

---

[31]"Caveat sibi ab omni tristitia et sollicitudine, inducatur ei gaudium et letitia cum omnibus rebus cum quibus contingit delectari." Taddeo Alderotti, *I "Consilia,"* ed. Giuseppi Michele Nardi (Turin: Edizioni Minerva Medica S.A., 1937), p. 22. On Taddeo and his *consilia* see also Nancy G. Siraisi, *Taddeo Alderotti and His Pupils* (Princeton: Princeton University Press, 1981). This richly informative book appeared too late to be of aid in writing this chapter.

[32]"Inducatur gaudium et letitia et solatium eundo spatiatim, videndo res pulcras et delectabiles sibi, audiendo cantilenas et instrumenta sibi placentia, et annuntientur et promittantur sibi magna lucra de mercationibus lucrativis, vel alio modo." P. 55.

plague in 1348) still retains something of Taddeo's perfunctory formulaic advice. His favorite recommendations concerning the passions are to avoid being alone and to become cheerful by conversing with friends. One *consilium* expands this somewhat: "Among other things, [the patient] should especially take care not to remain alone nor to plunge himself into sadness or heavy thoughts. To this end conversation with good friends works very well, as do a change of scenery, tackling things that seem challenging to complete, and hawking and hunting."[33] Here the list seems predicated on the idea of distraction and includes not only activities that might in themselves conduce to good spirits but also work that will take one's mind off unhealthy preoccupations. Later we will see Boccaccio naming some of the same pursuits as cures for melancholy, to which he adds the reading of the *Decameron*.

In a long *consilium* on a bishop's problems with his liver and other digestive organs, Gentile suggests something of his own attitude toward the efficacy of the sixth nonnatural as part of a regimen: "In regard to the accidents of the soul, it is easy to explain what may be helpful but not easy to see that it is carried out." He lists a variety of possible sources of cheerfulness for the patient, from thoughts of heaven to thoughts of earthly pleasures. Though convinced that the proper emotional attitude has a role to play in this instance, he is aware of the subjectivity of personal responses and the difficulty of instituting mental change in the way that one might institute a dietary regimen; doubtless this accounts, at least in part, for the wide variety of possible means to cheerfulness that he enumerates.[34]

---

[33]"Inter alia singulariter procuret non remanere solitarius nec profundare se ad tristitiam et cogitamina. Ad hoc multum valet conuersatio cum dilectis et mutatio de terra in terram et tentare aliqua que videantur difficilia in consecutione et aucupari et venari." Gentile says that regimen is particularly important in this case, a patient with digestive problems. *Consilia Cermisoni. Consilia Gentilis* (Venice, [1495?]), f. 63v. The *consilia* of Antonio Cermisone, printed with Gentile's in this volume, are predominantly recipes and show little interest in the *accidentia animae;* there is usually a more religious tone to his recommendations about mental attitude, e.g. "Mente letetur et speret in domino qui sibi sanitatem restituet" (f. 21). For bibliography on Gentile's *consilia,* see Lynn Thorndike, "*Consilia* and More Works in Manuscript by Gentile da Foligno," *Medical History,* 3 (1959), 8–19.

[34]"Circa accidentia anime quod sit vtile leuiter explicatur sed non leuiter executioni mandatur. Expedit enim vt euitentur in quantum possunt cogitamina tristia et intendatur gaudio et letitie et conuersationi amicorum et eorum

Like Gentile, Ugo Benzi frequently recommends conversation as a means of inducing cheerfulness. In one *consilium* he adds that such talk should take place "in beautiful and pleasant places, with delightful and sweet musical sounds (in locis pulchris et amenis cum sonis musicalibus delectabilibus et suauibus)," evoking an entire pastoral setting reminiscent of the gardens in the *Decameron*.[35] Often Ugo couples conversation with what seem like more distinctively literary activities, recommending in one case "conversing with friends and listening to pleasant things" (f. 20v), in another "hearing or reading delightful things" (f. 41v), in another "seeking out cheerful and amusing speech" (f. 11). His most detailed recommendation concerning the *accidentia animae* involves a case of melancholy in a noble youth who has come to fear that he is about to die. Here mental attitude is obviously crucial, and after naming the emotions to be avoided, Ugo turns to those to be promoted, adducing a variety of pleasure-creating activities that has many parallels to the list in the *Secretum secretorum:*

> There should be the most diligent effort made to instill liveliness and good hope in him, and to shift his thoughts on one day to some delightful and fitting thing, on another to something else. Such things include looking at various beautiful and entertaining decorations; hearing music and songs; reading something not too difficult, like a narrative or some other work he likes; perfuming or selecting clothes for himself; preparing houses, pleasure gardens, and estates; and other similar activities.[36]

In Ugo Benzi's mind, conversation with friends is closely linked to listening to discourses that most likely include the telling of

---

quibus delectatur, et rememorationi rerum amabilium et intuitui serenitatis celi et rerum preciosarum et innouationi vestium et eorum que delectationem afferunt et tristem cogitationem expellunt que sunt diuersa secundum diuersitatem hominum." F. 65.

[35]*Consilia Ugonis Senensis saluberrima ad omnes egritudines* (Venice, 1518), f. 4v.

[36]"Sed sit diligentissimum studium in dando sibi alacritatem et bonam spem et permutando cogitationes suas quadam die ad vnam rem delectabilem et honestam, alia die ad aliam. Et hoc aut videndo diuersa ornamenta pulchra vel ioculatoria, aut audiendo sonos et cantilenas, aut in legendo aliquid non difficile sed vel hystoriam vel aliam rem sibi caram, vel odorando vel ordinando sibi vestes, vel aptando domos et viridaria et possessiones, et aliis modis similibus." F. 13.

stories. Although words like "placita" and "sermones" are too general to allow specific inferences, the fact that such "delecta-bilia" can be read as well as heard must mean that they include forms substantial enough to be committed to writing. We are in that nebulous area of medieval discourse where it is difficult to distinguish between stories or anecdotes told casually as part of sophisticated conversation and narratives recited more formally as some kind of "official" entertainment. Ugo's advice to the young nobleman is less problematic: he recommends the medieval equivalent of "light reading," a narrative that will prompt immediate pleasure.

Some of the most interesting comments on the *accidentia animae* appear in Bartholomaeus da Montagnana, whose *consilia* number over three hundred in Renaissance editions. In certain cases he recommends that a patient follow a regimen that will increase the movement of *spiritus* and humors in his body, and he notes that a variety of passions will accomplish this end, including anger as well as delight. To gain delight he advises in one instance "delightful stories that may expand the *spiritus* and move bodily substances (historias delectabiles que dilatent spiritus et moueant materias)" and in another stories "distinctly oriented toward laughter (ad risum notabiliter inclinantes)."[37] Like Gentile, he is aware that dealing with the emotions is tricky and that there is a risk involved in trying to excite strong passions (f. 15v). He not only grants a therapeutic function to delightful stories but attributes adverse effects to other kinds of narrative. In a long *consilium* for a Dominican friar, whose many ailments are seen as a result of a combination of his natural complexion turning hot and dry and the accidental complexion of his brain turning cold and moist, Bartholomaeus recommends avoidance of all strong emotions and specifies that "this man should avoid distressing accidents of the soul, such as anxiety, melancholy, sadness, perverse ruminations, the reading of horrible stories depicting martyrdoms or death, and similar things."[38]

Perhaps it is his focus on the *movement* of bodily substances as a

[37]*Consilia Magistri Bartholomei Montagnane* (Venice, 1499), ff. 83v, 15v.
[38]"Ista vir euitet anime accidentia contristatiua, ut angstiam [sic], melancoliam, tristitiam, et meditationes prauas, et horribilium historiam [sic] lectiones representantes martyria siue mortes, et similia." F. 18; see f. 263v for the same reasoning in a *consilium* for a Franciscan.

result of the passions that leads him to treat material usually classified under the accidents of the soul as belonging to another nonnatural, motion and rest. Sometimes he runs the two categories together, apparently thinking in terms of a logical connection between bodily movement and the movements of the soul. In one *consilium* he mentions the study of moral or theological stories along with the singing of psalms as among the "exercises of the soul" that bring delight (f. 278). Possibly the more didactic, rational content of moral or religious narratives leads him to see them as an exercise for the soul rather than as simply an instigator of the passions, but in any case the idea that reflection on serious works can be part of a curative regimen suggests that the therapeutic powers of delight extend to more than purely entertaining literature. Another work treats listening to stories as exercise for the ear ("Aures vero exercitentur historias magnarum rerum audiendo"), as is attending to songs and instrumental music (f. 288v). Bartholomaeus also joins a long tradition in specifying singing or reciting aloud as a form of exercise, particularly good for the chest.[39] More than the other authors, he seems to think of activities we now classify as part of literature or the performing arts in terms of the variety of physiological and psychological purposes they serve.

The *consilia* are interesting for a number of reasons. They offer more immediate evidence of medical practice than academic treatises and regimens, and they show as well how theory and practice relate. Compared with their concern with medicaments, the amount of time they devote to the nonnaturals is relatively small, and within the sections on regimen the amount given to the *accidentia animae* is much smaller still. Even so, their reflections on mental attitude are intriguing and certainly point to a medieval awareness of a possible psychosomatic element in health and illness, an awareness not just theoretically

[39]See e.g. ff. 3, 18, 288v. For evidence from classical medicine recommending reading aloud, see Francesco di Capua, "Osservazioni sulla lettura e sulla preghiera ad alta voce presso gli antichi," *Rendiconti della Accademia di archeologia, lettere e belle arti di Napoli*, n.s. 28 (1953), 59–62, a reference I owe to Susan Noakes. In a regimen dated 1315, a physician of Valencia tells his two sons, away at school in Toulouse, that they can get exercise indoors in inclement weather. He includes dancing in this category; "eciam cantare est exercicium pectoris." Ed. Lynn Thorndike, "Advice from a Physician to His Sons," *Speculum*, 6 (1931), 113.

formulated in the concept of the nonnaturals but acted on in various attempts to recommend ways of altering a person's disposition.[40] In many of the cases cited, the physician's increased attention to the *accidentia animae* seems justified by the nature of the malady. But even the most detailed advice is usually quite conventional. Without a formal discipline of verbal psychotherapy, medieval physicians can do no more than list a number of possible causes of cheerfulness, acknowledge that there may well be others, imply that anything that will work is good, and occasionally admit to the difficulty of instituting successful mental regimens.

To pursue these issues further would demand more attention to complete cases than space allows and more medical knowledge than I have. We can, however, at least see the role that literature occupies in the *consilia*. Although it is not a large one, reading and hearing narratives appear as means of attaining the *gaudium temperatum* that normally stands as the desired mental attitude of a person in good health. The authors who mention literature specifically (we will meet more of them in a later chapter that treats *consilia* on the plague) seem to agree that delightful narratives promote cheerfulness. Literature, music, and conversation are grouped together as methods of properly disposing the emotions, in what may be the closest approach medieval medicine makes to recognizing psychosomatic factors in illness. By extension, reading or hearing stories, listening to music, conversing with friends in beautiful gardens—all those activities we see so often as part of the leisured social life of the later Middle Ages—play a role in hygiene as well as in therapeutics. The perspective of the regimens and *consilia* gives medical sanction to behavior that might otherwise be dismissed as the self-indulgence of the idle and the extravagant.

[40]Generally psychosomatic medicine is considered a modern discipline. But at times earlier thinking along psychosomatic lines is recognized as such. See e.g. Antoinette Stettler, "Zur Psychosomatik im Mittelalter," *Gesnerus*, 31 (1974), 99–106; Marek-Marsel Mesulam and Jon Perry, "The Diagnosis of Love-Sickness: Experimental Psychophysiology without the Polygraph," *Psychophysiology*, 9 (1972), 546–51. For broader historical background see Pedro Laín Entralgo, *Mind and Body*, trans. Aurelio M. Espinosa, Jr. (New York: P. J. Kenedy, n.d.), and L. J. Rather, *Mind and Body in Eighteenth Century Medicine: A Study Based on Jerome Gaub's De regimine mentis* (London: Wellcome Historical Medical Library, 1965). Rather's introduction and notes extend the range of his book beyond the eighteenth-century texts he prints.

The relevance of these hygienic ideas to literary theory will be clear, I hope, by the end of Chapter 4, when we have seen a number of works make reference to them by way of explaining their goals and usefulness. At this point, however, the view of literature implicit in the regimens and *consilia* may seem too distant from specific texts and specific literary theorizing to be accepted as a part of standard medieval critical thought. After all, one can recognize the use of poetry in therapy today but not think it appropriate to construct an elaborate poetics on the basis of that single limited function. Granted that physicians may have recommended literary entertainment as part of their medical advice, that in itself is no evidence that people more closely involved with literature gave such arguments weight or even accepted them. Hence in order to gain some initial assent to the presence of a medical view of the effects of fiction in medieval literary thought, I turn in the next section to two instances where what we would call literary criticism depends on the physiological ideas just presented. The first involves some twelfth- and thirteenth-century theorizing about the value of theatrics; the second, a much briefer example, involves a portion of Laurent de Premierfait's commentary on the *Decameron*, which will be discussed in full in a later chapter.

Theatrica

The idea of theatrics, a science of entertainments (*scientia ludorum*), appears first and fully developed in Hugh of St. Victor's *Didascalicon*, written in the late 1120s. One of its purposes is to categorize the various disciplines that constitute human knowledge. Knowledge is of four kinds: theoretical (which is concerned with truth and which includes theology, mathematics, and physics), practical (concerned with morals; includes ethics, economics, and politics), logical (concerned with words; includes grammar and argumentation), and mechanical (concerned with the works of human labor). Of the traditional seven liberal arts, the trivium appears within logic, the quadrivium within mathematics. Hugh finds a parallel to this pattern in the seven mechanical arts: three (fabric making, armament, commerce) are concerned with outer covering, as the trivium is concerned with words; four (agriculture, hunting, medicine, theatrics) are concerned with internal nourishment, as the quadrivium is concerned with interior mental concepts.[41]

Before considering Hugh's discussion of *theatrica* we must look at the preceding chapter on medicine, for the two are closely connected, as Glenda Pritchett has indicated (pp. 78–79). Hugh's treatment of medicine consists of a set of carefully selected passages from the *Isagoge* of Johannitius, simplifying its categorizations by dividing the discipline into *occasiones* and *operationes*. Operations are either interior (for example, the use of drugs, emetics) or exterior (for example, ointments, surgery). *Occasiones* are, as we have seen, the six nonnaturals, which Hugh enumerates. He attends particularly to the *accidentia animae*, quoting the *Isagoge* on the effects of various emotions on bodily heat.

He then defines the seventh mechanical art, and it is necessary to reproduce the entire discussion:

> The science of entertainments is called "theatrics" from the theatre, to which the people once used to gather for the performance: not that a theatre was the only place in which entertainment took place, but it was a more popular place for entertainment than any other. Some entertainment took place in theatres, some in the entrance porches of buildings, some in gymnasia, some in amphitheatres, some in arenas, some at feasts, some at shrines. In the theatre, epics (gesta) were presented either by recitals or by acting out dramatic roles or using masks or puppets; they held choral processions and dances in the porches. In the gymnasia they wrestled; in the amphitheatres they raced on foot or on horses or in chariots; in the arenas boxers performed; at banquets they made music with songs and instruments and chants, and they played at dice; in the temples at solemn seasons they sang the praises of the gods. Moreover, they numbered these entertainments among legitimate activities because by temperate

[41]*The* Didascalicon *of Hugh of St. Victor*, trans. Jerome Taylor (New York: Columbia University Press, 1961), pp. 61–82. My debt to Taylor's work will be obvious. Latin text ed. C. H. Buttimer (Washington, D.C.: Catholic University of America Press, 1939). On the sources and influence of Hugh's conception, see W. Tatarkiewicz, "Theatrica, the Science of Entertainment," *Journal of the History of Ideas*, 26 (1965), 263–72. On Hugh's understanding of the mechanical arts, see Pierre Vallin, " 'Mechanica' et 'Philosophia' selon Hugues de Saint-Victor," *Revue d'histoire de la spiritualité*, 49 (1973), 257–88.

motion natural heat is stimulated in the body and by enjoyment the mind is refreshed (temperato motu naturalis calor nutritur in corpore, et laetitia animus reparatur); or, as is more likely, seeing that people necessarily gathered together for occasional amusement, they desired that places for such amusement might be established to forestall the people's coming together at public houses, where they might commit lewd or criminal acts.[42]

Tatarkiewicz has rightly pointed out that, unlike the other descriptions of the mechanical arts, this one is in the past tense, apparently reflecting Hugh's reading in Isidore of Seville rather than his interest in contemporary pastimes. His implication seems to be that Hugh has added theatrics solely out of motives of intellectual completeness, appropriating an ancient source because it revealed certain activities with rules, hence valid arts, that needed to be dealt with somewhere in his system. Taylor, on the other hand, speculates that Hugh's "favorable attitude" toward theatrics is "perhaps not unconnected with the rise of liturgical drama in the twelfth century" (p. 206, n. 79). That suggestion is appropriately cautious, for nothing in the passage itself is explicitly contemporary. Yet I think Taylor's attempt to find a modern resonance is also true to Hugh's intent. For later in the *Didascalicon*, commenting on the different motives people have for studying the Bible, Hugh scorns those more interested in "marvels" than in "salvation":

They wish to search into hidden matters and to know about unheard-of things—to know much and to do nothing. . . . What else can I call their conduct than a turning of the divine announcements into tales (fabulas)? It is for this that we are accustomed to turn to theatrical performances, for this to dramatic recitations (sic theatralibus ludis, sic scenicis carminibus)—namely, that we may feed our ears, not our mind.[43]

Here we are in the present tense, but the idea of theatrics, a science that includes such *ludi* as plays and recitations, surely cannot be far away. Hugh may not have seen chariot racing,

[42]Taylor, p. 79; Buttimer, p. 44.
[43]Taylor, p. 134; Buttimer, p. 111.

but he and his audience would have had no trouble envisaging the public performance of "gesta," the presence of songs and music "in conviviis," or the Christian equivalent of singing praise in the temples. Hugh has a conception of entertainment that is relevant to his century as well as to classical culture; and even if we cannot identify precisely those stage entertainments he may have turned to in order to please his ears, we should think of his treatment of *theatrica* not just as a historical reconstruction but as a reasoned statement on entertainment applicable to his own era.

And when we do, we find that the rationale for theatrics is thoroughly physiological. Hugh ascribes the two arguments advanced—that temperate motion stimulates the body's natural heat, and that pleasure refreshes (or repairs) the mind—to ancient belief. But in fact they do not occur in Isidore's material on games (*Etymologiae,* XVIII, 16–69), which critics as long ago as Robert Kilwardby and as recently as Tatarkiewicz have named as his source. The arguments were obviously in Hugh's mind from his preceding chapter, where he had noted the effect of *gaudium* and other emotions on the natural heat. Here he explains the reactions somewhat more ambiguously: the temperate motion that promotes heat probably alludes to the physical endeavors of the participants, as Tatarkiewicz argues, though it is certainly possible that the line refers as well or instead to the emotions generated in the audience, since they too are movements that affect the body's natural heat. Later in the twelfth century, William Fitzstephen describes adult Londoners coming to watch boys play sports and having their natural heat raised simply by emotional identification with the children.[44] Hugh's second argument is not explicitly in the *Isagoge* but as we have seen is a familiar extension of its principles: the emotion of *gaudium* or *laetitia,* by expanding heat and *spiri-*

[44]"Elder men and fathers and rich citizens come on horse-back to watch the contests of their juniors, and after their fashion are young again with the young; and it seems that the motion of their natural heat is kindled by the contemplation of such violent motion and by their partaking in the joys of untrammelled youth (et excitari videtur in eis motus caloris naturalis contemplatione tanti motus et participatione gaudiorum adolescentia liberioris)." Text in J. C. Robertson, *Materials for the History of Thomas Becket,* Rolls Series, 67, p. III (London, 1878), p. 9. Trans. H. E. Butler, rpt. in *The World of Piers Plowman,* ed. Jeanne Krochalis and Edward Peters ([Philadelphia]: University of Pennsylvania Press, 1975), p. 31.

tus throughout the body, renders the mind as well as the members reinvigorated.[45]

Hugh's final alternative intimates that the physiological justification may be more rationalization than rationale, since he considers it "more likely" that the primary motive for the creation of places of entertainment was a moral and social one. He is certainly responding here to Isidore's association of theaters and brothels (XVIII, 42). But even if the origin of theatrics lay in the need for controlling wicked behavior, it is still true that people gathered for amusement "necesse," and Hugh thinks of that unavoidable need in medical terms. Theatrics is one of the mechanical arts that minister to bodily demands. Entertainment is justifiable because of its restorative value: it feeds the ears, satisfies the sensitive rather than the rational soul. As Hugh says elsewhere, there is a music of the body; it can be seen in the power of growth, in the mixture of humors, and "in those activities (the foremost among them are the mechanical) which belong above all to rational beings and which are good if they do not become inordinate, so that avarice or appetite are not fostered by the very things intended to relieve our weakness." Reason allows for a properly controlled satisfaction of physical and emotional needs. There are more important kinds of music, of course: of the soul, of the soul and body in harmony, of the universe itself. The proper human music "consists in loving one's flesh, but one's spirit more" (Taylor, p. 69). The *Didascalicon* as a whole is naturally more concerned with the latter; but its attention to the mechanical arts, and by implication to whatever literary activity is subsumed within the category of *theatrica*, rep-

---

[45]Cf. the revision of William of Conches's *De philosophia mundi*, which follows Hugh here but changes the terminology: "Two things are vitally necessary to man . . . movement to keep the mind from languishing, joy to keep the body from exhaustion by too much work (motus quidem ne animus tabescat, gaudium ne nimia exercitatione fatiscat corpus)." Trans. Taylor, p. 205, n. 68. Text in *Un brano inedito della "Philosophia" di Guglielmo di Conches*, ed. Carmelo Ottaviano (Naples: Alberto Morano, 1935), p. 34. The cause-effect relationships seem different from Hugh's, motion aiding the mind, joy the body; but since both involve the expansion of heat and *spiritus*, which has both mental and physical benefits, there is no fundamental disagreement. What is more significant for our purposes is that this work, like Hugh's, views theatrics in the context of the mechanical arts, which are a remedy for *infirmitas*, physical or psychological weakness, rather than for moral or intellectual frailty. On the kind of remedy provided by the mechanical arts, see Taylor, pp. 51–56, Ottaviano, p. 23.

resents Hugh's sensible and temperate recognition of the needs of the body.

His classification of the mechanical arts was highly influential. Tatarkiewicz points to its appearance in St. Bonaventure and in Vincent of Beauvais, while Roger Baron and Pierre Vallin cite other borrowings.[46] To these may be added the early thirteenth-century commentary on Alain de Lille's *Anticlaudianus* by Radulphus de Longo Campo. Like Hugh, Radulphus is concerned with categories of knowledge, and he discusses *mechanica* as one of four types of *scientia:*

> Mechanics is the science of human activities that serve bodily necessities. It has a countless variety of subdivisions, such as fabric making, armament, commerce, hunting, agriculture, surgery, and theatrics. Fabric making eliminates cold and produces the opposite; armament eliminates accidental death and preserves life; . . . theatrics removes displeasure by producing attentiveness and happiness. Thus it is clear that the mechanical arts remove a defect and produce bodily well-being.
>
> They are called mechanical, that is, adulterate, because they teach the spirit to serve the flesh, whereas conversely the flesh ought to serve the spirit. Hence the other three branches of knowledge are liberal, and this one alone is called servile.[47]

The list of mechanical arts follows Hugh, except that surgery replaces medicine, since Radulphus elsewhere classifies medicine as a subdivision of physics, which is part of theoretical philosophy (p. 41). Also, he treats the seven as exemplary rather than exhaustive. His definition of "mechanica" as "adulterina"

---

[46]See the notes to Baron's edition of the *Epitome Dindimi in philosophiam*, in *Opera propaedeutica Hugonis de Sancto Victore* (Notre Dame, Ind.: University of Notre Dame Press, 1966), pp. 220–21. Vallin, 286–88.

[47]"Mechanica igitur est scientia humanorum actuum corporeis necessitatibus obsequentium, cuius infinitae sunt species ut est: lanificium, armatura, navigatio, venatio, agricultura, chirurgia, theatrica. Lanificium quidem expellit frigus et informat contrarium; armatura expellit mortem casualem et conservat vitam; . . . theatrica removet fastidium informando attentionem et laetitiam. Patet ergo quod mechanica expellit defectum et informat valetudinem.

"Dicitur autem mechanica quasi adulterina. Docet enim spiritum servire carni cum e converso caro spiritui servire debeat. Cum igitur aliae tres filiae scientiae liberales sunt, haec sola servilis dicitur." *In Anticlaudianum Alani Commentum,* ed. Jan Sulowski (Wroclaw: Zakład Narodowy Imienia Ossolinskich Wydawnictwo Polskiej Akademi Nauk, 1972), p. 44.

comes from Hugh's false etymology (explained by Taylor, p. 191, n. 64), and his analysis of each art in terms of removing a defect and supplying a benefit corresponds to the *Didascalicon*'s focus in Book I on knowledge as a remedy for deficiency. Radulphus keeps Hugh's physiological perspective: the usefulness of theatrics is that it makes one more alert and cheerful, and these qualities are seen as part of "valetudinem," good health. His distinction between mechanical and liberal knowledge, framed in a pointed opposition that does not appear in the *Didascalicon*, further emphasizes *mechanica*'s application to the body alone and its inferior position among the sciences as a result. In short, Radulphus accepts and even sharpens Hugh's approach to entertainment as an art justified by its physical consequences.

St. Bonaventure alters Hugh's schema to make theatrics unique among the mechanical arts. The *De reductione artium ad theologiam* defines God's gifts to man in terms of four lights, ranging from the "light of grace and of Sacred Scripture" through the lights of philosophical knowledge and sense perception to the lowest, the "*external* light, or the light of mechanical skill." This light enables us to understand things created by human craft, which are intended to supply bodily needs ("propter supplendam corporis indigentiam"); it is external because it is in a sense "servilis" and lies below philosophical knowledge. Bonaventure then refers to Hugh's seven mechanical arts, but in a grouping different from his trivium and quadrivium:

> . . . every mechanical art is intended for man's *consolation* or his *comfort;* its purpose, therefore, is to banish either *sorrow* or *want;* it either *benefits* or *delights,* according to the words of Horace:

> "Either to serve or to please is the wish of the poets".

And again:

> "He hath gained universal applause who hath combined the profitable with the pleasing".

> If its aim is to afford *consolation* and amusement, it is *dramatic art,* or the art of exhibiting plays, which embraces every form

of entertainment, be it song, music, drama, or pantomime. If, however, it is intended for the *comfort* or betterment of the exterior man, it can accomplish its purpose by providing either *covering* or *food*, or by *serving as an aid in the acquisition of either*.

Bonaventure then explains how fabric making and armament provide covering, how agriculture and hunting provide food, and how commerce and medicine help in their acquisition. He ends with a reminder that "dramatic art, on the other hand, is in a class by itself (Theatrica autem est unica)."[48]

This is an intriguing passage, and interpretations of it vary.[49] For our purposes, we may note that Bonaventure seems perfectly content with Hugh's categorization of *mechanica* as ministering to bodily needs; his innovation, the separation of theatrics from the others on the grounds that it alone produces "solatium et delectationem" rather than "profectum," highlights the uniqueness of entertainment and its role in sustaining life, the banishing of sorrow. And it should be clear by now that, in a cultural context alert to mind-body relationships but without a separate discipline of verbal therapy, such a role is by no means trivial.

But not every thinker accepted *theatrica* so readily. About 1250, probably a few years before *De reductione* was composed, Robert Kilwardby, a Dominican who became Archbishop of Canterbury, wrote a treatise that, as its editor says, attempted to do for the thirteenth century what the *Didascalicon* did for the twelfth. In his analysis of kinds of knowledge, Kilwardby accepts Hugh's category of *mechanica,* an "art or practical science concerned with man's physical existence for the purpose of answering his material needs (ars vel scientia operativa circa res humanas corporales propter necessitates humanas corpo-

---

[48]*Saint Bonaventure's* de reductione artium ad theologiam, ed. and trans. Sister Emma Thérèse Healy (St. Bonaventure, N.Y.: Saint Bonaventure College, 1940), pp. 38–41.

[49]See Pritchett, pp. 70–72, and David L. Jeffrey, "Franciscan Spirituality and the Rise of Early English Drama," *Mosaic,* 8, no. 4 (1975), 23–25; also his *Early English Lyric and Franciscan Spirituality* (Lincoln: University of Nebraska Press, 1975), pp. 97–101. Jeffrey finds a "pedagogical theory of dramatic art" in Bonaventure's view of theatrics.

rales tollendas)."[50] He devotes a full chapter to summarizing Hugh's material on the seven mechanical arts and pointing out the fuller treatments in Isidore. Then, in chapter 40, he proposes some adjustments. Most are terminological, substituting more inclusive names for various arts.

His one change in substance is major: "It does not seem to me that *theatrica* should be given status among Christians; rather it should be hated and attacked (theatrica non videtur mihi ponenda apud catholicos, sed magis detestanda et impugnanda)." In support of his rejection of theatrics he cites Isidore's statement that Christians should have nothing to do with "impudicita theatri," "luxuria ludi," and similar forms of decadence (pp. 131–32). Hugh had omitted this and other passages in the *Etymologiae* which express disapproval of secular entertainments; but in light of much official Church opinion on these pastimes, Kilwardby's hard-line attitude should not be surprising. Still, not all recreations must go: "I think that those entertainments which are permitted to Christians, such as playing the cithara, trumpet, flute, and such, should have their standing as a part of medicine and be placed within that branch of medicine which deals with 'occasions.' "[51] He obviously saw and agreed with Hugh's statement of the physiological benefits of entertainment, so much so that he could reduce music to one of the *occasiones* of health and disease, that is, to its role in the sixth nonnatural, the *accidentia animae*, as a cause of *gaudium*. Presumably other entertainments, if they weren't so vile, would have a place there too, for all kinds of *ludi* minister to bodily demands. He proposes replacing *theatrica* with *architectonica* in order to keep the mechanical arts at seven.

Somewhere between Hugh's acceptance of a science of entertainment and Kilwardby's rejection of it except for certain kinds of music lie the views of Peter the Chanter and ecclesiastics associated with him. They do not discuss *theatrica* as a concept, but, as John W. Baldwin has shown, they reveal at least

---

[50]*De ortu scientiarum*, ed. Albert G. Judy, O.P. (Oxford: The British Academy and the Pontifical Institute of Mediaeval Studies, Toronto, 1976), p. 128.

[51]"Id autem quod de ludis licitum est catholicis, ut cithara, tuba, tibia et huiusmodi, pro loco et tempore aestimo esse reducendum ad medicinam ut collocetur sub illa parte medicinae quae considerat occasiones." P. 132.

some tolerance for certain kinds of entertainers.[52] In general their attitude toward performance is hostile; the Chanter says at one point that the acting profession alone "contains nothing of usefulness or necessity" (II: n. 196), a line that seems almost a direct refutation of Hugh of St. Victor's argument that *theatrica* meets a human need. But the condemnation is not complete. The canonist Huguccio accepts a limited kind of instrumental music if it is used for the praise of God, for legitimate church needs, or "for the health of the body (ad salutem corporis)," an essentially medical view of music's effects on people that may well have influenced Kilwardby's thinking (I: 202–3, II: n. 215). Thomas of Chobham, following another text of the Chanter, admits some kinds of narrative performance as acceptable. In a famous passage of the *Summa confessorum*, he distinguishes three kinds of *histriones*. After condemning the first two he turns to those performers who use musical instruments for people's delight ("ad delectandum homines"). Those who sing songs that move people to licentiousness are damnable; but others sing of heroic deeds and of saints' lives "and bring solace to people in their illnesses or in their mental discomfort (et faciunt solatia hominibus vel in egritudinibus suis vel in angustiis suis)." These "ioculatores" can be accepted as long as they do not engage in any of the damnable forms of behavior.[53]

In the context of our investigation, this statement of the *utilitas* of the one tolerable form of entertainment takes on some interest. Decent minstrels sing epics and saints' lives, and they bring "solatia" to people who are specifically in some kind of

[52]*Masters, Princes, and Merchants: The Social Views of Peter the Chanter and His Circle*, 2 vols. (Princeton: Princeton University Press, 1970), I: 198–204; II: chap. IX. nn. 174–235.

[53]*Summa confessorum*, Art. VI, Dist. IV, q. 2a, ed. F. Broomfield, Analecta Mediaevalia Namurcensia, 25 (Louvain and Paris, 1968), pp. 291–93. Other editions in Chambers, II: 262–63, and in Faral, *Les jongleurs*, with discussion, pp. 67–70. Often translated. For the source passages in Peter the Chanter, who tolerates warily *joculatores* who sing of noble deeds "for the purpose of recreation or possibly instruction (ad recreationem vel forte ad informationem)," see Broomfield's notes. On the presence of *chansons de geste* and saints' lives in the *jongleur* repertoire, see Faral, pp. 44–60. Similar to the views of Thomas and the Chanter is the opinion of Friar Thomas Docking, who distinguishes bad entertainers from those who create "solace to combat anger, sadness, tediousness, or sloth, or to combat bodily infirmities (solacium contra iram, tristiciam, tedium et accidiam, vel contra infirmitates corporales)"; quoted in Jeffrey, *Early English Lyric*, p. 218, n. 36, and see p. 176. See also Faral, p. 320, no. 253.

physical or emotional distress (the regimens sometimes list *angustia* among the accidents of the soul to be avoided). It is possible, given the paratactic grammar, that Thomas is thinking of "solatia" as amusing songs along with the more serious ones. But slightly later he restates his point more causally: entertainers may be tolerated who sing about the deeds of princes and other profitable matters "in order to bring solace to people (ut faciant solatia hominibus)." Stories of heroic deeds and other useful narratives are what produce comfort; there seems to be some kind of moral or religious component to the solace, for Thomas apparently sees *delectatio* as the more general term and *solatium* as a response restricted to worthwhile entertainments. But it is not possible, given the generality of the passage,. to infer much about Thomas's view of the profitableness of epic or hagiography. What is certain is his and Docking's belief that some kinds of narrative performance bring solace to people who need physical or mental relief. The only reason why they should qualify the audience in that way is the medieval tendency, observable in the theoreticians of *theatrica*, to think of entertainment as justifiable because of its hygienic or therapeutic effects.

Tatarkiewicz says that Hugh's concept of theatrics "fell into oblivion" after the thirteenth century until the Renaissance (269). That is exaggerated, but I know of no major theoretical treatment of the subject in the later Middle Ages. What is clear from the texts we have seen is that the idea of theatrics, as well as some views of performance not explicitly based on it, entails a medical understanding of the usefulness of entertainment, and that much of what is classified as entertainment seems to belong to what we call medieval literature. It is of course difficult to deduce from such highly theoretical discussions what specific works might fit within the conception. Certainly *theatrica* does not mean *poetica*. Hugh gives poetry a separate standing—but only, interestingly enough, as an appendage to the arts, something to be attended to after one's work on the liberal disciplines, if time allows (Taylor, pp. 87–89). Radulphus, as one might expect from someone commenting on a philosophical poem, makes *poesis* one of his major species of *scientia* (p. 44). But although theatrics does not include the *Anticlaudianus*, it does entail works distinctly "literary" in nature: recitations of *gesta,* songs, comedies, and tragedies. Arnulf of Orleans perceives the twelfth-century Latin elegiac comedy *Pamphilus* as an example of a love story presented "in theatro." His reference establishes the performance of that work and perhaps suggests one strain of literature that might be thought of as part of the theatrical art.[54]

The medieval classification of *theatrica* is based on circumstance and function rather than on the inherent characteristics of each type of presentation. To cite just one further example, Peter the Chanter notes that in various entertainments actors are chosen because they fit their parts; this happens not only in saints' plays but also "in festo stultorum in comediis et tragediis et in huiusmodi ludicris ac mimicis representationibus" (Baldwin, II: IX n. 234). This kind of grouping, which seems to include everything from full-scale drama to mime to the celebration of the Feast of Fools, makes perfect sense once we "widen the concept of theatre by including everything that is to-day known as the performing arts."[55] Any story told as part of a public performance, any scenario given whatever kind of stage presentation, any lyric sung—all these more or less literary presentations join music, dance, pantomime, even acrobatics, in the category of *theatrica.* Although we may not be able to know specifically what works Hugh and other writers on theatrics had in mind, and although any given work may well have had values unaccounted for by the general theory, the fact remains that the principal justification for a performance perceived as an example of *theatrica* was essentially medical: entertainment repairs the body and the mind.

If the example of theatrics is problematic because of the breadth of the conception and the generality of the theorizing, no such difficulties arise with my second example of physiological ideas in literary criticism. In the dedicatory letter to his translation of the *Decameron,* Laurent de Premierfait offers im-

---

[54]Bruno Roy, "Arnulf of Orleans and the Latin 'Comedy,'" *Speculum,* 49 (1974), 258–66. There is much controversy about how the Latin *comoediae* were presented and about theatrical knowledge in general in the twelfth century; for a good summary of these matters see Rosemary Woolf, *The English Mystery Plays* (Berkeley: University of California Press, 1973), pp. 25–38.

[55]Roy, 262, though he is speaking in a different context.

plicitly a critical interpretation of it, focusing particularly on its usefulness. A full examination of this text must come later, but it is relevant now to look at one portion of it. Laurent explains to the Duke of Berry that reading or listening to the *Decameron* will enable him and others to "acquire three profits that are mingled with three honest pleasures." He then defines these "prouffiz" that arise out of "plaisirs," and the last two have medical force:

> Second, after difficult and burdensome work, whether physical or mental, it is natural that everyone restore his energy either through the help of food or through some proper pleasure in which the soul takes delight. Third, since you and other earthly rulers represent divine power and majesty, I say that just as joyful and happy praise from the heart should be sung or spoken before the heavenly and omnipotent Lord, so is it proper before earthly lords that stories be told in an agreeable way and with proper language in order to gladden and cheer people's spirits. For in order to be more fully worthy in the eyes of God, rulers and all men may prolong their lives in any rational way consonant with God and nature.[56]

Laurent's view of the profits of the *Decameron* extends to more than intellectual or moral benefits. His second point is based on a parallel that is absolutely accurate to anyone thinking within the tradition of the nonnaturals. Work leads to weakness, whether of the body or the mind, and some kind of reinvigoration is necessary: food for the body, delight for the

---

[56]"Secondement, selon ordre de nature aprez griefues et pesantes besongnes traictees par labour corporel ou par subtillite d'engin il affiert que chascun homme refreschisse ses forces ou par confort de viandes ou par aucune honneste leesse en quoy l'ame prengne delectacion. Tiercement, puisque vous et autres princes terriens portez la representacion et figure de puissance et mageste diuine, je di que ainsi comme deuant dieu celeste et tout puissant doiuent estre chantees ou dictes loanges de cueur ioieux et esbaudi, aussi deuant les princes licitement peuent estre racomptees nouuelles soubz gracieuses manieres et honnestes paroles pour leesser et esbaudir les esperitz des hommes. Car pour plusamplement meriter enuers dieu il est permis aux princes et aussi a tous hommes alongner leurs vies par toutes voies consones a dieu et a nature acompaignee de raison." Bibliothèque Nationale MS f. fr. 129, f. 2v. Ed., with some errors in transcription, Attilio Hortis, *Studi sulle opere latine del Boccaccio* (Trieste: Julius Dase, 1879), pp. 745–46.

soul. Laurent thinks of both replenishments in terms of the role they play in restoring human energy. The *Decameron* does for the mind what a good meal does for the body. I don't think he is trying to be witty or cute here. He has a unified conception of refreshment that we will see in the next chapter embodied in the term "recreatio." He makes a perfectly natural and forceful comparison given the hygienic ideas discussed above, and only if we take it seriously can we appreciate some of the ways in which the Middle Ages thought about literary pleasure.

The third argument is even more explicitly hygienic. It is permissible to "gladden and cheer people's spirits (esperitz)," for such enjoyment leads to lengthening of life and hence to more opportunity to merit divine reward. Proper secular entertainment is the earthly counterpart of religious celebration, and even its outcome—the improved health that leads to longer life—is put in terms of a final cause, thus giving refreshment theological relevance. But just as interesting as the perhaps overly earnest fusing of secular and sacred here is the unspoken assumption that reinvigorating the *spiritus* will have a notable physical consequence: people who take entertainment live longer, apparently, than those who do not. Laurent's reference to "esperitz," like other literary claims we will see in Chapter 4, is quite likely specifically medical, referring to the *spiritus* that physicians assert to be at its optimum effectiveness for human well-being when one is in a state of temperate joy. Modern allusions to raising one's spirits, or being in good spirits, preserve the old terminology but, of course, without its scientific force. In the Middle Ages, a phrase like "esbaudir les esperitz" is not just a periphrasis for enjoying oneself: it is a precise statement of a desirable physiological consequence of entertainment.

Literature as *Confabulatio*

Thus far we have seen medical texts approach the usefulness of stories in terms of their connection with the accidents of the soul, as a means of attaining a desirable emotional state. There is one medieval book on health which discusses fiction in a different context, but the perspective remains equally physiological, and the attention given to the dynamics of literary response is more complete than in the regimens and *consilia* discussed above. The *Tacuinum sanitatis,* or *Tables of Health,* is a hygienic manual translated into Latin during the thirteenth century from the Arabic of Ibn Butlān, a Christian physician of the eleventh century who studied in Baghdad, practiced in Cairo, and eventually became a monk in Antioch. It should not be confused with the *Tacuinum morborum,* a set of therapeutic rather than hygienic tables by a different author, which was translated in 1296 for Charles of Anjou. The *Tacuinum sanitatis* is perhaps best known to art historians, for in the late fourteenth century a number of beautifully illuminated manuscripts of it were produced in Italy. A recent volume, *The Medieval Health Handbook,* now makes many of their illustrations readily available, and handsome facsimile editions of some of the manuscripts have appeared as well.[57]

From the illustrated versions we can see a view of health as holistic as that in the regimens, for like them the *Tacuinum* is based on the nonnaturals, as its introduction makes clear (see Arano, p. 6). Each page of the illuminated manuscripts offers a picture of something relevant to one's health, below which a text quite succinctly states pertinent information about its use, such as its nature (explained in terms of the four degrees of the four qualities of hot, cold, moist, dry), its usefulness, its dangers, and how to eliminate those dangers. The majority of the pages feature, as one might expect, various foods and herbs; but there are also a few illustrations of the other nonnaturals: entries relating, for example, to air (the four winds and seasons), motion and rest (walking, horseback riding, fencing), and the accidents of the soul (anger, joy, shame). In total more than 250 items appear, though no one manuscript has all of

---

[57]Luisa Cogliati Arano, *The Medieval Health Handbook,* trans. Oscar Ratti and Adele Westbrook (New York: Braziller, 1976). The introduction is principally from the standpoint of art history and is not especially lucid on the medical background, for which Léopold Delisle's "Traités d'hygiène du moyen âge," *Journal des savants* (1896), 518–40, is still useful. Facsimiles: Elena Berti Toesca, *Il Tacuinum sanitatis della Biblioteca Nazionale di Parigi* (Bergamo: Istituto Italiano d'Arti Grafiche, 1937); Luigi Serra and Silvestro Baglioni, *Theatrum sanitatis. Codice 4182 della R. Biblioteca Casanatense,* 2 vols. (Rome: La Libreria dello stato, 1940); Franz Unterkircher, *Tacuinum sanitatis in medicina. Codex Vindobonensis series nova 2644 der Österreichischen Nationalbibliotek,* 2 vols., Codices Selecti, vols. VI–VI* (Graz: Akademische Druck- u. Verlagsanstalt, 1967).

them. *The Medieval Health Handbook* reproduces most of the illuminated subjects, with English translations of the prose summaries, though unfortunately it does not include any representations of *gaudium*, which is illustrated by a woman and a man standing in a garden setting and which has the following explanation:

> Gaiety. Its nature is an expression of vitality and of the warmth resulting therefrom. Preferable: when it leads to a pleasant feeling. Utility: good for sad and endangered persons. Harm: when experienced too often, it leads to death. Removal of harm: by living with wise men. Especially advantageous to people with a cold temperament, to the weak, in cold seasons, and in cold regions.[58]

We have seen most of these details in the regimens, though expressed somewhat differently. I assume the value of wise men in moderating excessive joy means not that they are uniformly morose but that they are likely to use reason to temper extreme passions. Because of the purely sequential arrangement of the *Tacuinum*, there is no comparative treatment of the emotions, and hence, in contrast to the regimens, no summary statement about the advantages of moderate cheerfulness. But its value is implied elsewhere, for entries on singing, playing music, and dancing discuss the usefulness of these activities in terms of curing illness and inducing pleasure.[59]

Still, the principal interest of the illustrated versions of the *Tacuinum* is the art. The illuminations not only depict the subjects but usually create entire scenes around them, ranging, as do the illustrations of the months in the *Très riches heures* of the Duke of Berry, from views of peasants at work to studies of the leisured life of the upper classes. The terse prose descriptions occupy only a small portion of each page and could not have been the *raison d'être* of the manuscripts. One suspects that their chief contribution to the health of the people who could afford to own them was the *gaudium temperatum* instilled from contemplating beautiful pictures.

[58]Trans. C. H. Talbot, in Unterkircher, II: 137, with Latin text. For the illustration see Unterkircher, I: f. 104v or Serra and Baglioni, I: cciv.
[59]Arano, pl. 66; Unterkircher, II: 135–36.

It is a quite different story when we turn to the fuller, unillustrated *Tacuinum*, which is much less well known but much more medically informative. It too is constructed in a highly schematic manner, with each item of the nonnaturals numbered and defined according to *iuuamentum, nocumentum,* and so on. But the full-length prose text also groups each item within a table, thereby providing a somewhat more hierarchical structure than the one-by-one enumeration of the illustrated versions, and surrounds each table with some general commentary on the principal topics treated therein. Every table also includes a section that gives a paragraph-length discussion of each item; this information is omitted in the short prose summaries of the illuminated manuscripts. Table XXXI, for example, deals with music and the accidents of the soul; it has entries for certain emotions and also for singing, instrumental music, and dancing. Table XXXIV treats not only the general category of motion and rest but also such specific forms of exercise as horseback riding, hunting, and wrestling.[60] For a discussion of literary performance, though, one must turn to another nonnatural.

Table XXXII presents, in addition to some items relating to repletion and evacuation, four entries on the subject of sleep and waking. Two, simply enough, are *somnus* and *vigiliae,* with the usual recommendations about not overdoing either; the third, *confabulationes in somnis,* talking in one's sleep, notes the relevance of the phenomenon to both rational and emotional concerns. The fourth item is *confabulator,* and before we try to define what that means, we need to begin with the *Tacuinum*'s. more general discussion of sleep and how it is induced. Sleep comes from humid vapors released by the food one has eaten; it is valuable for the rest it gives the body and the aid it gives to digestion by moving the natural heat from the exterior to the interior.

[60]I base this description on two closely related fourteenth-century manuscripts at the British Library, Sloane 3097 and Add. 38689, in both of which the *Tacuinum* follows Bernard Gordon's *Regimen sanitatis.* The Renaissance edition of the *Tacuinum* (Strasbourg, 1531) groups the general commentaries on each table at the front, and adds some small illustrations of each item at the bottom of pages, but otherwise follows the tabular arrangement of the unillustrated MSS.

If the digestion of food is not successful, but becomes corrupted, the vapors of the heat thus released ascend to the
brain and cause wakefulness. Hence one needs conversations,
which may encourage sleep, since sleeplessness dries out the
body, harms the members and the brain, confuses the senses,
and prompts acute illnesses. For this reason doctors advise
people with cold hearts to have stories told to them that provoke anger, and those with hot hearts stories that entail pity,
in order that their constitutions may be moderated. The reason that conversations produce sleep is that the ear receives,
without any natural movement, certain qualities of sense data,
the more delightful of which it takes in and transmits to the
imagination, and the imagination to reason. The reason marvels at that which is before it and then tires from this wonder,
so that from repeated wonder at the imaginings it has taken
in and is fixed on, the faculty of hearing ceases to bring
forward what has been spoken. Thus the apparatus of hearing, along with the other senses, pauses from the apprehen-
sion of sense data, and sleep is induced, the senses resting
from perceptions made while awake. . . . Hence that which is
spoken should be delightful, with a fitting verbal adornment,
so that one may sleep deeply and not have bad dreams.[61]

Conversation is a means to sleep, and since sleep is essential
to well-being, conversation has a medical value. The description of how it contributes to sleep involves the familiar medi-

[61] *Tacuinum sanitatis* (Strasbourg, 1531), pp. 29–30, with emendations from
B.L. Add. 38689, f. 89: "Et si forte cibus digeri non ualeat sed corrumpitur,
uapores calidi ab eo resoluti cerebrum ascendunt, propter quod uigiliae acci-
dunt. Indiget enim propter hoc confabulationibus, quibus somnus prouocetur,
eo quod non dormire corpus dessicat, membris et cerebro nocet, sensum [*ed.*
sensus] permiscet, acutas aegritudines commouet. Qua de caussa praecipiunt
medici habentibus corda frigida recitari [*ed.* recitare] coram eis historias iracun-
diam prouocantes et habentibus corda calida historias misericordiam conti-
nentes, ut temperentur [*ed.* obtemperentur] complexiones ipsorum. Et caussa
in hoc est quod confabulationes somnum prouocant eo quod auditus recipit
absque motu naturali qualitates sensibilium, et quia auditus recipit delectabilius
ipsorum uel eorum quae audit, et imaginationi transmittit; imaginatio uero
rationi. Ratio uero admiratur de praesentatis donec fatigetur ex admiratione
praedicta, ita quod ex multiplicata admiratione imaginabilium receptorum quibus intenta est uirtus ipsa audibilis audibilia non praesentat; propter quod
quiescit instrumentum auditus ab apprehensione sensibilium, cum aliis sensibus. Unde prouocatur somnus, ipsis sensibus quiescentibus ab apprehensioni-
bus in uigiliis factis. . . . Sermones ergo qui recitantur, delectabiles debent esse
ornatu uerborum, ut somni prolixi fiant et dormientes non uideant somnia
timorosa."

eval psychology of perception, from *sensibilia* to *imaginatio* to *ratio*.[62] The *Tacuinum* invokes the principle that delightful words lead to a pleasant activity of the mind because of its interest in sleep and dreaming; but the psychology would explain as well why didactic literary theory values surface pleasure as a means of leading an audience to an understanding of rational content. The passage as a whole provides an explanation for some of the observations in the *consilia* on the emotional effects of different types of reading, and like them its view of "conversation" seems to include literary material as well, as the references to stories and verbal elegance suggest. But to see better what kinds of discourse belong to *confabulatio* we may turn now to the *Tacuinum*'s description of *confabulator* as one of the hygienic items in its table on sleep and waking:

> *Confabulator:* A teller of stories should have good discernment in knowing the kind of fictions in which the soul takes delight, should be able to shorten or extend his presentation of stories as he may choose, and to decorate, amplify, and arrange them as is fitting. He should not alter his appearance in conversation,[63] nor should the purpose of the *confabulator* be interfered with by too much talking. A *confabulator* should be proper in manner and courtesy, be able to stay awake, be a good judge of discourses (not only histories of great princes but also delightful stories that provoke laughter), and be conscious of verses and rhymes, so that through these things a

[62]See Murray Wright Bundy, *The Theory of Imagination in Classical and Mediaeval Thought*, University of Illinois Studies in Language and Literature, 12 (Urbana: University of Illinois Press, 1927), and Salman, 308–16. For the role of wonder (*admiratio*) in the process, and its connections with learning and pleasure, see J. V. Cunningham's chapter in *Woe or Wonder: The Emotional Effect of Shakespearian Tragedy*, reprinted in *Tradition and Poetic Structure* (Denver: Alan Swallow, 1960), esp. pp. 204–9.

[63]One of the standard ecclesiastical complaints about entertainers is that they misuse their bodies through contortions, gestures, clothing, etc. See Baldwin, I: 199. I think the prescription that one not "mutet suam effigiem" may be a means of distinguishing the *confabulator* from the *histrio* and other less savory performers. Geoffrey of Vinsauf, in the section on delivery in his shorter *Documentum de modo dictandi et versificandi*, says that one should vary voice, facial expression, and gesture according to the material, but he is careful to stress that all three should be elegant and restrained, not like the gestures of an actor ("gestus histrionis"). Ed. Edmond Faral, *Les arts poétiques du XIIᵉ et du XIIIᵉ siècle* (rpt. Paris: Champion, 1962), p. 318. See also Hermannus Alemannus, pp. 32–33.

prince may gain an abundance of pleasures. For his digestion
will improve because of them, and his *spiritus* and blood will
be purified, and he will be freed from all sorts of troubling
thoughts, and his memory sharpened for the common talk
and occurrences that swell up around him.[64]

Literally, a *confabulator* is simply one who converses; in the
illustrated versions of the *Tacuinum*, which show people sitting
around a fire in various stages of attention, the description of
its usefulness and dangers implies nothing more than ordinary
conversation.[65] But the longer prose version, as Delisle notes,
turns into a brief treatise on how entertainers should recite
stories for the amusement of the nobility. The *Tacuinum* translator expects a *confabulator* to bring pleasure to his prince
through a complex of literary and rhetorical skills that are the
subject of many a medieval art of poetry. Both serious historical narrative and humorous stories qualify as *confabulatio*. Such
verbal pleasure, besides inducing sleep, will have a variety of
other physiological and psychological benefits. This passage
brings a hygienic perspective to an activity almost always discussed only in social terms; if medieval people seem so fond of
after-dinner entertainments, at least part of their interest may
be due to the reasoned medical view that such behavior has
value in maintaining health.

A well-known passage in Froissart gives us a portrait of the
confabulator at work. The author has come to visit Gaston Phoebus, Count of Foix:

[64]"Confabulator: debut autem recitator fabularum boni esse intellectus in
scientiis ipsius generis fabularum in quibus delectatur animus, potens abbre-
viare et prolongare, cum voluerit, fabularum sermones, ipsos ornare, con-
tinuare et ordinare ut convenit. Nec mutet suam effigiem in ipsa confabula-
tione, nec prolixitate sermonum varietur confabulatoris intentio. Sit vero
confabulator ipse boni modi et bone curialitatis, potens sustinere vigilias,
scrutator sermonum, historiarum regum et sermonum delectabilium et risum
provocantium, et versuum et rithmorum conscius, ut propter ea rex assumat
plenitudinem gaudiorum. Nam propter hec melioratur digestio ejus, et mun-
dificabuntur spiritus et sanguis ipsorum, et vacabit a variis cogitationibus, et
efficitur bone memorie in rumoribus et eventibus supereminentibus ei." Ed.
Delisle, 534, from a number of Bibliothèque Nationale MSS; the British
Library MSS have a few different readings, the most interesting being "animus sapientis" for "animus" in the first sentence. Add. 38689, f. 89; Sloane
3097, f. 94.
[65]Arano, pl. 140; Unterkircher, I: f.100v and II: 132.

.... I had brought with me a book, which I made at the contemplation of Wenceslas of Boeme, duke of Luxembourg and of Brabant, which book was called the Meliador, containing all the songs, ballads, rondeaux and virelays, which the gentle duke had made in his time, which by imagination I had gathered together; which book the earl of Foix was glad to see, and every night after supper I read thereon to him, and while I read, there was none durst speak any word, because he would I should be well understood, wherein he took great solace, and when it came to any matters of question, then he would speak to me, not in Gascon but in good fair French.[66]

Froissart here exemplifies a number of characteristics specified in the *Tacuinum:* having arranged his material, he reads it to a prince after dinner while everyone else has been quieted down so that the featured speaker may be properly heard and understood. Froissart answers questions in the process, as the reading turns into something more like ordinary conversation. And, of course, the result of the performance is "soulas" for his host. This scene, doubtless typical of the way much medieval literature was presented, does not depict what we know today as a poetry reading; it gives us rather the reading of poems as part of conversational entertainment.

Don Juan Manuel, the fourteenth-century Castilian nobleman and author, confirms that the *Tacuinum*'s medical perspective on stories and sleep was a part of conventional literary theorizing. In one dedication, he notes that he has often been burdened with cares, leading to sleeplessness and resulting in a loss of bodily health, which he remedies by having some books

---

[66]II, c. 26, in the translation of Lord Berners, *The Chronicles of Froissart,* ed. G. C. Macaulay (London: Macmillan, 1904), p. 329. Text in *Oeuvres de Froissart. Chroniques,* ed. Kervyn de Lettenhove, vol. 11 (Brussels, 1870), p. 85: "je avoye avecques moy porté ung livre, lequel j'avoie fait à la requeste et contemplation de monseigneur Wincelant de Boesme, duc de Luxembourg et de Brabant, et sont contenus ou dit livre qui s'appelle de Meliader toutes les chansons, ballades, rondeaulx et virelais que le gentil duc fist en son temps: lesquelles choses, parmy l'ymagination que j'avoie de dittier et de ordonner le livre, le conte de Fois vit moult voulentiers. Et toutes nuits après souper je luy en lisoie, mais en lisant nulluy n'osoit sonner mot, ne parler, car il vouloit que je fuisse bien entendu. Certes, aussi il prendoit grant soulas au bien entendre, et quant il chéoit aucune chose où il vouloit mettre argument, trop voulentiers en parloit à moy, non pas en son gascon, mais en bon et beau franchois."

or stories read to him to alleviate his worries. Elsewhere he states that such reading will enable one either to escape from troublesome thoughts and fall asleep or, failing that, to learn something useful.[67] He seems to be thinking principally in terms of didactic material, but his interest apparently lies less in intellectual growth than in psychological comfort. In the context of reading to sleep, the question of pleasure or profit becomes subordinated to the immediate hygienic need; hence the *Tacuinum* would have the *confabulator* versed in everything from histories to comic tales. What counts is what most pleases and thereby unburdens one's prince.

What the *Tacuinum* says about the value of listening to stories would apply equally well to reading them, and its analysis of how the mind works on literary material from the point of view of falling asleep receives a witty exemplification in the early portions of Chaucer's *Book of the Duchess*. The narrator begins by pointing out, with much repetitiousness, that his central problem is that "I may nat slepe."[68] He is well aware of the medical dangers of this condition, which the *Tacuinum* and the regimens make clear. Since no earthly creature can live without sleep, he thus fears death, and this concomitant problem aggravates his condition; his mind is "mased" and depressed, and in this dulled state all life becomes flat, meaningless. He knows that such an existence is "agaynes kynde" (16), and that phrase may well suggest the *res contra naturam*, for the narrator's condition is in medical terms pathological.[69] He speculates on the cause of his sleeplessness, a mysterious eight-year sickness that is usually interpreted as love-longing, but after a few lines returns to his malady and how he tried to remedy it:

> So when I saw I might not slepe
> Til now late, this other night,
> Upon my bed I sat upright
> And bad oon reche me a book,

[67]Quoted and discussed, with additional evidence, by Ian Macpherson, "Don Juan Manuel: The Literary Process," *SP*, 70 (1973), 6–8.

[68]Line 3; also 5, 21–23, 25, 31, 44. Ed. F. N. Robinson, *The Works of Geoffrey Chaucer*, 2nd ed. (Boston: Houghton Mifflin, 1957). All subsequent references to Chaucer will be to line numbers of this edition.

[69]Cf. John M. Hill, "The *Book of the Duchess*, Melancholy, and That Eight-Year Sickness," *Chaucer Review*, 9 (1974), 35–50.

> A romaunce, and he it me tok
> To rede, and drive the night away;
> For me thoughte it beter play
> Then play either at ches or tables. [44–51]

The image of a man awake in bed is precisely that used in the illustrated versions of the *Tacuinum* to depict *vigiliae*,[70] though the parallel is probably due less to specific iconographic intent than to the lack of chairs and sofas in medieval bedrooms. The narrator reads to drive the night away, to pass the time, preferring literary entertainment to chess or backgammon. Later we will see Boccaccio's storytellers favoring narratives over board games for explicit, and I think seriously meant, psychological reasons. Chaucer's comparison is probably not as surprising or sly as it may seem to a modern audience, for, as we have often noted, narratives were perceived in the context of public or private entertainment and grouped with other similar sources of "play" such as music, dancing, and games. The narrator has "fables" of ancient "poets" brought to him because they are "beter play," more fully satisfying entertainment, not because they are great literature. Ovid fulfills a function now occupied by the late show on television or by the mystery story at one's bedside. At least that is how the narrator perceives it, and if ultimately we find that there is more to the story of Ceys and Alcione than he realizes, and by implication more to Ovid than just play, nevertheless we ought to see his reasoning here as perfectly natural.

The fables of poets are "To rede, and for to be in minde" (55). "Be" is not a forceful verb, but the line is more important than it may seem at first glance. The stories, once read, are to be held in the mind, retained by the memory so that the reason may have use of them. The line alerts us to think in terms of profit as well as pleasure, in the same way that the Canterbury pilgrims' belief that the *Knight's Tale* is "worthy for to drawen to memorie" (A 3112) signals the importance of that story. The speaker's immediate concern, however, is to find something interesting, and he does: "a tale / That me thoughte a wonder thing" (60–61). It is a story of love, death, and grief, and it

---

[70]Unterkircher, I: f. 101v; Toesca, f. 91.

happens to involve Morpheus, the god of sleep, prompting the narrator to think about the possibility of paying for his services in order to cure his insomnia:

> Whan I had red thys tale wel,
> And overloked hyt everydel,
> Me thoghte wonder yf hit were so;
> For I had never herd speke, or tho,
> Of noo goddes that koude make
> Men to slepe, ne for to wake;
> For I ne knew never god but oon.
> And in my game I sayde anoon—
> And yet me lyst ryght evel to pleye—. . . . [231–38]

In his morose state he is not inclined to be playful, yet somehow the fiction triggers a spirit of "game," an amused and amusing flight of thought, his offer of a feather-bed and other rewards to Morpheus or anybody else who can make him sleep. No sooner are the words out than "sodeynly, I nyste how, / Such a lust anoon me took / To slepe, that ryght upon my book / Y fil aslepe" (272–75). And in sleep he dreams a "wonderful" dream that is the center of the poem.

Much has been written about dream-vision poetry in the Middle Ages and Chaucer's relationship to it. Scholars acknowledge his innovativeness in using a literary text as a structural component in his early dream visions. But innovations have contributing causes, and however original and humorous Chaucer may be in describing his means of falling asleep, it is worth noting that his invention in the *Book of the Duchess* seems predicated on a psychology of reading and sleeping that is explained in the *Tacuinum*. From the sense data of the story Chaucer derives "wonder," the "admiratio" which the *Tacuinum* says is involved in reason's contemplation of the most interesting things that the imagination presents to it. Intent upon this wonder (having read the tale "wel" he went back and "overloked hyt everydel"), the narrator becomes actively involved in speculating on what he has found "delectabilius" in the story, the new knowledge of a god of sleep.[71] Thus, even though

[71]Lines 233–37. On wonder as a desire for knowledge, and as causative of pleasure because of the hope of attaining that knowledge, see Aquinas, *ST*, I–II, q. 32, a. 8, trans. Cunningham, pp. 207–9.

reflecting on the story's pathos causes him sorrow the following day (95–100), his mind's involvement at this point in one of its more delightful aspects has led him to a livelier, healthier state. The man burdened with a "sorwful ymagynacioun" (14) is now, thanks to Ovid's story, at least somewhat released from his "cogitationibus" and able to apply his mind "in my game." His sudden sleep is humorous, of course, because it suggests that his request has been miraculously answered by Morpheus. But it has really been answered by a fiction, which has activated his thinking through wonder and filled his brain with pleasant rather than depressing thoughts; with his mind fixed on those ideas, his senses rest. The phrase beginning with line 273 means "such a desire to sleep quickly seized me," but its syntax and the fact that "lust" also means "pleasure" make a second reading tempting if not likely: literary pleasure has indeed brought him to sleep.

The psychology of reader response does not form a large part of the *Book of the Duchess* and is not delineated with precision. Chaucer is after other, and more important, things. But the suggestions of the *Tacuinum's* logic in regard to stories and sleep give coherence to a section of the poem where Chaucer's humor has not always seemed consonant with its larger purposes. If we think of the playfulness as a therapeutic response to melancholy induced by the delights of fiction, its curative nature makes it a fitting part of the preparation for the dream itself.[72] For if Ovid is Chaucer's *confabulator,* then the narrator is the Black Knight's, and Chaucer John of Gaunt's. The narrator's role in the dream is to lead the knight to wholeness, to let him "ese [his] herte" by telling of his sorrow (553–57), and he does not speak except to further that end. But the work as a whole is all Chaucer's speech, and it is meant to comfort a prince. The relevance of the narrator's sorrow and the story of Ceys and Alcione to the remainder of the poem has been argued fully in many places. It requires the reader of the *Book of the Duchess* to see that there is more to Ovid's story than information about a god of sleep. Chaucer's focus on the dynamics of a man reading and thinking about a work of litera-

---

[72]Cf. Hill, 44–45, who views the narrator's response as a "defense" mechanism to avoid contemplating the more sorrowful aspects of Ovid's story.

ture, a man who benefits from a story even though his wonder
is fixed on one of its less important aspects, is thus both a
means of alerting his audience to what his poem asks of them
and an expression of hope for what it might be able to achieve
for the Duke of Lancaster.

To summarize very briefly the medical view of literature discussed in this chapter: literary delight is one species of the
delectatio that results from attaining a desired good; it instills
gaudium in the reader or listener, which when appropriately
moderated is the ideal emotional state, useful not only in preserving health but also in attaining the finest disposition of
mind and body. Thus literary pleasure promotes physical and
mental well-being. This is, to be sure, an argument made by
physicians, and when we hear them in regimens and *consilia*
recommending entertainment as a means of inducing cheerfulness, we may well ask whether their view of literature is anything more than one profession's use of an art form for its own
ends, whether some brief allusions in manuals of health really
have much to do with literary thought. But when we hear
scholars and theologians discuss theatrics as a remedy for
bodily weakness, and Laurent de Premierfait claim that the
Decameron will reinvigorate the Duke of Berry's *spiritus* and
hence prolong his life; when we see Don Juan Manuel explicitly
and Chaucer implicitly invoke the principles of *confabulatio* as a
means of unburdening the mind and promoting sleep, then we
have evidence for an answer to those questions, one that later
material in this book will confirm: the hygienic justification of
fiction is an important aspect of medieval literary theory.

3

The Recreational Justification

In the *Divine Comedy,* Dante uses the image of a bow and arrow to represent not only physical movement but also mental movement or inclination. In *Paradiso* XIII, 105, Aquinas refers to "the arrow of my intention." In *Purgatorio* XXV, 17–18, Virgil sees that Dante is eager to ask questions and tells him to "discharge the bow of your speech." But the ultimate archer is God, as Beatrice indicates when she explains to Dante that they are ascending to heaven by "the virtue of that bowstring . . . which aims at a joyful target whatsoever it shoots."[1] Arrows fly where archers aim; impelled by God, man's rational soul seeks its mark in union with Him, though it may not always fly straight or forcefully. Like the familiar medieval image of pilgrimage, the image of the bow and arrow is particularly apt for a culture and an author that perceive human life as a movement toward a goal that lies beyond. Both are teleologically oriented: you travel to get somewhere, you shoot to hit something. Deflection from the goal is error, hesitation truancy.

On occasion, Dante alters the image of bent bow and flying arrow in order to depict mental relaxation or breakdown. When he encounters Cacciaguida in Paradise, his ancestor is praising God in ways beyond mortal understanding; but the "bow" of the blessed soul's love becomes "relaxed" enough so that his speech can reach "the mark of our intellect" (XV, 43–45). In two other instances the relaxation of the bowstring im-

[1] *Par.* I, 125–26. Trans. Charles S. Singleton, *The Divine Comedy,* 3 vols. in 6 (Princeton: Princeton University Press, 1970–75). For commentary on the archery in this passage, see Singleton's notes to these lines and to line 119.

ages confusion or dereliction. Dante's breakdown when Beatrice demands a confession is compared to the breaking of a crossbow's cord when the force is too great and the consequent loss of power in the arrow (*Purg.* XXXI, 16–18). And when Marco Lombardo contrasts his generation to the corruption of Dante's, he does so by tersely noting that he "loved that worth at which all now have unbent the bow" (*Purg.* XVI, 47–48). For Dante, the bow ought always to be steadily bent; the target is heavenly felicity, and humankind must not slack in the effort to attain it. His imagery of bows and arrows, though not unique to him, is singularly appropriate to the directedness of the *Divine Comedy*, to its step-by-step movement from earthly confusion toward heavenly surety, to a place where the arrow of the soul can find its mark.

But not everyone in the Middle Ages had such an unyielding commitment to the tensed bow. In fact, the most popular image from archery throughout the period (aside from Cupid's arrows) makes a quite different point. In its most substantial and one of its most influential forms, it appears as an "old story" told by Abbot Abraham, one of the desert fathers whom John Cassian purportedly visited and whose wisdom he recorded, in the early fifth century, in a collection known at the *Collationes,* or *Conferences*:

> It is said that the blessed John, while he was gently stroking a partridge with his hands suddenly saw a philosopher approaching him in the garb of a hunter, who was astonished that a man of so great fame and reputation should demean himself to such paltry and trivial amusements, and said: "Can you be that John, whose great and famous reputation attracted me also with the greatest desire for your acquaintance? Why then do you occupy yourself with such poor amusements?" To whom the blessed John: "What is it," said he, "that you are carrying in your hand?" The other replied: "a bow." "And why," said he, "do you not always carry it everywhere bent?" To whom the other replied: "It would not do, for the force of its stiffness would be relaxed by its being continually bent, and it would be lessened and destroyed, and when the time came for it to send stouter arrows after some beast, its stiffness would be lost by the excessive and continuous strain, and it would be impossible for the more powerful

bolts to be shot." "And, my lad," said the blessed John, "do
not let this slight and short relaxation of my mind disturb
you, as unless it sometimes relieved and relaxed the rigour of
its purpose by some recreation, the spirit would lose its spring
owing to the unbroken strain, and would be unable when
need required, implicitly to follow what was right."[2]

Abraham is explaining that even though monks may wish
always to be solitary, occasional visits from their brethren have
advantages for both body and soul: "unless the strain and tension of their mind is lessened by the relaxation of some
changes, they fall either into coldness of spirit, or at any rate
into a most dangerous state of bodily health" (c. 20). The purpose of the Conference as a whole, though, is to promote the
renunciation of the world; the defense of recreation enters as
part of an explanation why anchorites should remain in the
desert with their brethren and not return to their homes. The
image of the bent bow appears as well in the *Verba seniorum*, a
collection of sayings of the desert fathers, this time imputed to
St. Anthony. Anthony's relaxation takes the form of "conversing with some brethren" rather than petting a partridge, and
he makes his point by asking the hunter to shoot a number of
arrows. "The hunter said: If I bend my bow all the time it will
break. Abbot Anthony replied: So it is also in the work of God.
If we push ourselves beyond measure, the brethren will soon
collapse. It is right, therefore, from time to time, to relax their
efforts."[3]

The *Verba seniorum* and the *Collationes* were popular texts in
the Middle Ages and gave the image of the bent bow, the mind
that cannot survive continual strain, widespread currency.[4]

[2]Conference XXIV, c. 21, trans. Edgar C. S. Gibson, in *A Select Library of
Nicene and Post-Nicene Fathers*, 2d series, vol. 11 (rpt. Grand Rapids, Mich.:
William B. Eerdmans, 1964), pp. 540–41.

[3]*The Wisdom of the Desert*, trans. Thomas Merton (Norfolk, Conn.: New Directions, 1960), p. 63.

[4]Bruno of Cologne uses it to justify taking pleasure in the delights of nature
in order to renew one's spirit for the contemplation of God; trans. R. W.
Southern, *The Making of the Middle Ages* (1953; rpt. New Haven: Yale University
Press, 1961), p. 168. The *Alphabetum narrationum*, an alphabetical collection of
exempla for use in preaching, includes both the John and Anthony stories; see
An Alphabet of Tales, ed. M. M. Banks, EETS o.s. 126, 127 (1904, 1905; rpt.
Millwood, N.Y.: Kraus Reprint, 1972), pp. 5–6, 274. John's version appears

That justifications of relaxation appeared for over a thousand years in the mouths of the desert fathers may seem an interesting historical irony, but it may also serve to indicate that even in some of its most ascetic moments medieval culture remained aware of the value of recreation. As V. A. Kolve has said, the story of the hunter's bow that needs release from tension "is one of the central images by which the Middle Ages understood the human psyche."[5] Later we will see it invoked in specifically literary contexts, but for now it may stand as an introduction to the subject of this chapter: the idea of recreation and its pervasiveness in later medieval thought. The concept is independent of poetics; once we have examined it fully, we will see in the following chapter how literary criticism and advertisement appeal to it, as well as to the hygienic argument, not in an attempt to create a separate category of aesthetic experience but as a means of giving psychological and ethical value to the enjoyment derived from storytelling.

Aristotle and the Secular Tradition

To write a thorough history of the idea of recreation, from classical through medieval thought, would require a book in itself. The closest thing we have to that book is the first chapter of Joachim Suchomski's *"Delectatio" und "Utilitas,"* which includes the idea of recreation in its survey of Christian attitudes toward jest and entertainment from the beginning of the Middle Ages through Aquinas. This chapter does not attempt to duplicate Suchomski's chronological survey but to consider some of the more important texts that influenced late medieval thinking on the subject. All the elements of the idea in its simplest form are present in the stories of John and Anthony, as they are in this verse from the immensely popular *Disticha Catonis:*

---

under his name but is also cross-listed under the heading "Recreacio interdum vtilis est religiosis" (p. 447; see also the following entry). G. G. Coulton cites some other instances of the image in *Five Centuries of Religion,* 4 vols. (Cambridge: Cambridge University Press, 1923–50), I: 532.

[5]*The Play Called Corpus Christi* (Stanford, Calif.: Stanford University Press, 1966), p. 129.

Interpone tuis interdum gaudia curis,
ut possis animo quemvis sufferre laborem.

Sumtyme among thi bysynesse
Melle [mix] solace, gamen and ioyowsnesse,
That thou may the lyghtlyker
With mery thouht thi trauayll ber.[6]

The causal relationship between the first line and the second is the key to understanding the ethical sanction of recreation. Human labor and intention direct themselves to an end, but like the bow the mind and body cannot sustain the pressure of unrelieved pursuit of that end. Relaxation in the form of *gaudia* offers a temporary release, enabling people subsequently to return to their work and continue it more effectively.

To understand the connections between relaxation and recreation more precisely, and to see the recreational argument in its most fully developed form, we must turn to Aristotle's *Nicomachean Ethics* and to the medieval commentaries on it. Here the earlier, highly limited ecclesiastical acceptance of entertainment becomes broadened and more tolerant; the influence of the *Ethics* helps shape a more liberalized view of recreation in the later Middle Ages, one usually expressed in secular, ethical terms rather than in explicitly Christian ones.[7]

[6]III, 6. Ed. Marcus Boas and H. J. Botschuyver (Amsterdam: North-Holland, 1952), p. 159. The Middle English translation was edited by Max Förster in *Englische Studien*, 36 (1906), 33. Its three equivalents to *gaudia* are relevant to understanding some of the literary terminology we will encounter in the next chapter. The distich appears frequently: it is in *Piers Plowman*, B text, XII, 20–25; the *Libro de buen amor*, c. 44; and is incorporated into the Anthony story in the *Alphabet of Tales* (n. 4). We will see it often throughout this book. The stanza advising "recreacion" in the "Mumming of the Seven Philosophers," ed. R. H. Robbins, *Secular Lyrics of the XIVth and XVth Centuries*, 2d ed. (Oxford: Clarendon Press, 1955), p. 112, is little more than an expanded paraphrase of the distich. For background material on the *Disticha*, see Richard Hazelton, "The Christianization of 'Cato': The *Disticha Catonis* in the Light of Late Mediaeval Commentaries," *Mediaeval Studies*, 19 (1957), 157–73.

[7]Cf. Suchomski, pp. 55–61. A full-scale history of the impact of the *Ethics*, not only on philosophy but on popular social and moral thought, remains to be written. For documentation of its appearance in academic circles, see Gordon Leff, *Paris and Oxford Universities in the Thirteenth and Fourteenth Centuries* (New York: John Wiley, 1968), passim. Its broader diffusion occurred through such channels as encyclopedias like Brunetto Latini's *Trésor* and treatises on moral behavior. The Aristotelian mean emerges as a frequent locus of value in late medieval writing; for one specific case, not concerned with recreation but useful for its evidence of the *Ethics's* influence, see Thomas H. Bestul, *Satire and*

In the *Ethics*, which for the sake of convenience we may consider in the text preserved in the commentary of Thomas Aquinas, Aristotle discusses the relationship between happiness and pleasure, and among others one specific form of pleasure, amusement. He concludes that for a good man "happiness does not consist in amusement (non in ludo ergo felicitas)," even though many people seem to desire it. He explains the proper relationship between desire for entertainment and virtuous behavior by making the former an instrument of the latter:

> to play in order to work better is the correct rule according to Anacharsis. This is because amusement is a kind of relaxation (requiei enim assimilatur ludus) that men need, since they are incapable of working continuously. Certainly relaxation is not an end (non utique finis requies), for it is taken as a means to further activity.

Hence, although "felicitas," the highest form of pleasure, involves delight, it is the joy that comes with virtuous activity, not the joy that comes with entertainment (cum gaudio, sed non in ludo).[8]

The commentary of Aquinas on this passage elaborates on Aristotle's reasoning; two points are pertinent to our interests. Aristotle's example of people's desire for amusement is that "tyranni" enjoy having witty people around them. Aquinas explains that Aristotle calls such "potentes" tyrants because they are more interested in their personal pleasures than in the public good. The fact that "princes devote their leisure" to amusements does not necessarily make recreation a cause of happiness. The shift from *tyranni* to *potentes* locates the discussion in the medieval world of princes and their entertainments, which, as we saw in the previous chapter, includes storytelling among other forms. Second, Aquinas stresses that such amusements ("delectationes ludicrae") belong to the category of bodily delights ("delectationes corporales") and hence cannot

---

Allegory in Wynnere and Wastoure (Lincoln: University of Nebraska Press, 1974), pp. 5–13. See also below, Chap. 5, n. 22.

[8]*Nicomachean Ethics*, X, 6. Trans. C. I. Litzinger, O.P., *Commentary on the* Nicomachean Ethics, 2 vols. (Chicago: Henry Regnery, 1964), II: 900–1. Text in *In decem libros Ethicorum Aristotelis ad Nicomachum*, ed. R. M. Spiazzi, 3d ed. (Turin: Marietti, 1964), L. X, lectio IX, p. 538. Henceforth I will cite page numbers of these editions.

pertain to properly human felicity since they appeal only to the
animal part of the soul (Litzinger, II: 903–4; Spiazzi, pp. 539–
40). This view of *ludus* as a source of bodily pleasure is consistent with the medical approach toward theatrics of other medieval thinkers. The particular kind of *gaudium* that comes *in
ludo* seems implicitly to be the cheerfulness of disposition which
conserves health. Here, as in other discussions of recreation,
the physiological understanding of delight tends to be assumed
rather than argued. The recreational approach usually presup-
poses the medical rationale discussed in Chapter 2 and spends
its time more on psychological and moral considerations.

These considerations occur in most detail in *Ethics* IV, 8.
Although both author and commentator are careful to distinguish pleasure in entertainment from true felicity, they do accord the former a legitimate place in human activity, as Aquinas spells out most fully:

> But amusement does have an aspect of good inasmuch as it is
> useful for human living. As man sometimes needs to give his
> body rest from labors, so also he sometimes needs to rest his
> soul from mental strain that ensues from his application to
> serious affairs. This is done by amusement. For this reason
> Aristotle says that, since there should be some relaxation for
> man from the anxieties and cares of human living and social
> intercourse by means of amusement—thus amusement has an
> aspect of useful good—it follows that in amusement there can
> be a certain agreeable association of men with one another, so
> they may say and hear such things as are proper and in the
> proper way. [Litzinger, I: 368]

Psychological needs prompt ethical concerns, the question of
propriety in entertainment. Aquinas follows Aristotle in distinguishing a mean, a proper degree of interest in amusement,
from two extremes: the excessive desire to create laughter (buffoonery), and the excessive harshness in those "who are not
mellowed by amusing recreation" (boorishness). The mean is
the virtue of *eutrapelia*, wittiness. This moral virtue, one of
those concerned with words and actions in social relationships
(outlined in *Ethics* II, 7), reveals itself not only in the moderate
frequency with which one takes amusement but also in the
nature of one's subjects and language: "It is proper to men of

this sort to narrate and listen to such amusing incidents (talia ludicra) as become a decent and liberal man who possesses a soul free from slavish passions" (Litzinger, I: 368–70; Spiazzi, pp. 236–37). Throughout this discussion the context is one of polite social conversation; Aquinas seems to be thinking in terms of informal jests and jokes. But we may remember from Chapter 1 that *ludicra* is also Gundissalinus's term for the works of poets that please rather than profit and that manuals of health group a variety of forms of discourse within concepts of *conversatio* and *confabulatio*. It is certainly possible that Aquinas's discussion of the virtue of *eutrapelia* implicitly includes story-telling; its principal relevance, though, is its delineation of a virtue connected with entertainment.

Aquinas pursues this matter more extensively in the *Summa theologica*, II–II, as part of a discussion of temperance and the moderation of bodily desires. Question 168 deals with modesty in bodily actions and is devoted principally to actions and speech made in play. Article 2 asserts that there can be a moral virtue *in ludis*, arguing that the soul, like the body, tires when strained excessively, in great part because intellectual effort requires the use of powers that operate through the body. Contemplation is most tiring of all, since it demands that a person rise beyond the "sensibilia" he is naturally attracted to, thereby inducing greater fatigue. Just as physical rest repairs bodily exhaustion, "so psychological tiredness is eased by resting the soul. . . . pleasure is rest for the soul (quies autem animae est delectatio)." Pleasure is to the mind what sleep is to the body.[9] Here Aquinas retells Cassian's story of the bent bow, but his own sense of *ludus* includes verbal as well as physical play: "Those words and deeds in which nothing is sought beyond the soul's pleasure are called playful or humorous (ludicra vel jocosa), and it is necessary to make use of them at times for solace of soul (ad quamdam animae quietem)."

This is the essence of the recreational argument. Play offers

[9]This analogy is pursued at greater length in a commentary on the *Ethics* by John Buridan, *Questiones Joannis Buridani super decem libros ethicorum aristotelis ad nicomachum* (Paris, 1513; rpt. Frankfurt: Minerva G.M.B.H., 1968), L. IV, q. 19; Utrum eutrapelia sit virtus moralis, ff. 88–89. Aquinas's discussion in q. 168 appears also in the *Summa theologica* of Antoninus of Florence, Pars IV, tit. IV, c. X, §3, cols. 165–66.

delight; delight is rest; and rest is necessary. Hence, to the objection that play cannot be virtuous since it is directed to no end but itself, whereas virtuous action involves choice directed to something else, Aquinas responds: "The activity of playing looked at specifically in itself is not ordained to a further end, yet the pleasure we take therein serves as recreation and rest for the soul (ad aliquam animae recreationem et quietem), and accordingly when this be well-tempered, application to play is lawful." Play is justified because of its value as recreation. *Jocosa verba* may have no intention beyond amusement, but the very amusement they provide has psychological usefulness, and such activity comes within the province of ethics insofar as it needs proper rational control. As Aquinas puts it in the *responsio* of the third article, "playful and jesting words and actions lie within the field of reason."

Article 3 concerns the sinfulness of excessive play. One of the reasons advanced why *superfluitas ludi* ought not be considered sinful is that actors, *histriones,* spend all their time playing but are not therefore in a state of sin. To this Aquinas replies that as long as they play moderately, without scurrilous words or behavior and at the proper times, their art is indeed lawful. For although they do not have another profession, they do engage in "other serious and virtuous activities" in the eyes of God, such as praying and being charitable. Aquinas accepts the principle that "the acting profession, the purpose of which is to put on shows for our enjoyment (ad solatium hominibus exhibendum), is not unlawful in itself." This "solatium" is that which Bonaventure and others impute to theatrics and which physicians explain as contributing to the desirable psychological state of temperate cheerfulness. By discussing the function of performance in the context of the morality of play, Aquinas extends the conception of legitimate recreation to kinds of discourse more elaborate than spontaneous jokes and witticisms.

In question 168 Aquinas sets the limits of legitimate play. He cites Cicero and Ambrose to point out that the "delectatio" offered by amusement must not be indecent, must not dissipate all "gravitas animae," and must be ordered according to the proper circumstances— -time, place, person (a. 2, resp.). In his discussion of whether insufficient playing is sinful, he follows Aristotle in arguing that "too little playing is less wrong than too much" and suggesting that only a little recreation "suffices to give flavour to living, just as a little salt suffices for food" (a. 4, resp.). The dietary analogy is revealing and reminds us that behind the ethical concerns about proper play lies the physical reality of a body and soul needing recuperation. The entire question in fact is part of a discussion of the need to control bodily desires. The moral problem is to give play its due without turning it into an end in itself; the idea of recreation, predicated on an Aristotelian ethics, accomplishes just that: it legitimizes entertainment on psychological grounds, gives it a human value that is far from negligible, but at the same time puts it into a hierarchy of values that transcend it. For work is more important than play, and the felicity of contemplation a greater pleasure than recreational enjoyment.

It would be possible, but certainly not refreshing, to explore the idea of recreation further in Aquinas and in later discussions of the *Ethics* such as John Buridan's *Questiones* and Nicole Oresme's translation and commentary. Nor is it necessary, since the basic arguments do not change. But one other philosophic defense of recreation is worth some attention, since it incorporates so many central ideas and commonplaces. In the section on moral philosophy of the *Opus majus,* Roger Bacon explains at some length why people must take recreation:

> Since according to Scripture the body which is corrupted burdens the soul, and our earthly habitation is depressing to the sense that is cognizant of many things, for peace of mind, therefore, human frailty must necessarily relax the mind at times through the comforts and recreations necessary for the body (solacia et recreaciones corpori necessarias). For otherwise the spirit becomes anxious, dull, fitful, and gloomier than it should be, languid with the tedium of goodness, complaining, and prone to frequent fits of impatience and anger.

Here, as elsewhere, the need for refreshment is tied to man's frailty; it is a concession to corruption. But it is a worthwhile, indeed a necessary, one, and Bacon goes on to note that even the holiest men took time out from their ascetic routine, citing Cassian on John the Evangelist and putting the story of the bent bow into the mouth of St. Benedict. Bacon then turns to an important classical source for the idea of recreation, Seneca's *De tranquillitate animi,* citing in passing the first line of Cato's famous distich. He quotes Seneca at length, who includes in his list of "solacia" such activities as giving the mind over "ad iocos," drinking wine, and dancing. Such "animis remissio" results in a more acute mind later, whereas uninterrupted strain leads to "languor," just as a field will lose its fertility if it is constantly forced to be productive. Seneca notes that people are naturally attracted to "lusus" and "iocus" but warns against the dangers of overindulgence. Bacon repeats his examples of properly ordered recreations—the establishment of certain holidays each month, the refusal to conduct business after a certain hour each day. He discusses wine, its relaxing effects and its association with poetic madness. Even though Bacon is working primarily from Seneca rather than from Aristotle, which produces a somewhat greater emphasis on private indulgence than on public moderation, his view of recreation is essentially similar to what we have seen in Aquinas: it is an activity dangerous if pursued extensively but necessary at times and useful when taken with restraint.[10]

At this point some distinctions may be in order. The idea of recreation is in one sense an attempt to fit play into an ethical framework. It invites consideration of the idea of play itself, which has been the topic of some well-known theoretical treatments, particularly Johan Huizinga's *Homo ludens,* and has fostered a number of literary studies which rely in one way or another on theories of play and game, one of the most notable being Kolve's interpretation of the cycle drama (pp. 8–32). In some respects medieval views of play are reasonably close to modern ones, but in general they tend to treat the subject from an ethical perspective rather than from a psychological, sociological, or anthropological one. I prefer to stay with medieval theorizing here, especially since its point of view, as we will see, is more directly related to medieval literary claims and criticism than are modern play and game theories.

[10]Trans. Robert Belle Burke, *The* Opus majus *of Roger Bacon,* 2 vols. (Philadelphia: University of Pennsylvania Press, 1928), II: 783–86. Text in *Moralis philosophia,* ed. F. Delorme and E. Massa (Turin: Thesaurus Mundi, 1953), pp. 181–84.

We have already seen how broad a range of activities the term "ludus" encompasses, as does the modern word "play"— depending on the context, it may refer to sports, theatrical performances, games, entertainment in general, or any words or actions that can be distinguished from normal "serious" behavior ("I said it in play"). Medieval theorizing recognizes different types of play, principally on the basis of motives or ends. Aquinas argues a threefold *distinctio,* which Robert Holcot echoes in his popular commentary on the Book of Wisdom: a "base and improper play" that is sinful, a "play of devotion and spiritual joy," and a "play of human consolation, the mean of which is called *eutrapelia.*" The *Summa theologica* attributed to Alexander of Hales offers a fourfold classification of dance and play: one sinful, one spiritual, one taken for the recreation of human nature ("ad naturae recreationem"), one taken for physical exercise.[11] Aside from this separate category for exercise, the distinctions are parallel, recognizing a vicious play that proceeds from base motives, a virtuous kind that proceeds from spiritual joyfulness (here the example is always David's dancing in front of the ark), and a kind of play intended for people's *recreatio* or *consolatio.* Holcot's reference to the virtue of *eutrapelia* in connection with this type makes it obvious that he is thinking of the kind of entertainment discussed in the *Ethics* and that the morality of this sort of play depends on the degree to which one adheres to the mean in its use.

We may use the distinction between recreative and spiritual play to contrast briefly the idea of recreation and the idea of leisure. Superficially they are closely related in that both refer to a state of nonwork. But recreation, as we have seen, is always discussed as the necessary rest to enable man to return to work;

[11]For Holcot and the source in Aquinas see Siegfried Wenzel, "An Early Reference to a Corpus Christi Play," *Modern Philology,* 74 (1977), 390–91. The fifteenth-century *Summa angelica,* s.v. *ludus,* echoes this distinction, defining play as either "spiritualis," "humanus," or "diabolicus." Human play is not sinful when done in the proper circumstances and when intended for honest recreation or the exercise of body or mind. (Lyons, 1519), ff. 289v–90v. For Alexander of Hales, I cite the Quaracchi edition (4 vols., 1924–48), II, Pars II, inq. III, tract. III, sect. III, q. 1., c. 1, solutio, p. 471. Such distinctions are useful, incidentally, in understanding the examples of and attitudes toward play in the Lollard *Tretise of Miraclis Pleyinge,* which George R. Coffman found so confusing; see Kolve, pp. 18–19.

play, seen in this context, is a lesser good that must be valued below the serious efforts it restores one for.[12] *Recreatio* is etymologically a re-creation, a re-constituting of one's normal physical and mental health which has flagged because of work and natural human frailty. This is a valuable service, but obviously subordinate to the ongoing business of one's life. Leisure, on the other hand, is historically superior to man's work. It is the goal of personal or civic activity, a state of fulfillment. Michael O'Loughlin has discussed the classical manifestations of the idea, perhaps best known through Horace, and has argued that the Christian monastic ideal is a transformation of the classical notion of civic leisure. With its attendant activity of contemplation, leisure is a mode of existence allowing for the fullest realization of the potential of the human soul.[13]

True, contemplation and recreation share similarities. Aquinas says that contemplation can be compared to play for two reasons: each gives delight, each is taken up for its own sake.[14] These similarities allow Huizinga to claim as play everything from games to religious ceremony. Though valid for its own purposes, his approach ignores a crucial medieval distinction: the end, the final cause of the activity. The *finis* of recreative play, as we have seen, is improved ability to work, regardless of the fact that one might not be thinking of that end when one plays. The *finis* of Christian contemplation is joy in God, the only truly sufficient *quies* for the unquiet heart. The Middle Ages did not confuse the two activities, and it is significant that for the best modern statement of the distinction one must go not to theorists of play but to the Catholic philosopher Josef Pieper, who, although he does not treat the idea of recreation per se, distinguishes leisure and festive time from those pauses in routine which serve merely to prepare one for further

[12]Thus John Buridan, f. 88v: "Just as waking is superior to sleep and is its end, so serious work and steady application are superior to mental divagation and sportive activity (ludicris operationibus) and are their ends."
[13]*The Garlands of Repose: The Literary Celebration of Civic and Retired Leisure.* (Chicago: University of Chicago Press, 1978), esp. pp. 166–88. For discussion of the reemergence of the classical idea of leisure in the Renaissance, contrasting medieval and humanist views of contemplation, see Klibansky, Panofsky, and Saxl, pp. 243–45.
[14]Quoted and discussed by de Bruyne, III: 295.

work.[15] In this he is following the logic of *Nicomachean Ethics* X, 6, and its medieval Christian commentaries.

One commentary on that chapter will aid us in a further distinction. When Nicole Oresme translated the *Ethics* in 1370 and completed the passage arguing that felicity does not consist in play but that the "repos" of play is for the purpose of activity, he added an explanation in his annotations to make clear that the "repos" Aristotle is talking about is not the same thing as the heavenly rest promised in the Bible. "Aristotle means that [recreational] rest is for the sake of work in this life in which idleness is wicked." However, "in eternal glory there is not a rest which is the cessation of all activity," for there is constant "operacion" among the blessed in their experience of God. The "repos" of heaven only abolishes that kind of activity which is "cheerless, enervating, and arduous."[16] Oresme's distinction here between kinds of "repos" introduces the idea of idleness. In the work of the active life idleness is a sin; how can one discriminate between valid recreational "repos" and mere slothfulness? Recreation involves some kind of activity, some form of *ludus* which creates physical refreshment or mental *quies* through *delectatio*, thereby reinvigorating the psyche. It is thus possible for recreational activities to be seen as remedies against idleness. The *Castle of Perseverance* articulates the morality of play not in terms of Aristotelian ethics but in terms of the Christian categories of the deadly sins and their opposing virtues. Besynesse urges Mankind to avoid Slawthe with good works and adds that he should always be occupied with something:

[15]*Leisure the Basis of Culture*, trans. Alexander Dru (New York: New American Library, 1963), esp. pp. 38–45.
[16]*Le livre de* Ethiques *d'Aristote*, ed. A. D. Menut (New York: Stechert, 1940), p. 517. Cf. Oresme's related distinction between play and contemplation in his translation of and commentary on Aristotle's *Politics*, 1337b–1338a, ed. A. D. Menut, *Transactions of the American Philosophical Society*, 60, part 6 (1970), 341–42; since the work of the active life enervates the spirits and the inner and outer senses, causing sadness, the "delectation" afforded by games and music is an appropriate remedy, "just as laxatives offer a remedy against repletion of humors," for it renders the body's spirits refreshed and strengthened. But contemplation does not need "such exterior delights" because of its own "delectations tres merveilleuses." The medical analogy testifies further to the physiological view of entertainment discussed in Chap. 2.

Do sumwhat alwey for loue of me,
Þou þou schuldyst but thwyte a stycke.
Wyth bedys sumtyme þe blys.
Sumtyme rede and sumtyme wryte
And sumtyme pleye at þi delyte.
Þe Deuyl þe waytyth wyth dyspyte
Whanne þou art in idylnesse.[17]

Reading, writing, whittling, praying, playing—a wide range of human endeavor, all of it seen here as part of *solicitudo* in the fight against idleness.

But activity by itself cannot always be sufficient to make the distinction. The monastic tradition stresses work as the remedy for sloth, *acedia*.[18] What some might call recreative play others might see as inanity, the furthering of idleness. There are questions of intent as well, as implied in Guillaume de Deguileville's *Pèlerinage de la vie humaine*, in an episode that has interesting literary implications. In this allegory, the pilgrim at one point meets Youth, a damsel covered with feathers, symbolizing Youth's flightiness. She likes only to "go sportë me" and to live "In merthe only, & in solace," and she lists her favorite entertainments: various kinds of games, hunting, listening to "song & menstralcye," and reading "no storyes but on ffablys, / On thyng that ys nat worth a lek"—no sober histories, just trivial fictions.[19] Youth leads the narrator to a fork in the road, with a woman "off lytel bysynesse" on the left and a "besy" man on the right (11254–67). The old man harrangues against idleness. The lady explains that lovers come her way, echoing the opening of the *Roman de la rose* in which the porter of the garden of Deduit is Idleness. She says that she teaches the lovers to dance, to make "Balladys, Roundelays, vyrelayes," to play music, "To spendë al the day in ffablys," to play games— "And to al swych maner play, / Thys the verray ryhtë way" (11603–26).

[17]Lines 1647–53, ed. Mark Eccles, *The Macro Plays*, EETS o.s. 262 (London: Oxford University Press, 1969), p. 51.
[18]See Siegfried Wenzel, *The Sin of Sloth: Acedia in Medieval Thought and Literature* (Chapel Hill: University of North Carolina Press, 1960), pp. 21–22; also pp. 59–60 for later acknowledgment of the value of variety and relaxation.
[19]Trans. John Lydgate, *The Pilgrimage of the Life of Man*, ed. F. J. Furnivall, EETS e.s. 77, 83, 92 (1889, 1901, 1904; rpt. Millwood, N.Y.: Kraus Reprint, 1973), lines 11178–212. I will cite line numbers hereafter.

Youth's proclivities are the domain of Idleness, as the almost exactly parallel catalogues suggest. Deguileville allows no conception of recreation to intrude here, not because the activities named might not be legitimate entertainment (later in this chapter we will see hunting explained on recreational grounds, and in the next some late medieval lyrics on the same principle) but because in the context of youthful aimlessness they have become an end rather than a means. Youth wants a life of "merthe" and "solace" *only*. Presumably the grieving knight in Chaucer's *Book of the Duchess,* though he too was young and in love, had somewhat more moral awareness. For although he fell in love at a time when "Yowthe, my maistresse, / Governed me in ydelnesse" (797–98), his love for good fair White prompted him to do his "besynesse / To make songes" in order to "kepe me fro ydelnesse" (1155–57). His thinking here perhaps parallels that of the musical theorist Johannes de Grocheo, who, enumerating types of songs popular around the turn of the fourteenth century, says of the *stantipes* that it "causes the souls of young men and girls to concentrate because of its difficulty and turns them from improper thinking."[20] The formal intricacy of a ballade or rondel would serve equally well to channel the young knight's energies along artistic lines. In any case, the different perspectives on lyric composition in Deguileville and in Chaucer are a succinct reminder of the dangers of postulating a unitary late medieval attitude toward certain forms of secular activity. From the perspective of man's pilgrimage through life, youthful love lyrics are idle trifles; from the perspective of a young man in love with a noble and ennobling lady, self-expression through poems is a valid activity that combats idleness and its attendant brooding and improper thinking. Later in this chapter we will see Gaston Phoebus make much of the dangerous thoughts that arise in idleness, for which his remedy is another recreation, hunting; and in Chapter 6 we will see the same idea play a major role in Boccaccio's explanation of the value of his *Decameron* distractions.

The conflicting attitudes of Deguileville and the grieving knight point to perhaps the most difficult problem in dealing

[20]*Concerning Music (De Musica),* trans. Albert Seay, 2d ed. (Colorado Springs: Colorado College Music Press, 1974), p. 17; repeated in regard to the purely instrumental *stantipes* on p. 20.

with the morality of recreation, the question of intent, one raised as well in the *distinctiones'* separation of evil from recreational play. On the one hand, play, as Aristotle and Aquinas say, has no other end but itself; on this level one's intent in playing is to enjoy it, to gain the *delectatio* offered by the satisfying completion of a chess game, a hunt, or a well-told tale. But as a part of one's moral life play can only be justified to the extent that it promotes one's capacities for serious endeavor: work, study, contemplation. It is on this level that the ethical judgment of play usually takes place. One's intent within the play is delight; one's intent concerning the play should be recreative but may be libertine. Distinguishing this kind of intent is not always easy. Doubtless many people in the Middle Ages felt that the recreational argument tended to be a smokescreen for self-indulgence, and hence we get passages like Deguileville's which do not even allow it to be considered. But his voice is by no means the only "official" one.

Related to the problem of intent and the validity of recreation is the question of proper play. The tradition of the *Ethics* and its commentaries gives substantial attention to the need for decency in play if it is to be acceptable entertainment. Jokes, for example, should not be vulgar or cruel, though Aquinas makes the interesting point that in regard to social amusement, "talking and listening are very different, for a man properly listens to things he could not properly say" (Litzinger, I: 368), an ethical attitude that seems consistent with what we know about the enjoyment of some rather coarse fabliaux and *novelle* among people of more than minimal refinement. The recreational argument thus loses force when applied to pastimes that are patently immoral. Dice playing in particular comes in for severe attack. "Recreacion may not excusen pleying at þe dice," says a Lollard tract on the topic.[21] When Chaucer's Pardoner harrangues against the tavern sins, he notes apropos of "hasard-rye" that "Lordes may fynden oother maner pley / Honest ynough to dryve the day awey" (*CT* C 627–28). The wicked game stands condemned, not all forms of recreation.[22]

[21]British Library MS Add. 24202, f. 22.
[22]Robert A. Pratt has shown that much of the Pardoner's homiletics is based on John of Wales's *Communiloquium*, and he notes John's "somewhat parallel" line to 627–28: "There is play that is socially proper, intended for recreation

The Pardoner's reference to "Lordes" is doubtless prompted by his examples of dicing among kings and nobility, and
it serves to remind us of one of the major sources in the
later Middle Ages for the distinction between honest and
dishonest play, manuals for princes. The long version of the
Secretum secretorum includes a chapter on the "disports" of
rulers, justifying them on primarily physiological grounds but
warning against overindulgence.[23] Much more detailed is the
advice of Philippe de Mézières to Charles VI, in the third
part of his long allegory *Le songe du Vieil Pelerin* (The Dream
of the Old Pilgrim). Queen Verite discusses the topic of
"esbatemens," entertainment, acknowledging that after the
arduous tasks of royal government one needs some "honneste recreacion." She mentions as proper entertainments
("esbatemens raisonnables") some physical pastimes like archery and dancing, though the latter requires strict moderation.
She instructs her charge to avoid dishonest games prohibited
by the Church, such as dicing and all games based on the
desire to win money. She is careful to stress that "all your
entertainments must be regulated according to time and
place," the kind of concern with appropriate circumstances
which we have seen in Aristotle and Aquinas. Her advice to
hold to the mean ("tenir le moyen") in all recreations evokes
a whole Aristotelian morality. Her concern for limiting indulgence in entertainment prompts a concluding story about the
nephew of St. Cyril, who died at eighteen, appeared to his
uncle in a vision, and explained that he was condemned to
hell for delighting too much in entertainment and for not
making confession before he died "concerning my games and
my excessive entertainments."[24]

---

and relief from fatigue (Item est ludus socialis honestatis, scilicet ad recreationem et relavamen laboris)." "Chaucer and the Hand That Fed Him," *Speculum*,
41 (1966), 632.

[23]See Manzalaoui, pp. 318–19; Steele, pp. 15, 58, 140–41.

[24]Ed. G. W. Coopland, 2 vols. (Cambridge: Cambridge University Press,
1969), II: 212–16. What might the nephew's confession have sounded like had
he remembered to make one? In *The Sin of Sloth*, pp. 198–99, Wenzel prints a
formula for confessing sloth that concludes with a view of overindulgence in
entertainment as a part of that sin. The penitent is to say: "I have often allowed
myself frivolous and worthless thoughts and have let my mind wander amidst
them. I have become accustomed to speaking idle and scurrilous or foul words.
I have been too interested in mimes and shows or in hunting. I have habitually

The *Songe* dates from 1389. Less than twenty years later another Frenchman, the Augustinian Jacques Legrand, wrote an encyclopedia, the *Sophilogium*, which includes a chapter "De ludis principum."[25] He too follows the standard line: there is nothing blameworthy if one "refreshes his spirit in proper recreation (in honesto solatio spiritum suum recreet)," but princes are wrong to spend all their time on games or to devote themselves to wicked ones. He cites a variety of authorities on the dangers of dicing and paints a vivid picture of how such dissipation affects one's rule—the sort of material Shakespeare's Henry IV would have used to lecture Prince Hal. When he turns to "ludi honesti" he cites, as Bacon did, Seneca's *De tranquillitate animi,* and retells Cassian's story of John and the partridge. Legrand subsequently translated the *Sophilogium* into two French works, and this chapter became part of the *Livre des bonnes meurs,* a treatise on moral behavior that was very popular during the fifteenth and sixteenth centuries and was translated into English by William Caxton as the *Book of Good Manners.*

As we have seen, although the idea of recreation is itself relatively simple, the ethical questions it engenders are not. There is perhaps no better summary of the medieval notion of recreation and the moral concerns it prompts than that in a Renaissance play, John Redford's *Wit and Science,* which turns many of the principles and problems discussed above into personification allegory.[26] Wit seeks to marry Science, the daughter of Reason and Experience. At the beginning of the play Reason recognizes that Wit cannot "hold owte" on his journey to this marriage, that is, to the attainment of learning and knowledge, without some "solas" to "refresh" him (29–33). The main obstacle to Wit's achieving his goal is Tediousnes, and when Wit arrogantly thinks he can beat back Tediousnes by

---

played dice, chess, and similar games and taken too much delight in them. (Cogitaciones frivolas et inanes sepe admisi et permisi animum in talibus vagari. Verbis vanis et scurrilibus vel turpibus assuetus fui. De ludis mimicis et theatralibus aut venacionibus me nimis intromisi. Ad aleas et scaccos ut huiusmodi ludere consuevi et in hijs nimis delectatus sum.)" Note that even in the confessional context the focus is not on the entertainments themselves but on how often or how excessively the penitent has pursued them, thus implying a legitimate level of delight in recreations.

[25]*Sophilogium,* IX, c. 8 (Lyons, 1495), ff. 134–134v.

[26]I cite line numbers from the text in David Bevington's *Medieval Drama* (Boston: Houghton Mifflin, 1975), pp. 1030–61.

himself, he is felled. But Honest Recreacion, the "best phy-
sicke" in order to attain "consolacion" (228–30), revives him,
having been sent to Wit by Reason. Reason now recommends
that Wit send Recreacion and her companions (Cumfort,
Quicknes, and Strength—both physical and psychological restoration) home, since they have done their job; but in an amusing
exchange, the previously earnest Wit now turns casual, telling
Reason not to be too "hastye" and assuring him that he will get
to his daughter "all at leiser" (275–77). Seeing that Wit does
not want to leave Honest Recreacion, Reason departs. Wit decides that he would rather marry his new companion than Lady
Science, and to prove himself worthy of her begins to dance, at
the end of which he falls into the lap of Idlenes. Honest Recreacion is appalled, but Wit is interested only in his "ese" at
this point (342), and Idlenes helps to blind him to the difference between them by accusing Honest Recreacion of promoting all sorts of entertainments, evil as well as decent (371–85).
Wit falls asleep and is unable to hear Honest Recreacion's pro-
testations that Idlenes has blurred a crucial distinction. As a
result of his slide from recreation into idleness, Wit takes on
the appearance of Ignorance, is rejected by Science, and ultimately has to win her again by fighting Tediousnes, this time
with the aid of Diligence and Instruccion, as he should have
previously.

It is all there: the values of recreation, its pleasures, and its
dangers. Although the educational concerns of the play are
notably Renaissance, *Wit and Science* gives dramatic shape to a
view of the role of *ludus* in life that obtained in earlier centuries
as well as its own. More than the statements of principle by
moral philosophers, it treats sympathetically both the need and
the difficulty of knowing when vacation turns into truancy.

Monastic *Recreatio*

Thus far we have been considering the idea of recreation principally in a secular context, using material from the
realm of moral philosophy, ethics. The medieval attitude toward entertainment that emerges seems, though guarded, certainly more tolerant than is often thought. Although G. G.
Coulton and others have documented substantial clerical hostil-

ity toward entertainment, I have tried to show that for the later Middle Ages as a whole the dominant attitude is shaped by an essentially ethical tradition out of Aristotle. Still, there is some testimony from monastic life that is relevant as well.

The Rule of St. Benedict, recognizing that idleness is an enemy of the soul (chap. 48), prescribes manual labor and religious reading as countermeasures. It does not formulate an idea of recreation and throughout rejects anything suggestive of casual entertainment: "But as for buffoonery or idle words, such as move to laughter (scurrilitates vero vel verba otiosa et risum moventia), we utterly condemn them in every place, nor do we allow the disciple to open his mouth in such discourse."[27] But by the later Middle Ages, some members of religious orders—and not only sensualists like Chaucer's Monk—must have seen that rule as old and overly strict. The concept of recreation, which we have found to be present even in the desert fathers, affects interpretations of proper behavior in the cloistered life. The ordinances in 1300 for the Benedictine priory of Ely allow, upon permission, walks outside the cloister for recreation ("causa recreacionis") though not for wanton trifling ("causa lasciuiendi"). In the fourteenth century, the prior of the monastery at Durham had a country house to which monks would come on occasion "for recreation or *ludi.*" In the fifteenth, the nuns at St. Helen's, Bishopsgate, were instructed "that all daunsyng and reuelyng be utterly forborne among yow, except Christmasse and other honest tymys of recreacyone among yowre self."[28] Although John of Whethamstede, abbot of St. Albans, chided a brother for wanting to leave the abbey for Christ Church, Canterbury, where among other seductions there was, "in regard to recreation," too much conversation, he nevertheless maintained a cell at Redburn where the brothers went to spend some time "in solatiis." In 1423 he had to warn them that such privileged time was not appropriate to

[27]*The Rule of St. Benedict,* ed. and trans. D. O. H. Blair, 5th ed. (Fort Augustus, Scotland: Abbey Press, 1948), c. 6, pp. 38–39. This attitude appears elsewhere in the Rule.

[28]For Ely, see Evans, pp. 12–13. For Durham, see Dom David Knowles, *The Religious Orders in England,* 3 vols. (Cambridge: Cambridge University Press, 1948–59), II: 246, 324–25, and Chambers, II: 240–44. For St. Helen's, Eileen Power, *Medieval English Nunneries* (rpt. New York: Biblo and Tannen, 1964), p. 309; see also p. 384 and n. 1.

those "who do not know how to place proper limits on their pleasures," and he explicitly forbade excessive "vigilias," which led to neglect of religious duties.[29]

This evidence reveals a view of recreation which acknowledges a legitimate need for loosening the strain of monastic discipline. In fact, the term "recreatio" in the context of the cloister means "a temporary but intentional relaxation of the normal monastic regime of silence, prayer, work and seclusion."[30] Thus at Durham, special occasions on which the monks could eat meat were known as "recreationes"; the custom of periodic bloodletting came to involve a kind of recreational time during which certain freedoms from normal regulations were permitted; holidays at certain manors and hunting extended the principle to activity outside the monastery.[31] Recreation in this sense involves the idea of refreshment in its widest possible application: any alteration of behavior that will reinvigorate, whether it involve diet, medicine, psychology, or exercise. That range of meaning is evident also in the English noun "recreation," which in the *Oxford English Dictionary* has senses that run from "refreshment through partaking of food" (Gower often uses it in this way) to refreshment through amusement to refreshment through spiritual consolation. Such semantic range is further testimony to the link between hygiene and entertainment previously explored. It is epitomized in the title of a late medieval work, the *Summa recreatorum*, whose five parts consist of a variety of "refreshers" ranging from information on foods and diet to discussion of worthwhile laws to "delightful stories and songs." The inclusion of scientific, moral, and entertaining material as part of banquet behavior is in-

---

[29]*Annales Monasterii S. Albani a Johanne Amundesham . . . conscripti,* ed. H. T. Riley, 2 vols., Rolls Series 28, pt. 5 (London, 1870–71), I: 89, 113. See II: xx–xxiv for discussion and partial translation, and for some minor corrections, E. F. Jacob, " 'Florida Verborum Venustas': Some Early Examples of Euphuism in England," *Bulletin of the John Rylands Library,* 17 (1933), 272.

[30]Knowles, II: 245.

[31]See ibid., I: 283–85, II: 245–47; Knowles, *The Monastic Order in England,* 2d ed. (Cambridge: Cambridge University Press, 1963), pp. 455–56, 461–62; Huling E. Ussery, "The Status of Chaucer's Monk: Clerical, Official, Social, and Moral," *Tulane Studies in English,* 17 (1969), 10. Regulations for chantry priests reveal a similar range of allowable *recreationes;* see K. L. Wood-Legh, *Perpetual Chantries in Britain* (Cambridge: Cambridge University Press, 1965), pp. 256–60.

debted to Macrobius's *Saturnalia,* as the *Summa*'s prologue acknowledges, but it is perhaps a more distinctly late medieval view of *recreatio* that accounts for the work's title and its inclusion in a manuscript containing other scientific and medical texts.[32]

Even the Benedictine Rule's firm stand against frivolous talk that induces laughter could be tempered. The fifteenth-century confessional manual of Antoninus of Florence poses the following question to be asked about the behavior of religious:

> Has the person been too frivolous in conversation or prompted others to levity or to laughter with words or actions or entertainments? Sometimes these things can be done without sinning for the purposes of recreation or of relieving oneself or others from slothfulness. Rarely, however, is this sort of thing proper for religious.[33]

The legitimate uses of levity are very carefully circumscribed here, but that comes as no surprise considering that Antoninus is concerned with people in religious orders. What is revealing is that even in such circumstances there is allowance for amusement provided that it serves recreative purposes or that it aids in alleviating *acedia*. This latter function reminds us of the harsher realities of religious discipline; spiritual sloth, in a variety of manifestations, was a genuine problem, and insofar as occasional levity might help one cope with it, *solatii* could be justified even within the walls of the cloister. Thomas Walsing-

[32]For a summary of the work, which can be dated before 1412, and its relation to the later and better-known *Mensa philosophica,* see Brian Lawn, *The Salernitan Questions: An Introduction to the History of Medieval and Renaissance Problem Literature* (Oxford: Clarendon Press, 1963), pp. 107–11. For information on the Vienna manuscript and on the contents of the section of stories and songs, which range from religious and moral pieces to lighter verse, see Alfons Hilka, "Zur *Summa recreatorum.* Liste der poetischen Stücke und Abdruck von vier Marienliedern," in *Studien zur lateinischen Dichtung des Mittelalters. Ehrengabe für Karl Strecker,* ed. W. Stach and H. Walther (Dresden: Wilhelm und Bertha v. Baensch, 1931), pp. 97–116. I owe this reference to George Rigg.

[33]*Summula confessionis,* Interrogatorio, Pars III, c. 13 (Venice, 1473), f. 77v: "Si conuersando fuit nimis leuis uel alios inducens ad leuitatem uel risum uerbis gestibus uel solatiis; que aliquando sine peccato fieri possunt ad recreationem uel subleuandum se uel alios ab accidia, raro tamen decet huiusmodi religiosos."

ham, monk and chronicler, has this psychological concern in mind when he distinguishes the kinds of usefulness his *Historia Alexandri* provides. Readers in general will learn of actions and values worthy of glory. For people in the cloister the narrative is "utilis" because of the *delectatio* it generates; such pleasure may dispel *acedia* and alleviate tediousness, thereby forestalling unprofitable restlessness.[34]

Though not widely different from secular ideas, monastic views of recreation tend to perceive it more as a relationship than as a set of specific amusements. Recreation is the relaxation of a rule, the unbending of the bow, and recreational activity thus defines itself as whatever a temporary dispensation allows one to do that normal routine does not. Eating meat may be recreative from this point of view, even though it would not appear in a conventional list of *ludi*. Such an approach, which points up a feature only implicit in the secular material we have considered, is important because it helps us avoid the oversimple equation of recreation with triviality. To perceive a work of literature as recreative is not necessarily to judge it as inconsequential but rather to consider it as standing in a certain relationship to other kinds of endeavor.[35] Take the case of a request for a book made by the abbot of St. Augustine's Abbey. His letter asks a friend to lend him a story of Godfrey de Bouillon's conquest of the Holy Land, noting that it is one of those works "you have been accustomed to read in order to mix entertainment with your duties (ex quorum lectura interponi solent solacia curis vestris)" and that he too will receive pleasure and consolation

---

[34]Quoted in *Thomae Walsingham de archana deorum*, ed. Robert A. van Kluyve (Durham: Duke University Press, 1968), pp. xi–xii: "Religiosis insuper et in claustris residentibus non erit hec compilatio minus utilis, quia ex processu delectationem non modicam generabit et fortassis talium personarum tollet accidiam et tedium relevabit. Et cum sit generativa letitie lectio huius hystoria, occasiones vagandi inutiliter aufert et efficaciter primiet et extinguet." On the dangers of *acedia* see Wenzel, *The Sin of Sloth*, passim, and the article by P. Alphandéry he cites on p. 205, n. 5; Power, pp. 293–97.

[35]I have adopted this idea from H. Wagenvoort, "Ludus Poeticus," in his *Studies in Roman Literature, Culture and Religion* (Leyden: Brill, 1956), pp. 30–42. He argues that the classical, especially Horatian, use of "ludus" to describe poetic composition does not mean that poetry was viewed "as a mere game" but that the term is "a relative notion" comparing lesser to greater seriousness and/or achievement.

from it.[36] The sentence explicitly echoes *Disticha Catonis* III, 6: "Interpone tuis interdum gaudia curis." It treats the reading of a *chanson de geste* as the sort of pleasure which a person needs to intermingle with his more serious work. But surely the story of one of the nine worthies is not simply escapist adventure, not without some moral value; in medieval theorizing such histories are said to offer examples of noble deeds and qualities to be imitated, and doubtless this one of fighting for the faith contributes to Christian purposefulness. Why then does the letter define such reading in recreational rather than didactic terms? Because relative to the abbot's (and presumably his friend's) ongoing concerns, the responsibilities of a life devoted to the service of God, such activity is more immediately pleasurable, a respite from workaday strain. John Mason thinks of Cato's distich, probably, not because he believes the narrative of Godfrey's adventures to be merely a trivial pastime but because he perceives, properly enough, that the activity of reading it is relaxation from official duties. To at least some extent, recreation is always a relative term, saying less about the inherent quality of whatever it is that brings *delectatio* than about its standing vis-à-vis other concerns.

Walter Map's *De nugis curialium,* written nearly two centuries earlier than John Mason's letter, defines itself in a similar way, in this case in a secular context. At the beginning of his miscellany of stories, anecdotes, observations, and satire, Map says that he will treat his material "so that the reading may please and the edification contribute to morality." Here is the familiar division of literary response into pleasure gained from narrative or stylistic features and profit derived from an intellectual core. The book thus advertises itself as a complete literary enterprise, combining the two values, and in a later passage suggests that even though a story may appear "friuola" one can profit from it. Yet the collection as a whole is given purely recreational status, as Map makes clear in his prologue to Part III, addressing a patron:

[36]Text and discussion in W. A. Pantin, "The Letters of John Mason: A Fourteenth-Century Formulary from St. Augustine's, Canterbury," in *Essays in Medieval History Presented to Bertie Wilkinson,* ed. T. A. Sandquist and M. R. Powicke (Toronto: University of Toronto Press, 1969), pp. 216–17.

When our counsellors leave the business of counselling, wearied by the greatness of a king's tasks, they take pleasure in unbending to join converse with the lowly, and in lightening with jests the weight of serious affairs. In this way it may please thee, after thou hast rested from the counsel of a book of philosophy, or, it may be, of the divine book, to hear or read for the sake of pastime or pleasure (recreacionis et ludi gracia) the savourless and sapless trifles of this book. For it is not of the contests of the courts or of the magnitude of a philosopher's maxims that I am going to treat.[37]

The modesty of this claim is not inconsistent with Map's Horatian goals. His collection offers instruction *ad mores*, yet relative to philosophy and theology its material consists only of trifles, *nugae;* it is worthwhile, yet royal business is more important (or at least more importunate). What cannot be disputed is the need for relaxation and the pleasure people take in entertaining stories. The concept of recreation enables Map and others to locate with some honesty the role of literary entertainment in medieval life.[38] It is also, of course, a role literature has played in other eras; the idea of recreation defines rather well the complex status of a form of discourse that is relevant to the ongoing concerns of life yet valued and enjoyed in great part as a withdrawal from them.

Recreation in Medieval Life: Two Examples

The evidence assembled above, ranging from learned commentary on Aristotle to popular tags and anecdotes, not only explains the idea of recreation but also gives some indication of its pervasiveness throughout the later Middle Ages. Yet since the context has thus far been principally theoretical, it will

[37]*De nugis curialium,* ed. M. R. James (Oxford: Clarendon Press, 1914), pp. 18, 122, 104. Trans. Frederick Tupper and M. B. Ogle, *De nugis curialium (Courtiers' Trifles)* (London: Chatto & Windus, 1924), p. 130. See also James Hinton, "Walter Map's *De nugis curialium:* Its Plan and Composition," *PMLA,* 32 (1917), 81–132.

[38]Cf. the later example of Christine de Pisan, who sends to Guillaume de Tignonville, provost of Paris, texts of the well-known *debat* on the *Roman de la rose,* noting that, amidst his laborious efforts on important affairs, he might take pleasure, "soulas," in the exchange. Ed. C. F. Ward, *The Epistles on the Romance of the Rose and Other Documents in the Debate* (Chicago: University of Chicago, 1911), p. 36.

be useful to see the idea in application, to see how people used it to understand or justify certain kinds of behavior. Although one could document the appearance of the recreational argument in medieval discussions of almost any pastime—dancing, for example[39]—the remainder of this chapter will survey only two places that often feature its use: observations on student life and treatises on hunting.

It is natural to expect that concerns about student behavior would prompt some reflection on the relationship between study and play. Failure to recognize the limits of a student's, particularly a young student's, powers of concentration could be harmful. Writing early in the twelfth century, Guibert of Nogent criticizes the teacher he had as a boy for working him without restraint, because unrelenting mental stress dulls "the natural powers of grown men, as well as of boys" and turns "energy" into "apathy." Guibert then offers a better pedagogical technique: "when the mind has been fixed exclusively on one subject, we ought to give it relaxation from its intensity, so that after dealing in turn with different subjects we may with renewed energy, as after a holiday, fasten upon that one with which our minds are most engaged."[40] He speaks in terms of "variety" and "change" in one's endeavors rather than play, but the principle of necessary respite from strain, mental vacation, governs the reasoning. Not surprisingly, we find that manuals for young students permit play. One, a fifteenth-century set of typical student dialogues, envisages an after-school scene of game playing in the churchyard in which children's minds are refreshed ("recreatur puerorum animus"). Another from later in the century permits play for recreation ("causa recreandi"), though it restricts time, place, and type of game, and insists to boot that the students always speak Latin.[41] A

[39]For some medieval commentary on dancing, see Coulton, *Five Centuries,* I: 531–38. He tends to ignore secular testimony that is less censorious, and the paragraph on Antoninus of Florence, p. 533, distorts his position, which does admit cases where dancing is not sinful; see *Summa theologica,* II, tit. VI, c. 6 (Verona, 1740), cols. 785–87.

[40]*Self and Society in Medieval France: The Memoirs of Abbot Guibert of Nogent,* trans. C. C. Swinton Bland, rev. and ed. John F. Benton (New York: Harper & Row, 1970), pp. 46–48.

[41]Charles Homer Haskins, *Studies in Mediaeval Culture* (1929; rpt. New York: Ungar, 1965), pp. 80–81, 90–91.

fourteenth-century treatise spells out the medical and psychological rationale for recreation, affirming a causal relationship
between physical invigoration and mental acuity:

> Nor should the scholars be always kept intent upon their
> books and writing tablets, but they should be given an occa-
> sional recess and set at suitable games, so that their spirits
> may be raised and their blood stirred by the pleasure of play
> (ut spiritus exaltentur et sanguis sublimetur ludi delecta-
> tione). For thus the boys' minds which before were fatigued
> by the tedium of classes are refined and refreshed (ingenia
> subtiliantur et recreantur).[42]

The passage represents a practical application of medical principles discussed in Chapter 2—the delight produced by play
promotes the improved operation of blood and *spiritus* in the
body, which in turn promotes improved mental activity.

Older students need holidays too. A fifteenth-century collection of letters includes one in which a son requests his father to
have a horse sent so that he can return home for the Feast of
Corpus Christi. He justifies the vacation at length using the
familiar recreational argument, complete with allusions to the
Cato distich and the image of the bent bow.[43] A good deal
more subtle is the sixth chapter of the *Manuale scholarium*, a
1481 treatise in dialogue form designed to acquaint students
with life at Heidelberg. It involves two students talking about a
break in studies. Camillus asks Bartoldus if he would like to
take a walk, but Bartoldus thinks he should keep studying.
Camillus argues that too much work makes the mind collapse,
and Bartoldus agrees that some relaxation is proper. They
head out to the fields and spend time discussing the scenery. In
a meadow Bartoldus admits that they have found as pleasant a
place as paradise: "The flowing of the brook greatly refreshes
(recreat) me, and it delights the eye to see the fish darting
hither and yon." With good Petrarchan earnestness he decides
to bring his books out to the meadow, "for the mind ought to

[42]Ed. and trans. Lynn Thorndike, *University Records and Life in the Middle Ages*
(1944; rpt. New York: Norton, 1975), pp. 225, 426.
[43]W. A. Pantin, "A Medieval Treatise on Letter-Writing, with Examples,
from the Rylands Latin MS. 394," *Bulletin of the John Rylands Library*, 13 (1929),
379–80.

be greatly improved here." Camillus agrees that it is a good place for study; he has taken such delight in it that Bartoldus has to remind him that it is time to return to town.[44] Like *Wit and Science*, this chapter gives dramatic life to intellectual concerns about the proper use of one's time. Its viewpoint seems to be somewhat more humanistic, more evocative of classical and Renaissance notions of leisure and contemplation, than most medieval testimony. Like Petrarch's attitudes, which we will examine in Chapter 6, its interest in having the students use the meadow for intellectual reflection tends to blur the separation of recreation and study announced at the beginning of the episode. *Delectatio* and *recreatio* are attained not through games but through observation of natural beauty and harmony; as in Guibert of Nogent (and in Bruno of Cologne, cited above, n. 4), the focus is more on varying one's attention than on defending amusement.

If there is a kind of academic pastoral ideal at work in this scene, it is one that seldom appears in medieval discussions of student conduct. Generally they acknowledge the need for recreation but immediately narrow the ways in which students should take it. There is no inconsistency between such acceptance and all the medieval censuring of disreputable student behavior, especially the preference for tavern over classroom. Abusing the principle of recreation does not invalidate it. When a father writes to his son, "I have recently discovered that you live dissolutely and slothfully, preferring license to restraint and play to work (ludicra seriis anteponas),"[45] his distress stems from the belief not that all *ludicra* must be rejected but that his son has been excessive in their use—*antiponere* rather than Cato's *interponere*. For all the adverse opinion voiced in the Middle Ages about student revelry, the authorities do not deny that some disport is permissible and desirable. And for the students' point of view we have only to read "Omittamus studia" from the *Carmina Burana* or the similarly

[44]Trans. Robert Francis Seybolt, *The Manuale Scholarium* (Cambridge, Mass.: Harvard University Press, 1921), pp. 50–53. Text in Friedrich Zarncke, ed., *Die Deutschen Universitäten im Mittelalter* (Leipzig: T. O. Weigel, 1857), 17–19.

[45]Haskins, pp. 15–16. As Haskins and Pantin both point out, medieval letters reflect medieval attitudes whether written as personal communications or as models of style.

exultant lyric on the end of term edited by Peter Dronke, both of which detail the afflictions to mind and body caused by prolonged study.[46]

The idea of recreation reaches its acme in the late medieval hunting manuals, some of which are so intent on turning game into earnest that the recreational argument becomes but a small part of their elaborate self-justification. Viewed from one perspective, they appear as a most un-Aristotelian extreme in the medieval interest in entertainment, part of that exaggerated, ritualized self-indulgence of an aristocracy whose values were becoming increasingly irrelevant amidst social and technological change. Viewed from another, less common, perspective, they are fascinating testimony to one way in which secular values could be articulated and maintained in the court culture of the later Middle Ages.

Basically, the Middle Ages thought of hunting as a sport and hence as a kind of play, though, as Hugh of St. Victor's list of mechanical arts makes clear, it could also be seen as a necessary occupation in the production of food. Hunting and hawking appear in William Fitzstephen's description of the many types of *ludi* of twelfth-century Londoners, and some two hundred years later the *Ménagier de Paris* includes a treatise on hawking as part of a category of "games and entertainments pleasing in part for the sake of learning how to speak to and associate with people."[47] Here the pleasures of the sport seem subordinate to the pleasures of being in the right "compaignie" (one thinks of the elegant hawking party in the illumination for August in the *Très riches heures*), but the fundamental point remains: hawking is a game, an entertainment.

Hunting was so popular in the later Middle Ages that it engendered a number of treatises and a set of rationales that went far beyond whatever simple recreational claims one might

[46]Text and trans. of the former in Helen Waddell, *Mediaeval Latin Lyrics* (1929; rpt. Baltimore: Penguin, 1968), pp. 214–17. Dronke, *Medieval Latin and the Rise of the European Love-Lyric,* 2d ed., 2 vols. (Oxford: Clarendon Press, 1968), II: 400–2.

[47]Robertson, p. 12. *Le Ménagier de Paris,* ed. Jérôme Pichon, 2 vols. (Paris, 1846), I: 7. The treatise itself is in II: 279–326. Chapters on the other "jeux et esbatemens" announced in the author's introduction, which he identifies as various kinds of "demandes," have not survived.

make on behalf of a pastime.[48] Some thirteenth-century works
focus on hunting or hawking as an *ars,* a discipline that requires knowledge and practice. This perspective is evident in
Frederick II's treatise on falconry and in the earliest vernacular
hunting manuals. Still, these treatises are aware that people
pursue the art for the pleasure it brings. Frederick distinguishes varying motives for falconry, ranging from baser in-
stincts like gluttony and avarice and "the joy of the eye (causa
delectamenti visus sui)" to the nobler purpose of "having the
best birds of prey," from which come both "surpassing fame
and honor" and the great delight ("magnum delectamentum")
of having excellent birds. (Frederick's disapproval of the joy of
the eye as a motive makes an interesting contrast to the great
hunting treatises a century later, which, in debates on the relative merits of hunting and hawking, include appeals to the
senses as a positive value.) The earliest French vernacular treatise on hunting, *La chace dou cerf,* though almost entirely concerned with such technical matters as tracking and brittening
the deer, begins with a list of other secular activities: some
people like to compose verses ("rimer"), either for honor or
money; others take interest in love or in tournaments. An honest spirit takes pleasure in many things ("En plusors choses se
deduit / Loious cuers"), and one such "deduit," of course, is
hunting.[49] "Deduit" has a wide variety of meanings in French:
pleasure, often sexual pleasure; amusement; sport; and sometimes, as we will see, it is used as a synonym for hunting.
Though not etymologically related, it seems to have much the
same semantic range as *delectatio,* and I think we are justified in

[48]The best short treatment of the sport and its manuals is Marcelle
Thiébaux, "The Mediaeval Chase," *Speculum,* 42 (1967), 260–74; see also her
Stag of Love: The Chase in Medieval Literature (Ithaca: Cornell University Press,
1974), which is principally about literary uses of the hunt. Two early works
have valuable bibliographic material on medieval and Renaissance hunting
treatises: Edward, Second Duke of York, *The Master of Game,* ed. William A.
and F. Baillie-Grohman (London: Ballantyne, Hanson, 1904), pp. 213–72; and
The Art of Hunting or, Three Hunting MSS, ed. Alice Dryden (Northampton:
William Mark, 1908), pp. 141–57. The 1904 edition of the *Master of Game* was
limited to 600 copies, and its extensive supplementary material was omitted in
the more easily available 1909 edition that I cite later.

[49]Text and translation of Frederick II in Haskins, p. 113. *La chace dou cerf,*
ed. Gunnar Tilander, Cynegetica 7 (Stockholm, 1960), p. 16. For other "purely
instructive" manuals see Thiébaux, *Stag of Love,* p. 26.

imputing to defenses of hunting on grounds of "delectamentum" or "deduit" some kind of understanding of the recreational rationale that justifies the temporary attainment of *quies* through delight.

When we move to the middle of the fourteenth century, hunting manuals claim to offer not only technical but moral instruction. They come equipped with a host of narrative and allegorical trappings. Leading the way is *Les livres du roy Modus et de la royne Ratio*, by Henri de Ferrières. I will discuss this intriguing text in more detail in Chapter 5, for it is most fully related to my concerns there. Here we can at least note that the first part of *Modus et Ratio* is a treatise on hunting, that King Modus is in charge of giving the rules for hunting as he is of all other "gieux" and "esbatemens," that he promulgates his *Livre des deduis* ("deduis" here means hunting) in order that people not be idle, and that his very proper sport is distinguished from vicious ones, such as dice playing. In short, we have in narrative form a panoply of recreational ideas to justify hunting: the need for properly controlled play, the distinction between good and bad entertainment, the justification of recreational activity as combating idleness. In addition, Queen Ratio's moralizations of the animals of the hunt introduce a good deal of religious and ethical instruction.[50]

The combination of secular pleasure and moral earnestness in *Modus et Ratio* sets the pattern for two other important treatises. Gace de la Buigne began his *Roman des deduis* in 1359 while in captivity in England with the King of France, Jean le Bon, whom he served as chaplain. He addressed it to the King's fourth son, Philip, Duke of Burgundy, who had also been captured at the Battle of Poitiers, so that he "might learn of these delights [of hunting] in order to avoid the sin of idleness and to be better instructed in manners and in virtues."[51] Certainly anyone who makes his way through all of Gace's twelve thousand lines of verse could not be accused of

[50]For the text, see below, Chap. 5, n. 29. Though his work is based on outdated scholarship, there is a sympathetic summary of the contents of the first part of *Modus et Ratio* in D. H. Madden, *A Chapter of Mediaeval History: The Fathers of the Literature of Field Sport and Horses* (1924; rpt. Port Washington, N.Y.: Kennikat Press, 1969), pp. 49–81.

[51]*Le roman des deduis*, ed Åke Blomqvist, Studia Romanica Holmiensia 3 (Karlshamn, 1951), p. 93. Hereafter I will cite page numbers of this edition.

idleness, and the poem's mixture of hunting advice and ethical instruction justifies the double claim that Philip will learn both the art itself and the principles of good behavior. To accomplish this dual purpose, Gace uses the seven deadly sins as a framework, showing how a good sportsman must avoid them. For example, a "debauched glutton" could not be a good falconer because he might hurt the bird while carousing (p. 152). Gace provides a battle of vices and virtues, and with the victory of the latter comes an after-dinner debate (inspired by the shorter debate in *Modus et Ratio*) between Deduit de Chiens and Deduit de Oyseaulx, whose supporters argue at great length the relative merits of hunting and hawking. Both sides want the title of "Deduit" alone, which would prove superiority, but the King who judges the debate decrees that each must keep his surname.

It is not a great work of literature, but it has some felicities. In spite of the heavy moralizing, there is a vein of humor throughout, especially in the debate, which pokes a certain amount of fun at the spokesmen, Amour de Chiens and Amour de Oyseaulx, for their longwindedness and overenthusiasm. At the end both Raison and Verité note the dangers of excessive fondness for such *deduis*. Gace seems to be both serious about the moral dimensions of his favorite sport and aware of the fact that it is, after all, just a recreation. At one point he alludes to Cato's distich (p. 116), and at another, in a charming passage spoken by Amour de Oyseaulx, he defends his own proclivities for falconry, arguing that he is inclined that way by nature and citing Aristotle in regard to the influence of lineage on one's personality (p. 288). Gace gives us further autobiography. He had a falcon as a child. Later, after becoming a priest, he would go out hawking once or twice a week with an expert falconer, but, he hastens to add, only after mass was said and his religious duties fulfilled (p. 289). Even as chaplain to three French kings he continued to enjoy hawking:

> . . . for he went, if you would know the truth, in order to take recreation, which is permitted to a priest, for neither in canon law nor in the Bible can one find a prohibition against having recreation, nor does canon law consider it foolish

when there is a need for it. However, if he did it too often, then the law would bring him down.[52]

The self-consciousness points to an awareness of criticism, or potential criticism, though the appeal to recreation is surely not entirely defensive. Like his contemporary Guillaume de Machaut, one of whose works we will consider in Chapter 5, Gace de la Buigne is a man of religious vocation who is at home with secular culture and values. Yet perhaps not completely at home. The very need to graft moral instruction onto a hunting treatise, the retreat, when pressed, to a stock defense of hunting as permissible recreation, certainly distinguish Gace's brand of secularism from later, more thoroughly naturalistic, ones. The recreational argument seems to be almost a kind of refuge, a convenient solution to his own somewhat ambivalent feelings about his passion for hawking.

We have already seen theoretical and literary understanding that the recreational argument is not absolute, that its appropriateness depends on motives and circumstances. The issue of clergy and hunting in the fourteenth century, which the *Roman des deduis* raises, supplies a historical example of the moral questions surrounding one type of recreation as practiced by one particular group. Father Beichner, in an article that takes a more charitable view of Chaucer's Monk, who "lovede venerye," than most critics do, has supplied evidence of various contemporary clerical hunters.[53] The attitude toward them, or theirs toward the hunt, seems to be at best ambiguous. John

---

[52]"Car il aloit, sachiés de voir, / Pour recreacion avoir, / Laquel chose a prestre est lisible, / Car n'est trouvé n'en droit n'en Bible / Qu'il y ait prohibicion / Pour avoir recreacion, / Ne que droit tiengne a niceté / Quant il en est necessité, / Maiz, se trop souvent y aloit, / Adonques droit le reprendroit." Pp. 289–90. Gace puns on *reprendre*, which has both a general meaning (to seize, reprove, censure) and a technical one in hawking (to make one's birds return; see p. 630). He goes on to mention the relevant text in canon law, of which Blomqvist prints excerpts in his notes. For further texts and background on the Church's attitude toward clerics hunting, see Rudolph Willard, "Chaucer's 'text that seith that hunters ben nat holy men,' " *Texas University Studies in English*, 26 (1947), 209–51. H. Gourdon de Genouillac, *L'église et la chasse* (Paris, 1886), has some interesting information on the Middle Ages but unfortunately very little documentation. See also G. G. Coulton, *Medieval Village, Manor, and Monastery* (1925; rpt. New York: Harper & Row, 1960), pp. 508–12.

[53]Paul E. Beichner, C.S.C., "Daun Piers, Monk and Business Administrator," *Speculum*, 34 (1959), 611–19. The texts I cite are on 617–18.

Peckham says that the canons of St. Augustine's at Coxford should have liberty to hunt, but not on foot and only when the prior is "indulging in such at the time." Why did he choose "indulgere" rather than "ludere" or "recreare"? The famous hunting abbot William de Cloune, according to the chronicler Henry Knighton, said privately that he did not delight in the "frivolous hunting" he participated in with the nobility for the sake of their favor. The abbot of St. Albans, says another chronicle, maintained hunters and hawkers for the enjoyment of his friends but personally execrated all forms of play. Hunting may have recreational justification, and yet these respected prelates, unlike Gace, do not advance it. In the case of Chaucer's Monk, to move from history to satire, the lines clearly rule out a defense on the basis of permissible play: "Of prikyng and of huntyng for the hare / Was *al* his lust, for no cost wolde he spare" (*CT* A 191–92, my italics). Recreation has become an end rather than a means, the temporary *delectatio* of hunting (here charged with sexual innuendo as well) a substitute for the permanent *quies* to be found elsewhere.[54]

But outside the ecclesiastical context the attitude toward the chase was not so ambiguous, though there was some criticism, and the celebration of hunting reached a kind of apotheosis in 1378 when Gaston Phoebus, Count of Foix, began his *Livre de chasse*. Though it draws heavily on *Modus et Ratio* and slightly on the *Roman des deduis*, according to Thiébaux, the book is in one sense a return to the more technical treatises, for it abandons narrative allegory in favor of direct instruction in the art of hunting, aided by some marvellous illuminations. But Gaston's preface makes as much of hunting in a few pages as Henri de Ferrières or Gace de la Buigne did in hundreds. He argues the value of hunting on the following grounds:

> . . . hunting causeth a man to eschew the seven deadly sins. Secondly men are better when riding, more just and more understanding, and more alert and more at ease and more

[54]Cf. the related argument of David E. Berndt, "Monastic *Acedia* and Chaucer's Characterization of Daun Piers," *SP*, 68 (1971), 435–50. See also the case described in a letter by Peter of Blois, trans. Willard, 247–49, where, in spite of the general harrangue against hunting, the addressee's sin is not that he hunts but that he hunts excessively, especially considering his advanced age.

undertaking, and better knowing of all countries and all passages; in short and long all good customs and manners cometh thereof and the health of man and of his soul. For he that fleeth the seven deadly sins as we believe, he shall be saved, therefore a good hunter shall be saved, and in this world have joy enough and of gladness and of solace, so that he keep himself from two things. One is that he leave not the knowledge nor the service of God, from whom all good cometh, for his hunting. The second is that he lose not the service of his master for his hunting, nor his own duties which might profit him most.[55]

Both sacred and secular systems are invoked here to establish the moral worth of hunting. Though Gaston does not use the term "recreation," it is clear that he is thinking within the context of a properly ordered hierarchy of activities when he subordinates the sport to proper obedience to earthly and heavenly lords and to one's serious occupations.

The rest of the preface justifies Gaston's initial assertions. A hunter flees the seven deadly sins by not being idle and thereby avoiding the "evil imaginations" that come with inactivity and prompt the other sins (p. 5). Gaston depicts the daily routine of the hunter, rising early, staying busy, going to sleep promptly because of his weariness. "Wherefore I say that such an hunter is not idle, he can have no evil thoughts, nor can he do evil works, wherefore he must go into paradise" (p. 8). The chain of thought is more explicit in the French, and the conclusion more striking: "Since a hunter is not idle he cannot have evil imaginings, and if he does not have evil imaginings, he cannot do evil things, for imagination comes first. And if he does not do evil things, he must go straightaway to heaven (puisque veneur n'est ocieux il ne puelt avoir males ymaginacions et s'il n'a males ymaginacions, il ne puelt fere males euvres; quar l'ymaginacion va devant; et s'il ne fet males euvres, il fault qu'il s'en aille tout droit en paradis)" (p. 5).

[55]Quoted from the translation by Edward, Second Duke of York, *The Master of Game*, ed. William A. and F. Baillie-Grohman (London: Chatto & Windus, 1909), pp. 4–5. Edward's translation dates from 1406–13. It is modernized in this edition; the Middle English is available in the 1904 text (see n. 48). For the original I have used *La chasse de Gaston Phoebus Comte de Foix*, ed. Joseph Lavallée (Paris, 1854). Subsequent citations will be from these editions.

Apparently Edward, for all his love of the sport, when he came to Gaston's "tout droit," could not quite accept the proposition that a good hunter would never even have to put in any purgatorial time.

Next Gaston turns to the assertion that hunters live "more joyfully" in this world than do other people. He paints a deservedly famous picture of the natural pleasures of a beautiful morning and the delights of the hunt, repeating several times that these things bring "great joy" and "great pleasure" to the hunter (pp. 8–11). Finally, he argues out his assertion of hunters' good health, noting that they eat less and get more exercise than others, thereby living longer. The fusion of secular and sacred values emerges once again: "men desire in this world to live long and in health and in joy, and after death in the health of the soul. And hunters have all these things" (p. 12). It is no incongruity that in Bibliothèque Nationale MS f. fr. 616, the *Livre de chasse* is followed by Gaston's prayers in Latin and French. For he seems to have believed that it is possible to have the best of both worlds; and the best of this one is a recreation elevated into a way of life.

Huizinga has argued that the coexistence of worldiness and devoutness in Gaston and in other late medieval French aristocrats depends on "the absolute dualism of the two conceptions."[56] Gaston's own logic seems to be more gradualistic than dualistic. The secular delights of hunting are, at least in theory, subordinate to more serious matters, as recreational morality would dictate. Yet one senses, in Gaston and in the other fourteenth-century treatises, that the idea of legitimate recreation is being asked to encompass more than Aristotle or Aquinas ever meant it to. Their efforts to explain that hunting is not just a pastime but a valuable pursuit in itself have something of the earnestness and defensiveness of the pronouncements of college football coaches on how their sport makes athletes into good citizens. There is a point at which an activity ostensibly recreational becomes so significant culturally, emerges as an embodiment of so many social preoccupations, that simply to call it "play" no longer suffices. In the fourteenth

[56]*The Waning of the Middle Ages,* trans. F. Hopman (1924; rpt. Garden City, N.Y.: Doubleday, 1954), p. 181.

century, in certain circles, that seems to have happened to hunting. It becomes a locus of important secular values and as such transcends its status as a mere pastime. In Chapter 5 we will see some of those values discussed and affirmed in works that use orderly recreation as an image of social stability in the face of plague. Here we may briefly note another, the emphasis on hunting as opposed to idleness (and thus to lecherous and other wicked thoughts), a dominant theme in the treatises and one that, as Thiébaux has pointed out, is evoked with such urbanity in the third part of *Sir Gawain and the Green Knight*.[57] It is one thing to argue, as the *Castle of Perseverance* does, that play has a part in *solicitudo:* it is quite another to intimate that a sporting activity by itself constitutes all the daily busy-ness man needs to save his soul. It is not hard to see how a leisured class might well develop such an argument as a justification for its favorite sport.

Yet the principle of recreation still remains, in King Modus's rulership over games and entertainment and in Gace's defense of his hawking. It offers a means of handling the secular assertiveness implicit in the treatises by conceptualizing it in a way that traditional, especially ecclesiastical, thinking can accept. In later centuries the delights of sport, and the delights of literature, will be talked about as pleasures valid in and of themselves; in the hunting manuals of Henri de Ferrières, Gace de la Buigne, and Gaston Phoebus, we sense a bourgeoning secularity that approaches such a point of view but never lets go of the theory that contains earthly delight within the limits of allotted recreation. This is a phenomenon that has its most obvious literary parallel in the *Decameron,* a work that seems to offer a naturalistic ethic in some of its tales and in Boccaccio's fourth day defense but which encases the tales in a framework based on traditional recreational and therapeutic ideas. We will consider the *Decameron* at some length later. It is time now, having examined the idea of recreation in the later Middle Ages as it derives from Aristotelian ethics, to look at some less complicated evidence of its use in literary thought.

[57]Thiébaux, *Stag of Love,* pp. 76–81.

4

Some Literature
for Solace

The ideas that moderate joy promotes well-being and that time out for entertainment is a necessary part of human life are independent of literature. They become a part of medieval literary thought only insofar as theory relies on them to explain the function of certain works or fictions appeal to them for purposes of justification. Though we have already seen a few such instances, such as the understanding of *theatrica* as ministering to bodily weakness and the assignment of *De nugis curialium* to the category of recreation, we have yet to survey the more substantial evidence of literary material invoking the ideas. This chapter supplies that evidence by considering some later medieval works and genres that allude, for one purpose or another, to hygienic or recreational principles.

I begin with some literary theorizing by Boccaccio and Petrarch, both of whom in their Latin writings make substantial claims for literature's capacity to profit, usually relying on allegorical approaches. But they impute other powers to literature as well. In 1338 Petrarch wrote a letter to a good friend describing his solitary life at Vaucluse. Acquaintances, he says, avoid the place because of its austerity; he has only his dog and his servants, and some of the latter are leaving. But he can also take joy in his "secret friends":

> They come to me from every century
> And every land, illustrious in speech,
> In mind, and in the arts of war and peace. . . .
> Now these, now those I question, and they answer

Abundantly. Sometimes they sing for me;
Some tell me of the mysteries of nature;
Some give me counsel for my life and death;
Some tell of high emprise, bringing to mind
Ages long past; some with their jesting words
Dispel my sadness, and I smile again;
Some teach me to endure, to have no longing,
To know myself. Masters are they of peace,
Of war, of tillage, and of eloquence,
And travel o'er the sea. When I am bowed
With sorrow, they restore me; when I meet
With Fortune's favor, they restrain my pride,
Reminding me that the days of life are fleeting.[1]

This passage of tranquil bibliophilia is much less well known than most of Petrarch's more polemical remarks on the value of literature, but it is more revealing than many of them about the variety of benefits that come from reading: one learns about the natural world, about oneself, about history, about the transitoriness of life. And mixed in with these intellectual and spiritual rewards is the power of "jesting words" to relieve sadness. Some reading, it appears, is playful rather than serious, but it too has a useful function to perform, one that seems to be a sort of therapy, helping to deal with emotional letdown. This role is, of course, that assigned to pleasurable reading and conversation by the physicians studied in Chapter 2.

Since Petrarch tends to be aggressively serious in almost all his writing (we will later see his somewhat snobbish treatment of the *Decameron*), it is rare to find him so receptive to the merely amusing. What kinds of jests would a man who craved the laurel crown deign to praise? Certainly not frivolous and vulgar *favole*. Perhaps he is thinking of urbane *joca* he might have encountered in various classical works; perhaps, as another letter suggests, Roman comedy:

> Recently I was reading some charming stories by Plautus for the sake of fleeing boredom and relaxing my mind (*fugiendi fastidii et relaxandi animi gratia*), and thereby for a short moment with the help of the ancient poet avoided the heavy

---

[1] *Epistolae metricae* I, 6, trans. Ernest Hatch Wilkins, *Petrarch at Vaucluse* (Chicago: University of Chicago Press, 1958), pp. 9–10.

cares of life. It is certainly astonishing how many pleasant
stories and elegant pieces (nugas) I have found therein, and
what trickery of servants, what old wives' tales, what flattery
of harlots, what greed of panders, what voraciousness of
parasites, what anxieties of old men, and what youthful loves.
I am now less astonished at Terence for having achieved such
great elegance following such a leader.[2]

Note how pleasure and profit mingle here. Petrarch's own
intentio in reading is thoroughly recreational; something entertaining will both bring him relaxation, the necessary *quies*
that will allow him to return to his "heavy cares" later, and
keep him from boredom, that is, keep his mind occupied
and thus not prey to the ennui that comes from idleness. But
Plautus, he finds, has other virtues as well; he writes elegantly, and he portrays different types of characters and
hence leads one to an understanding of life, a consequence
implicit from the rest of the letter, where Petrarch cites a
remark from Plautus's *Casina* that he finds applicable to his
own problems with servants.

Petrarch's reading of Plautus seems to be a perfect illustration of what Boccaccio, in the great defense of poetry in the
Genealogy of the Gods, suggests about the value of one kind of
fiction. Boccaccio specifies four types of *fabula:* the first two
correspond roughly to Macrobius's categories II.A and II.B
(see Chap. 1, n. 18), where truth is veiled by either a totally or a
partially fictitious surface; the third "is more like history than
fiction"; the fourth "contains no truth at all, either superficial
or hidden." The terminology here generally follows the allegorical tradition in separating a narrative from the truth it
embodies. But Boccaccio's third kind of fiction, which includes
Virgil and Homer, who have a "hidden meaning" beneath their
historylike surfaces, also encompasses Plautus and Terence:
"they intend naught other than the literal meaning of their
lines. Yet by their art they portray varieties of human nature
and conversation, incidentally (interim) teaching the reader

[2]*Familiari* V, 14, trans. Aldo S. Bernardo, *Rerum familiarium libri I–VIII*
(Albany: State University of New York Press, 1975), p. 267. Text in *Le
familiari,* ed. V. Rossi and U. Bosco, 4 vols. (Florence: Sansoni, 1933–42), II:
34–35.

and putting him on his guard."[3] This is a deservedly well-known passage in medieval literary criticism, and to explore all of its implications is beyond my purposes here. If we remember from Chapter 1 the easy relegation of Plautus and Terence to that category of fiction made *causa delectandi,* Boccaccio's assertion of their profitableness marks a major rise in their literary stock.[4] Still, that "interim" is intriguing. Boccaccio does not seem to think that the moral intentions of even the best comedy are as great as those of the works that allegorically veil truth, and elsewhere he is quick to dismiss much comic poetry as unworthy of defense. Petrarch's comments on Plautus may verbalize some of what the *Genealogy* leaves unsaid: that although Roman comedy shrewdly examines human nature and is thus relevant *ad mores,* its principal usefulness is as a source of relaxation and enjoyment. At the end of this book we will see another early humanist, Laurent de Premierfait, take the same view of Roman comedy and use it to explain the nature of the *Decameron.*

Although the *Genealogy* does not mention *delectatio* here, it is not at all disdainful toward the recreative powers of literature. After defining the four types of fiction and showing that the three worthwhile types all appear in the Bible, Boccaccio goes on to defend literature's efficacy. It has been used in "quelling minds aroused to a mad rage."

> By fiction, too, the strengths and spirits of great men worn out in the strain of serious crises, have been restored. This appears, not by ancient instance alone, but constantly. One knows of princes who have been deeply engaged in important matters, but after the noble and happy disposal of their affairs of state, obey, as it were, the warning of nature, and

---

[3]*Genealogia* XIV, 9, trans. Charles G. Osgood, *Boccaccio on Poetry* (Indianapolis: Bobbs-Merrill, 1956), pp. 48–49; for more on the third kind, see p. 63. Text in *Genealogie deorum gentilium libri,* ed. Vincenzo Romano, 2 vols. (Bari: G. Laterza, 1951), II: 707.

[4]Terence, however, had been valued throughout the Middle Ages for his observations on human nature, though they were often abstracted from the plays. See Curtius, p. 437; Paul Theiner, "The Medieval Terence," in *The Learned and the Lewed,* ed. Larry D. Benson, Harvard English Studies 5 (Cambridge, Mass.: Harvard University Press, 1974), pp. 231–47; and, for earlier opinions similar to Boccaccio's, Suchomski, pp. 85–89. Plautus was respected in some twelfth-century circles; see Woolf, pp. 26, 28.

revive their spent forces by calling about them such men as will renew their weary minds with diverting stories and conversation (qui iocosis confabulationibus recreent animos fatigatos). Fiction has, in some cases, sufficed to lift the oppressive weight of adversity and furnish consolation, as appears in Lucius Apuleius; he tells how the highborn maiden Charis, while bewailing her unhappy condition as captive among thieves, was in some degree restored through hearing from an old woman the charming story of Psyche. [Osgood, pp. 50–51]

Fiction also makes the mind "slipping into inactivity" become "more vigorous," and to prove it Boccaccio tells the story of the learned King Robert of Sicily, a reluctant student until Aesop's fables "lured" him into diligent study.

This last example is clearly based on the didactic theory of the fictional surface as sugarcoating. The other arguments are based on principles explained in chapters 2 and 3. Boccaccio fully proclaims literature's restorative power: it improves both physical and mental condition. And these effects, it would seem, are not restricted to any one kind of fiction; certainly the "diverting stories and conversation," like the conversations discussed in the *Tacuinum sanitatis,* involve a variety of forms of discourse. Boccaccio earlier in the chapter had associated *fabula* with *confabulatio* in an effort to give fiction making the same naturalness and usefulness as ordinary human speech, and here he associates them again. Whatever sort it may be, whether it veils truth or not, fiction, like conversation, brings recreation and health to its audience. In the *Genealogy* as a whole Boccaccio spends much more time on its didactic import, but in this passage at least he reminds us that there is more to its usefulness than instruction alone. Francesco Tateo has argued that Boccaccio's emphasis on the natural need for refreshment gives a value to fiction it does not have in scholastic explanations that stress recreation as mere time out from seriousness.[5] I do not think he aggrandizes the recreative value of fiction beyond what we have seen in some philosophical and medical testimony and what we will see in other literary justifications; but it is true that in choos-

---

[5]"Poesia e favola nella poetica del Boccaccio," *Filologia romanza,* 5 (1958), 330–32.

ing to assert the hygienic and psychological functions of *delecta-tio* in the midst of a discussion of the major values of literature, Boccaccio gives a greater dignity to these benefits than they usually had in earlier humanistic literary thinking.

Turning from theory to practice, we can find similar claims in various works of literature. *Kyng Alisaunder,* a Middle English romance of the late thirteenth or early fourteenth century, translated from the French, begins with a number of lines about the "Bysynesse, care and sorou3" that beset people every day, whether through sickness, poverty, or other adversity. Nobody can avoid "ennoy3e/ Jn many cas" while alive.

> Ac is þere non, fole ne wys,
> Kyng, ne duk, ne kni3th of prys,
> Þat ne desireþ sum solas
> Forto here of selcouþe cas;
> For Caton seiþ, the gode techer,
> Oþere mannes lijf is oure shewer.

Some people, though, prefer "ribaudye" to a story of God or Mary, or would rather drink ale than hear a "gode tale." The "noble geste" of Alexander is not for those whose "wille" lies "in þe gut and in þe barel." It is the story of a conqueror who triumphed throughout the Orient, and its presentation of the "wondres of worme and beest" will be "deliciouse" to hear.[6] One can see the concepts of pleasure and profit behind these arguments: the presentation of unusual material serves an educational function, one commended by the *Disticha Catonis,* while at the same time providing the pleasure of wondering at exotic animals. Both effects produce "solas," and what is most striking about this introduction is not its statement of literary intentions nor its rejection of cruder entertainments but the recreational context in which it locates itself. The daily grind of life wears one down; everybody needs refreshment, and that is what *Kyng Alisaunder* will provide.

More famous, and more distinctively therapeutic in its claims, is the thirteenth-century *Aucassin et Nicolette.* Calling itself a

[6]Ed. G. V. Smithers, 2 vols., EETS ỏ.s. 227, 237 (London: Oxford University Press, 1952, 1957), I: 3–5; see Smithers's notes, II: 65, for parallels to the contrast between bad and worthwhile stories.

chantefable, for it is told in a combination of prose narrative and verse meant to be sung (the music survives in the sole manuscript), it is a charming story of young love finally winning out over a variety of obstacles. At the same time, as most recent criticism has stressed, it is a sophisticated parody of a great many conventions of courtly romance. Its introduction asserts no profound treatment of love or fortune but does argue that this entertaining composition ("bons vers . . . del deport"), which recounts Aucassin's pains and prowess in the course of his love for Nicolette, has merit.

> Nus hom n'est si esbahis,
> tant dolans ni entrepris,
> de grant mal amaladis,
> se il l'oit, ne soit garis
> et de joie resbaudis,
>   tant par est douce.[7]

> There is no one so perplexed, so grief-stricken, miserable, or beset with illness, who upon hearing it will not be improved in health and cheered up through joy—it is that pleasant.

An altogether remarkable assertion. Doubtless it, like much else in the fiction, is not to be taken with full seriousness. Yet in light of the medical backgrounds we have explored, the claims are certainly not nonsensical; the pleasures of literary enjoyment produce *gaudium,* which helps restore physical and psychological well-being, both of which are explicitly mentioned in the passage. *Aucassin et Nicolette,* a blend of song and story, laced with adventure and comedy, begins with the hero grieving (VII, 2) and ends with both hero and heroine happy as they had never been before (XLI, 4, 10); the comic movement from unhappiness to delight and joy (XLI, 21–22) embodies in narrative form the change from grief to "joie" promised to the audience.

There is, in fact, a minor medical theme throughout the work. Aucassin's frustrated love is a malady, Nicolette the medicine which can make him cured, "garis" (XVIII, 30–31;

----

[7]I, 10–15, ed. Mario Roques, 2d ed., CFMA (rpt. Paris: Champion, 1965), p. 1.

XX, 16–17; XXII, 36–37). At one point the author humor-
ously turns the metaphor into reality by having Nicolette put
Aucassin's shoulder back in socket (XXVI).[8] The beloved as
physician is a familiar image in medieval love literature, parallel to, but not necessarily meant as a moral parody of, biblical
and patristic imagery of Christ as physician; one might not
make so much of it were it not for the comic twist, the claims at
the beginning that the work will make its audience "garis," and
its attention elsewhere to relationships between *psyche* and *soma*.
In one episode, Nicolette, needing to escape after secretly visit-
ing Aucassin in prison, has to slide down the rocky wall of a
moat, bruising and bloodying her hands and feet; yet because
of her "great fear" she feels neither "pain nor grief" (XVI, 18–
19). Later, as Aucassin rides through heavy woods to find his
beloved, the sharp underbrush bloodies him, "but he thought
so much about Nicolette, his sweet love, that he felt neither
pain nor grief" (XXIV, 7–8). And when he finds her, though
his shoulder is injured, he feels neither "pain nor grief" because they are now together (XXVI, 8). The extreme emotions
of fear and love make the protagonists forget their physical
injuries and suffering. This perfectly valid psychosomatic observation, though its formulaic repetition is probably humorous
considering the work's other parodic exaggerations, invites us
to reflect on *Aucassin et Nicolette*'s first assertion of the power of
emotion, the therapeutic value of the "joie" brought to an audience by this delightful *chantefable*. It too, apparently, can abol-
ish physical and mental distress. One suspects that the author's
prefatory claims are deliberately overstated, part of the urbane
playfulness and parody that permeate the whole work; but
even if they are, such wit would have had point only if the
audience of *Aucassin et Nicolette* was familiar with therapeutic
claims on behalf of literary entertainment.

Fabliau and Court Lyric

Let us turn from individual works to genres, and first
to that most notorious of medieval types, the fabliau. To what

---

[8]Eugene Vance, "The Word at Heart: *Aucassin et Nicolette* as a Medieval
Comedy of Language," *Yale French Studies*, 45 (1970), 49, notes this detail as an
example of the author's "downgrading" of courtly conventions.

end were the fabliaux created? "Let us examine the prologues of the fabliaux. They speak with a single voice: a fabliau is nothing but an amusing trifle." Thus Joseph Bédier summarized fabliau purposes, in line with his still standard definition of the genre as versified tales for amusement ("contes à rire en vers").[9] The fabliaux in fact do not respond with the unanimity he suggests, for some claim moral purposes and most have little or nothing to say about their intentions. But a number do, in one way or another, point up their power to entertain, and in so doing ally themselves with the theories of delight we have examined.

The simple introduction to one fabliau makes a typical case:

> Raconter vueil une aventure
> Par joie et par envoiseüre;
> Ele n'est pas vilaine à dire,
> Mais moz por la gent faire rire.[10]

> I want to tell a story for the sake of joy and pleasure. It is not shameful to tell but meant to make people laugh.

The tale produces laughter, which promotes joy, and we know the values of *gaudium*. The third line is coy, since the story involves an extended metaphor for sex; the introduction fends off questions of propriety by stressing the work's *intentio* of amusement. In addition to others claiming to delight or to make people laugh (e.g. II: 24; V: 157), some fabliaux imply this purpose in their conclusions by bringing on personages of high social rank who function as judges of the tales' actions; their responses are usually laughter and appreciation of the wit of the trick that has been recounted (e.g. III: 174, 206–7; V: 64; cf. the conclusion of Chaucer's *Summoner's Tale*). It is fair to

[9]*Les fabliaux*, 6th ed. (Paris: Champion, 1964), pp. 309, 30. Similarly, a much more recent work argues that the nature of fabliau humor is essentially that of the joke; see Thomas D. Cooke, *The Old French and Chaucerian Fabliaux: A Study of their Comic Climax* (Columbia: University of Missouri Press, 1978), pp. 137–69. Many of the quotations in the next few paragraphs appear in Bédier's discussion of fabliau intentions, but he does not consider their theoretical implications.

[10]*Recueil général et complet des fabliaux*, ed. Anatole de Montaiglon and Gaston Raynaud, 6 vols. (Paris: Librarie des Bibliophiles, 1872–90), IV: 199. Subsequent references to this collection in the text will cite volume and page numbers.

infer that such delight and laughter would contribute to one's cheerfulness, and also to infer from another fabliau's concern not to bore (III: 46) that its end is the opposite of ennui, the passing of time in an entertaining way.

A few tales claim not only to delight but also to refresh. The author of *Des trois avugles de compiegne* states the case briefly: "Fablel sont bon à escouter: / Maint duel, maint mal font mesconter / Et maint anui et maint meffet" (I: 70). (Fabliaux are worth hearing: they make one overlook much grief, sickness, anxiety, and injury.) Another tale associates its capacity to cause laughter with a lessening of anger, anxiety, and irritability, concluding that "quant aucuns dit les risées, / Les forts tançons sont obliées."[11] In other words, a good humorous story functions to regulate destructive emotions. These claims to beguile troubles may seem superficial and escapist, but that is probably because we have institutionalized forms of verbal therapy that deal much more directly and thoroughly with personal feelings. For the Middle Ages, I suspect, claims to lead people away from emotional problems are assertions of therapy rather than detours around it, as the evidence of the *consilia* in chapter 2 suggests.

One of the longest proclamations of fabliau virtues occurs at the beginning of *Du chevalier qui fit les cons parler:*

> Now fabliaux have grown so many,
> they've pocketed a pretty penny,
> those by whom they're told and done,
> because they bring a lot of fun
> where carefree, idle people gather,
> as long as folks aren't there to blather;
> even grouches never fail,
> on hearing read a clever tale,
> to feel immediate relief
> and put aside the care and grief
> and woes from which they agonize.[12]

[11]II: 114, but see the better reading of line 2 in R. C. Johnston and D. D. R. Owen, eds., *Fabliaux* (Oxford: Basil Blackwell, 1965), p. 44 and n. p. 97. Trans. Cooke, p. 106.

[12]Trans. Robert Harrison, *Gallic Salt* (Berkeley: University of California Press, 1974), p. 219; text p. 218. Cf. *Recueil*, VI: 68.

This argument combines elements of the hygienic and recreational justifications. Its latter lines echo the fabliau assertions just discussed of providing emotional therapy. The earlier portion seems to rely more on recreational ideas: storytelling brings "confortement" to the "oiseus," solace to the idle, but only as long as the audience does not become "noiseus," troublesome. Fabliaux meet the need for recreational activity or engagement in opposition to sloth, and the warning against excessive unruliness puts the entertainment, at least ostensibly, in the category of honest as opposed to dishonest play. The preface to a shorter version of *Du chevalier* which appears in MS Harley 2253 invokes the recreational justification more directly: stories produce "solas," and solace produces "releggement," mental relaxation and repose (VI: 198).

Nowhere, perhaps, is the relationship between theory and practice more open to questions of motive than in the case of the fabliaux. Clearly these fictions invoke recreational and therapeutic ideas to justify themselves. In light of the traditions we have discussed, their claims to alleviate mental or physical discomforts cannot be automatically shrugged off as desperate, far-fetched efforts at respectability. On the other hand, a great many fabliaux are just dirty stories, and *Du chevalier* is among the most outrageously vulgar of the group. Are not its claims to provide "confortement" or "solas" more than a little disingenuous, like the appeals of pornographers to First Amendment rights? At what point does an argument become an excuse? We have seen this problem implicitly acknowledged by theorists, in such places as Aquinas's careful delimitation of acceptable, decent recreation; one can probably assume that he did not have telling *Du chevalier* in mind as an example of *eutrapelia*. Yet it seems to me fruitless to try to draw hard-and-fast distinctions between types of literature which make valid claims to recreate and types which use recreational ideas more or less cynically. "Acceptability" in any given case must have been dependent on a variety of factors, few of which we can locate with precision in regard to any given text. If certain quarters would have regarded *Du chevalier* as obscene and offensive, *scurrilitas* of the worst sort, others must have found it good entertainment, for it is one of the most popular fabliaux in terms of manuscript survival, and its appearance in Harley 2253 suggests an audience for it that can hardly be called churlish in all its tastes. Ever since Per Nykrog challenged Bédier's thesis about the bourgeois basis of the fabliaux, and responses to Nykrog challenged his exclusively aristocratic thesis, careful consideration of fabliau texts has pointed to a wide social spectrum of audiences.[13] A similar variety of taste in regard to fabliau comedy must have existed as well, certainly not determined by social status alone. There is substantial evidence that some medieval people, at least, enjoyed frivolous and even obscene stories as well as more serious fiction, and given this range of toleration (and the purposes of this book) it is probably wisest simply to note where the recreational arguments appear rather than to attempt to sort out the motives that might lie behind them.

The status of the fabliau in relation to more earnest composition emerges as an aspect of some later prefaces. Although the genre is principally a thirteenth-century one, Bédier discusses a trio of early fourteenth-century trouveres, writers primarily of allegorical and didactic poems, who on occasion return to it.[14] It is instructive to see how they talk about their fabliaux in light of their other, less purely entertaining, work. The evidence in Jacques de Baisieux is minimal. Of his five surviving poems, one, *Li dis de le vescie a prestre*, is a fabliau, best known as the only full-scale analogue to Chaucer's *Summoner's Tale*. At the end the author says that he translated it from Flemish into French "because of the trick, which he liked (Por la trufe, qu'il a amee)" (Thomas, p. 112). "Trufe" may refer specifically to the trick performed in the tale, but as the term is used by the two other trouvères it tends to acquire generic force, to denote

[13]Fundamental here is Jean Rychner, *Contribution à l'étude des fabliaux*, 2 vols. (Geneva: Droz, 1960). See also his "Les fabliaux: Genre, styles, publics," in *La littérature narrative d'imagination*, Colloque de Strasbourg, 23–25 avril 1959 (Paris: Presses Universitaires de France, 1961), pp. 41–52, in which Rychner suggests, among other things, that the fabliau genre might be defined more properly on the basis of its social role than on the basis of purely formal criteria. Such an approach is consistent with medieval habits we have seen elsewhere of classifying works by pragmatic function rather than by structural or generic principles.

[14]Pp. 418–26. The work of Watriquet de Couvin and Jean de Condé can be dated with certainty between 1310–40. Making Jacques de Baisieux their contemporary is highly conjectural, as Bédier admits and as Jacques's most recent editor stresses; see Patrick A. Thomas, ed., *L'oeuvre de Jacques de Baisieux* (The Hague: Mouton, 1973), pp. 24, 45–47.

the narrative which relates the trick. To the extent that one can
work from such a brief reference, the word suggests that
Jacques perceives his tale as a trifling but entertaining narrative, not the more substantial subject matter he seeks elsewhere
for his elegant compositions ("biaz dis") (pp. 72, 94).

Watriquet de Couvin is more expansive in discussing his fabliau, *Des trois chanoinesses de Couloigne*. At the beginning he notes
that people who tell "aucunes truffes" find their work as well
received as do those who write "uns sarmons." So he will tell "a
little madcap tale, provided that everyone will laugh at it if they
find it well told (.i. poi du reverie / Par covent que chascuns en
rie / S'il i a mot qui bien le vaille)." His conclusion confirms this
purpose: "These are jests (risées) to entertain (esbatre) kings,
princes, and counts." There are as well "risées" within the
story, first when Watriquet recites some to amuse the three
canonesses, who have explained to him that "we don't want
anything noble, just something that can make us laugh," and
later when the women themselves, urged by one to tell jokes
and jests ("gogues et risées"), produce a series of wishes so
offensive that someone censored them out of the sole surviving
manuscript.[15] The narrative gives us layers of levity. The
stories within the frame amuse the women, and Watriquet recites the entire "aventure" to amuse the court. Much of his
poem's humor depends on the canonesses' shameless ribaldry,
but whatever one may think of their taste in entertainment, the
logic of the fabliau as a whole, presented to a secular audience,
is unexceptionable: jests produce laughter, and laughter produces a state of amusement—"esbatre" appears in a French
translation of the *Disticha* and probably carries with it here
implications of the full recreational argument.[16] Watriquet's
other fabliau, *Des trois dames de Paris*, lacks such extensive self-
analysis but suggests its status obliquely at the start by claiming
to be a true but unusual "aventure" and clearly at the end by

[15]*Dits de Watriquet de Couvin,* ed. Auguste Scheler (Brussels: Victor Devaux,
1868), pp. 373–74, 379, 377–78. References to Watriquet will be to page numbers of this edition. For more on *Des trois chanoinesses* and structurally similar
tales, see Roy J. Pearcy, "The Genre of William Dunbar's *Tretis of the Tua Mariit
Wemen and the Wedo,*" *Speculum,* 55 (1980), 58–74.
    [16]"Entremet toy de jouer et d'esbatre / Aucunes foiz pour tes cures abatre, /
Si que puisses mieulx porter en courage / De cest monde le labour et l'orage."
Ed. J. Ulrich, *Romanische Forschungen,* 15 (1904), 91–92.

referring to its action, like that of *Des trois chanoinesses,* as "reverie" (pp. 381, 390).

But the simple division between "truffes" and "sarmons" is not the whole story. Watriquet's tone at the end of *Des trois chanoinesses* is somewhat defensive, I think, and his poetics in general not very tolerant of the merely amusing. In prefatory remarks to the *Dis de la cygoigne* he notes that many people are entertained ("esbaudiz") and take pleasure in hearing good compositions, but they do not profit from them if they do not assimilate deeper meanings. Such people, who gather more pleasure "from a *fatras* or a trifle" than from worthwhile stories, come to disregard virtue and turn to vice.[17] As Bédier and others have shown, Watriquet and his contemporaries draw a firm distinction between the edifying material proffered by good minstrels and the disreputable amusements produced by bad ones; the minstrel who has become a dignified court maker looks down on vagrant entertainers. Watriquet sincerely wants to edify, though that desire need not exclude elements of professional rivalry and aggrandizement in his posture as well. Throughout his work he prefers "sarmons" to "truffes"; yet he wrote two fabliaux, and in spite of the disparaging allusion to "fastras" he is the only fourteenth-century author whose verses in the genre of the *fatras* have survived. According to the manuscript rubric, he recited them (obscenities and all, apparently) before King Philip of France.[18] It is not difficult to construct a critical theory for Watriquet which accommodates his professions as well as his practice: although it is wrong to be merely "esbaudiz" by material meant to instruct, and to prefer "risées" to more substantial literature, amusement is proper on those limited occasions when a work's only intent is to entertain its audience. But he was probably never quite so categorical about it, and the evidence suggests a kind of "situation poetics," the court maker pulled in varying directions by his own convictions and interests and by audience demands, trying to accommodate them all.

[17]Pp. 283–84. The passage is partially quoted and discussed in *Preface to Chaucer,* p. 61. Cf. Douglas Kelly, *Medieval Imagination: Rhetoric and the Poetry of Courtly Love* (Madison: University of Wisconsin Press, 1978), pp. 108–10.

[18]Lambert C. Porter, *La fatrasie et le fatras: Essai sur la poésie irrationnelle en France au Moyen Age* (Geneva: Droz, 1960), pp. 72–73, 97; text pp. 145–59 and in Scheler, pp. 295–309. Although the *fatras* form was later used for pious subjects, both it and the *fatrasie* seem to have originated as virtuoso amusements.

Jean de Condé, a minstrel at the court of Count William II of Hainault, whose daughter Philippa became Queen of England when she married Edward III, offers additional evidence of the tendency to separate trivial from serious writing, even though, like the others, he never uses the term "fabliau" to characterize his tales in that tradition. At the beginning of one story he distinguishes between jesting and serious literature, "truffe" and "auctorité," offering the former this time since some people prefer it.[19] The introduction to *Li dis dou pliçon* also rings with terminology like Watriquet's: "There are many people who take more pleasure in hearing jests (risées) and clever japes than they do in sermons (siermons), so I have often been urged to put jests into rhyme; and therefore I want to set about rhyming a true incident" (II: 127). A third fabliau, *Des braies le priestre*, mentions its literary status only in passing: Jean offers a new story about a lecherous priest to add to the "maint lait reviel" (II: 121), the many off-color pleasantries, already told on the subject. In all these fabliaux, neither Jean nor Watriquet makes explicit reference to theories of refreshment, and their remarks about furnishing what their court audiences demand are usually taken to indicate disdain for the merely entertaining. But it is possible that the allusions to people's preferences for entertainment over edification constitute a somewhat more objective recognition of simple psychological and social facts. A nobleman might legitimately seek "risées" in order to recreate himself, and a court maker functioning as *confabulator* would appropriately supply such material.

There is, if we look further, certainly no disapproval of entertainment per se in another of Jean's poems, *Le sentier batu*. Though always classified as one of his fabliaux, it is not so much a story as a recounting of an exchange of witticisms. The context is a game known as "The King Who Does Not Lie," a social pastime related to the tradition of the *demandes amoureuses*. In this instance a woman has been chosen Queen. She

[19]*Dits et contes de Baudouin de Condé et de son fils Jean de Condé*, ed. Auguste Scheler, 3 vols. (Brussels: Victor Devaux, 1866–67), III: 197. All references to Jean's works are to volume and page numbers of this edition, though his fabliaux, like Watriquet's and Jacques's, also appear in the *Recueil général*. There is a thorough study of Jean's work by Jacques Ribard, *Un Ménestrel du XIVᵉ siècle: Jean de Condé* (Geneva: Droz, 1969).

asks a question of each of her companions, they answer, and she responds to their answers. Then all the other players have a chance to put a question to her and comment on what she has said. In the episode told by Jean, the Queen's question and response to one participant, a knight she had once refused to marry, cast aspersions on his sexual prowess; in the second round, he takes revenge with a question and remark implying her promiscuity. Jean tells the story, he says, to show that "it is not wise to make fun of others or to say things that grieve people or make them ashamed. . . . Nor is it good to make earnest of game." At the end he repeats his warning against "voir gas," earnest game, play that is too close to a painful truth. The tale is interesting principally for its close connection with a society pastime that can be documented elsewhere; it suggests how easily conversational play can turn into literary narrative.[20] And as well, it reveals the special status of *gab:* jesting, a legitimate facet of secular life, becomes dangerous when it is misused in the attempt to cause "anui" rather than to relieve it. Game ought not be earnest. *Le sentier batu* is in one sense an exemplum based on the distinction in *Nicomachean Ethics* IV, 8, between proper amusement and improper jest, which turns play into insult. It is also, implicitly, an illustration of the social circumstances that justify Jean's own forms of *gab,* the "truffe," "risées," and "reviel" that are his fabliaux.

These social circumstances emerge through argument rather than dramatization in *Li dis des Jacobins et des Fremeneurs*, a defense of some kinds of minstrelsy against the attacks of friars and, by way of reciprocation, an assault on the corrupt state of

[20]III: 299–303. Trans. Robert Hellman and Richard O'Gorman, *Fabliaux: Ribald Tales from the Old French* (New York: Thomas Y. Crowell, 1965), pp. 23–26. Text and verse translation in Harrison, pp. 138–47. For background on the game, see Elizabeth Daverman, "New Finds on the Courtly Game, *Le jeu du Roi qui ne ment,*" a paper presented at the Fourteenth International Congress on Medieval Studies, Western Michigan University, May 4, 1979. Another court pastime with literary manifestations, the cult of the flower and the leaf, seems also to have been intended essentially as recreative entertainment, at least in the eyes of Charles d'Orléans. His two ballades on the subject note that while with a "compaignie" on the first of May he participated in the game; he remains detached from it, preoccupied with the death of his lady, but he recognizes that it exists "to alleviate melancholy" and "for entertainment (pour esbat)." George L. Marsh, "The Sources and Analogues of 'The Flower and the Leaf,' " *Modern Philology*, 4 (1906–7), 131–33.

the Dominicans and the Franciscans. Jean begins by adducing examples to show that, contrary to the clerical charge, minstrelsy is not in league with the devil. His first instance is David's harping before Saul, which is able to "conforter" the king (1 Kings 16: 14–23). After other religious evidence he turns to the demands of secular court life. It is right for "cheavaliers" to have abundant pleasure ("envoisement") because their role demands upholding the ecclesiastical and the secular order, which involves fighting against any opponents of either church or state. Hence they must be physically and mentally at their peak; think what would happen, says Jean, if they became depressed. Accordingly, they should frequent the court, mix with other people, "bring themselves great joy and solace (Mener grant joie et grant soulas)"—of course, it must be "joie houneste." Listening to minstrels is a means of attaining this necessary *gaudium temperatum:* "It is appropriate that refreshment take the form of joy through minstrelsy (Or couvient il que resbaudie / Soit joie par menestraudie)." Jean goes on to discuss the psychological changes, from worry to cheerfulness ("D'anui à joie"), that minstrelsy prompts (III: 249–53; cf. Ribard, p. 149). Later in the poem, after attacking the friars, he returns to the defense, noting that he himself is a minstrel and that his work reproves vice and inculcates virtue. The work of good minstrels ought not be confused with that of "enchanteurs" and other less worthy entertainers (III: 257–59). Although Jean maintains, as he usually does elsewhere, that his goals are both pleasure and profit, the explanation of the nobility's need for recreational *joie* may be applied to anything that provides legitimate play, including the fabliaux and court games that bring enjoyment to knights and ladies. Jean's commendation of good minstrelsy for its restorative powers offers a thorough theoretical justification for his and his fellow trouvères' fabliau entertainments.

Later in the fourteenth century another, much greater, writer turned also to the tradition. Chaucer's fabliaux are so much richer than what survives in Old French that many critics see them as transcending rather than extending the genre.[21] But

---

[21]For a recent overview, see Beryl Rowland, "What Chaucer Did to the Fabliau," *Studia Neophilologica,* 51 (1979), 205–13.

for all their artistic sophistication, they represent a literary intention which he identifies as different from that of his more serious work. Chaucer's thinking is based more or less on the broad Horatian formula, which appears in varied terminology throughout his work. In the *Parlement of Foules* the narrator reads books for "lust" and "lore" (15); at the beginning of the *Canterbury Tales* Harry Bailly proposes to reward the pilgrim who tells "tales of best sentence and moost solaas" (A 798); later he asks Chaucer for a story that will offer either "som murthe or som doctryne" and warns the Monk that "sentence" without "desport ne game" will not appeal to an audience (B² 2125, 3979–92). The end of the *Nun's Priest's Tale,* whatever Chaucer's purpose in raising the theoretical issue, offers a standard allegorical version of *delectare* and *prodesse,* in which the literal level of the fable becomes "chaf" and the "moralite" the profitable "fruyt" (B² 4628–33). It is with this conceptual habit in mind that we must read the last line of the apology before the *Miller's Tale,* where, after a series of witty gambits that call attention to the forthcoming "harlotrie" without really offering a satisfactory defense of it, Chaucer advises that "men shal nat maken ernest of game" (A 3186). This line needs to be taken in light of the tradition of literature seeking to please rather than to profit; "ernest" and "game" are another Middle English equivalent of the Horatian polarity, translating the two different goals of fiction into the distinction between frivolous and serious matter, a tendency we have seen throughout the Middle Ages.²² Chaucer here affirms that the tales of the Miller and the Reeve, and by implication other similar "harlotrie," are more playful than the rest of the *Canterbury Tales,* meant essentially to delight rather than to give moral instruction.

Of course, things are seldom simple in the *Canterbury Tales.* Although in one sense Chaucer belongs to a tradition of court makers, his learning and genius are such that we are reluctant to accept at face value the easy dichotomy of pleasure and profit which he establishes to explain his fabliaux just as Watriquet de Couvin and Jean de Condé did to explain theirs. The apology occurs in a dramatic context. Might not this be the

---

²²Cf. Gower, *Confessio amantis,* VII, 3109; elsewhere, of course, Chaucer uses the terms "ernest" and "game" without literary implication.

pilgrim rather than the poet speaking? Might not A 3186 be just another ploy, one designed to alert us to precisely the opposite kind of reading? Can we really accept the *Miller's Tale*, brilliant work of art that it is, as a mere "game"? To deal with the first two questions is beyond the scope of this book, since they involve detailed consideration of some of the most complex aspects of Chaucer's art. We can say, however, from the standpoint of medieval literary thought, that a straightforward reading of A 3186 is certainly possible, for the line makes perfect sense as an expression of a substantial tradition acknowledging and valuing literature for pleasure rather than profit. If court makers with as much pretension to seriousness as Watriquet and Jean could write more trivial verse, there is no reason to assume Chaucer could not as well. To the third question I would say only that an exceptionally general theoretical distinction about literary purpose is not the same thing as a sympathetic understanding of the intricacies of a literary work. There is much in the *Miller's Tale* of great artistry in plotting and characterization, much of religious resonance. In that sense it is certainly not a trifle. Yet I believe that Chaucer ultimately would have thought of it and his other fabliaux as less serious, less worthy of being held in the mind, than the *Knight's Tale* or the *Clerk's Tale*. It is much like the distinction Graham Greene made at one time between his "entertainments" and his "novels," a distinction based on intent at a very basic level. There is no reason why we might not find an author's "game" or "entertainment" more satisfying artistically, perhaps even wiser morally, than some of his more explicitly serious work. The Horatian polarity has nothing to do with aesthetic quality, nor with human insight. For these matters we need different criteria, and although one can find them in other medieval and modern literary thought, they are simply not the criteria Chaucer chooses to invoke in regard to his fabliaux. He remains medievally pragmatic in explaining only their most apparent *utilitas,* their provision of the "game," the *delectatio,* that brings solace and joy to an audience. And it is not difficult to imagine why: presenting the "cherles termes" (A 3917) and vulgar action of the fabliaux to an audience that knew him as the author of the *Book of the Duchess* and the *Troilus,* Chaucer would naturally seek to locate such tales in a context that his listeners or readers could readily accept and appreciate.

Turning from the coarseness of the fabliau to the grace and decorousness of the late medieval court lyric involves major changes in form and sensibility but not, as it turns out, in the perception of the genre's usefulness. Since I have written about the poetics of the fixed form lyrics at some length elsewhere, I present here only a very brief look at the most pertinent evidence and refer the reader to three related articles for fuller documentation and discussion.[23]

From the perspective of literary theory the key text in understanding the myriad of late medieval ballades, roundels, and virelays is Deschamps's *Art de dictier*, dated 1392, a manual for would-be versifiers describing the formal properties of the lyric types in vogue. All such compositions, according to Deschamps, belong to the category of music, even if they are recited rather than sung. And music occupies a special place within the liberal arts:

> [It is] like the medicine of the seven arts. For when the energy and spirit of men intent on the other arts named above become wearied and tired of their labors, music—through the sweetness of its art and the melody of its voice—sings to them . . . so that through its delightful melody the hearts and *spiritus* of those who have become overworked, sluggish, and tired through thinking, imagination, and bodily labor directed toward the other arts are medicined and refreshed and better able subsequently to study and work at the other six arts previously mentioned.[24]

[23]"Deschamps' *Art de dictier* and Chaucer's Literary Environment," *Speculum*, 48 (1973), 714–23; "Making and Poetry in the Age of Chaucer," *Comparative Literature*, 31 (1979), 272–90; and "Toward a Poetics of the Late Medieval Court Lyric," in *Vernacular Poetics in the Middle Ages*, ed. Lois Ebin (Kalamazoo: Medieval Institute Publications, forthcoming 1982).

[24]"Musique est la derreniere science ainsis comme la medicine des .VII. ars; car quant le couraige et l'esperit des creatures ententives aux autres ars dessus declairez sont lassez at ennuyez de leurs labours, musique, par la douçour de sa science et la melodie de sa voix, leur chante . . . tant que par sa melodie delectable les cuers et esperis de ceuls qui auxdiz ars, par pensée, ymaginaison et labours de bras estoient traveilliez, pesans et ennuiez, sont medicinez et recreez, et plus habiles après a estudier et labourer aux autres .VI. ars dessus nommez." *Oeuvres complètes*, ed. Le Marquis de Queux de Saint-Hilaire and Gaston Raynaud, 11 vols., SATF (Paris: Firmin Didot, 1878–1903), VII: 269.

I do not know of any precisely similar categorization of music. Instead of treating it as part of the quadrivium, Deschamps gives it separate status among the liberal arts, in a way reminiscent of St. Bonaventure's separation of mechanical arts into six which aim at *commodum* and one, theatrics, at *solatium*. Whatever prompted this approach, it is clearly based on recreational principles. Serious mental or physical labor leaves people weakened; delight produces rest and refreshment; and with refreshment comes renewed diligence. It is reasonable to give "esperis" a precise scientific meaning, since the passage as a whole relies on a medical analogy and hence invites recollection of the exact hygienic benefits of being delighted. Twenty years earlier Nicole Oresme had given instrumental music the same recreational value, and the relationship between music and medicine was a familiar idea throughout the Middle Ages.[25]

Similar views of music, as an element of lyric poetry, occur in Machaut, in the fourteenth-century Provençal treatise, the *Leys d'amors,* and in other French testimony from the period.[26] It is possible, as Douglas Kelly argues, to separate music and words as independent aspects of the fixed form lyrics and to find different functions for each, music affording emotional pleasure, language artistic and moral satisfactions. But in the *Art de dictier,* at least, Deschamps stresses the musical values of pleasure and solace as the fundamental result of lyric composition, whether sung or spoken. Pleasure is therapeutic, and it is no accident that Deschamps later cites, as an example of instances where recited verses are preferable to ones sung, the case of a person reading "a book of these pleasing compositions to someone who is ill" (VII: 272). Music would be too loud; the spoken lyric can by itself, apparently, help ease a sick person's misery.

Deschamps's view of lyric as natural music involves the logical fusion of hygienic and recreational ideas. The power of music (taken broadly to include the aural and rhythmic pleasures of spoken verse) to repair mind and body is the medical fact that justifies the ethical inclusion of refreshment as a legitimate ac-

[25]See Chapter 3, n. 16; Chap. 2, n. 28. For Renaissance texts on music as therapy, see Gretchen Ludke Finney, "Music, Mirth, and Galenic Tradition in England," in *Reason and the Imagination,* ed. J. A. Mazzeo (New York: Columbia University Press, 1962), pp. 143–54, a reference I owe to Glenda Pritchett.
[26]"Deschamps' *Art de dictier,*" 718–21; Kelly, pp. 239–56.

tivity within the framework of liberal pursuits. Hence lyric performance becomes, in theory as well as practice, a type of social entertainment; and abundant evidence, some of which appears elsewhere in this book, testifies to the late medieval perception of fixed form verse in this way. Occasionally, as in a chapter of the biography of Marshal Boucicaut, the full recreational argument appears in order to justify such literary pleasures. The author, describing Boucicaut's hatred of idleness and his constant labor at good works, notes that a life without any recreation through entertainment ("aucune recreation de quelque esbatement") is dangerous to one's health. He explains the mental and physical problems that result "when the imagination becomes strained by many things piling up one after the other." Today we call it stress. Because of his concern for Boucicaut's well-being, the biographer devotes the rest of the chapter to an explanation of the value of recreation, retelling the bent bow story to show that it is not at all displeasing to God to "recreate and refresh" the body. Moreover, he mentions some examples of entertainment which reinvigorate one's spirit: listening to songs, playing musical instruments, hearing "merry talk that is neither offensive nor indecent, or something that is humorous (paroles joyeuses sans peché, ne vice, ou quelque chose qui face rire)."[27] He is enumerating typical courtly entertainments, doubtless thinking of the fixed form lyrics among them. He invokes the re-creative pleasures of lyric as Deschamps defines them for a very practical hygienic end, the continued health of a man he admires.

Hostile Witnesses

All the literary claims discussed thus far view the recreational and therapeutic values of pleasure positively. But there are some instances in which these values, without others, are made to appear as rather trivial ones. The late twelfth-century Anglo-Norman life of St. Edmund by Denis Piramus opens with a fascinating prologue that suggests the competition for court attention between secular entertainment and more

[27]*Le livre des faicts du bon messire Jean le Maingre, dit Boucicaut*, ed. C. B. Petitot, 2 vols., Collection complète des mémoires relatifs à l'histoire de France, 6–7 (Paris, 1819), II: 214–18.

overtly pious narrative. The author begins with ostensible autobiography, though his pose is part of a literary tradition. He
has lived much of his life foolishly, serving the court with songs
and rhymes; as old age approaches he will jest no more and will
turn to a better kind of work. But before we discover what that
work is, he discusses audience response to some literature different from his, the romance *Partonopeus de Blois* and the lays of
Marie de France. These compositions are patently untrue in
content, though artfully composed, and court audiences love
them. Women hear the lays "de joie." The nobility enjoy delightful stories "because they remove and discard sadness, tedium, and weariness of heart, and they make people forget
their anger and banish troublesome thoughts." Denis knows
that his audience likes such pleasure ("deduit"), so he offers a
"deduit" that is more worthwhile than exotic romance, for it is
not only "delightful to hear" but leads to the salvation of one's
soul. It is the true story of the life and miracles of St. Edmund,
offering a good example to noblemen, and decent people
ought to want to hear such stories and hold them in their
memories.[28]

A similar prologue, but without the autobiographical opening, occurs in the early fourteenth-century *Roman du Comte
d'Anjou,* the story of a woman who endures a variety of misfor-
tunes with steadfast faith, intended as an "examplaire" to lead
people to persevere in good behavior. The poem begins with a
catalogue of various literary efforts to which people devote
themselves: "fables" and "aventures," stories of heroes like
Tristan and Roland, "pastourelles," songs with instruments including lays and ballades "to entertain people who are ill (Pour
esbatre ces gens malades)." All such works are "trufles," yet
their makers seem to do rather well for themselves, even
though they provide nothing for the soul but merely "drive
away tedium of spirit (l'anui des cuers enchacent)." This story
will not only offer "plesance" through the beauty of its rhyme

---

[28]*La vie seint Edmund le Rei,* ed. Hilding Kjellman (Göteborg: Elanders, 1935),
pp. 3–6. Denis is probably referring to the court of Henry II. For the tradition
of rejecting vain youthful writing, see Olive Sayce, "Chaucer's 'Retractions':
The Conclusion of the *Canterbury Tales* and Its Place in Literary Tradition,"
Medium Aevum, 40 (1971), 230–48, esp. 238–43.

and through its being true rather than fictitious, but it has a profitable "fruit" as well.[29]

Both these prologues deprecate species of secular literature on the grounds that they lack moral relevance. It is not just that they are lies, fabrications, but that they have no spiritual value whatsoever. (The degree to which this accusation is true or not is, for our purposes here, beside the point.) But neither author is blind to the real attractions of romance and lyric, and they define those attractions in recreational terms. Fictions bring delight, alleviate tedium and anxiety, and induce joy. Maillart's reference to the use of songs as entertainment for people who are ill reveals a therapeutic view of music and lyrics that Deschamps articulates at greater length later in the century. Such benefits are freely acknowledged: pleasure does have this kind of utility. What disturbs the authors is that the public seems so content with these limited values, that audiences freely reward writers of the merely pleasurable and need to be urged to listen to narratives of more spiritual import. Somewhat like Watriquet de Couvin and Jean de Condé, they do not condemn amusement per se but imply that audiences are excessive in their desire for the merely entertaining. The prologues are most interesting, perhaps, because they do not simply dismiss secular entertainment as seduction of the ears; even as they condemn its moral triviality they acknowledge its recreational benefits.

We learn of the recreational justification also from testimony even more antipathetic toward the activities it defends than are Denis Piramus and Jehan Maillart toward romance and lyric. The well-known condemnation of the Feast of Fools by the Faculty of Theology at the University of Paris in 1445 censures the event for its depravity and impiety. Its proponents claim that the actions are all done in play, not in earnest ("joco, et non serio"), that without some time for levity they would mentally burst, like casks in which the pressure of fermenting wine is not occasionally released, and that time out for entertainment enables them to return to their studies with more diligence. The Faculty perceives this argument merely as an ex-

[29]Jehan Maillart, *Le roman du Comte d'Anjou*, ed. Mario Roques, CFMA (Paris: Champion, 1931), pp. 1–3.

cuse for their sins; the principle of recreation cannot justify activity against God and the Church. Jean Gerson's condemnation of the Feast argues similarly: to those who say the activities are only "games and entertainments," he responds with the proverbial wisdom that faith is one of the things that ought not be denigrated through play.[30] But the evidence supplied by Chambers reveals that the Church's attitude could not always have been so unrelievedly hostile, that the celebration of the Feast of Fools, if not its excesses, was tolerated in many quarters; and in any rationale for it the recreational argument must have been the most natural and convincing one.

The argument was advanced also to explain the religious drama, as we learn from the Wycliffite *Tretise of Miraclis Pleyinge*. This tract condemns the drama principally because it represents *invisibilia* by means that appeal to the senses; but it does deal with other justifications advanced by proponents of miracle plays, including this one: "Also summe recreacioun men moten han and bettere it is, or lesse yuele, þat þei han þeyre recreacioun by pleyinge of miraclis þan by pleyinge of oþer iapis." To this defense the treatise responds:

> . . . verry recreacion is leeueful, ocupiynge in lasse werkis, to more ardently worschen grettere werkis. And þerfore siche myraclis pleyinge ne þe siȝte of hem is no verrey recreasion but fals and worldly, as prouyn þe dedis of þe fautours [supporters] of siche pleyis þat ȝit neuere tastiden verely swetnesse in God, traueylynge so myche þerinne þat þeir body wolde not sofisen to beren siche a traueyle of þe spirite, but as man goiþ fro vertue into vertue, so þei gon fro lust into lust þat þei more stedefastly dwellen in hem. And þerfore as þis feynyd recreacioun of pleyinge of myraclis is fals equite [righteousness], so it is double shrewidnesse, worse þan þouy þei pleyiden pure vaniteis. For now þe puple ȝyueþ credence to many mengid [confused] lessyngis for oþere mengid trewþis and maken wenen to been gode þat is ful yuel. And so ofte siþis lasse yuele it were to pleyin rebaudye þan to pleyin siche myriclis.[31]

[30]*Chartularium Universitatis Parisiensis*, ed. H. Denifle, IV (Paris, 1897), p. 653. English trans. in Thorndike, *University Records*, p. 345. Gerson, *Oeuvres complètes*, ed. Glorieux, VII (Paris: Desclée, 1966), p. 411. The standard treatment of the Feast of Fools remains Chambers, I: 274–335.

[31]*Selections from English Wycliffite Writings*, ed. Anne Hudson (Cambridge: Cambridge University Press, 1978), pp. 100, 103. Hudson does not print the

It meets the recreational argument head-on, with the uncompromising spirituality typical of Lollard thought. Recreation is valid only insofar as its lesser activities lead to more significant work. But what spiritual improvement does one see in the supporters of the drama? They are so caught up in works of the body (the appeal of the plays to the senses, provoking bodily rather than spiritual delight, is a frequent theme of the tract, and it reminds us of the physiological view of *theatrica* discussed in Chapter 2) that they are unable to rise to the true delights of God. Hence any claims to recreate must be false, since there is no evidence of the lesser activity, the playing, leading to any genuinely contemplative life. In fact, because of the hypocrisy of the recreational argument and the misrepresentation of spiritual truths by sensuous means, it might even be better to indulge oneself in "vaniteis" and "rebaudye"—at least in that case one would not be pretending to acquire righteousness nor misleading people about abstract realities. Genuinely valid "recreacioun" lies elsewhere: after "holy contemplacioun" in church, one's "recreacioun shulde ben in þe werkis of mercy to his neyebore" and in other necessary deeds that "reson and kynde" demand (p. 103). As a treatise against dice playing from the same manuscript puts it, there is "fer more myrþe" and "more recreacioun" in "deuoute werkis" that please God than in any which offend Him.[32] There was medieval criticism of the religious drama for its secular, impious tendencies, but that is not the point made here by the *Tretise*. It focuses instead on the relationship between game and earnest, recreation and inner life, demanding that the former be consistent with a spiritually pure form of the latter, and rejecting the notion that the lesser delights of recreation have to entail any bodily indulgence at all.

We have seen the medieval explanation of why they do, and the views of the *Tretise of Miraclis Pleyinge* are those of an uninfluential minority. By listing all the arguments it does not accept, the tract tells us that recreational ideas were part of the justification of a major form of medieval artistic enterprise,

---

full treatise, for which one must go to the new edition by Clifford Davidson, but what she omits is not directly relevant to our purposes. Important discussions of what we can learn from the treatise about medieval attitudes toward drama are in Woolf, pp. 84–101, and Kolve, passim.

[32]British Library MS Add. 24202, f. 22. On the MS see Hudson, p. 179.

that the religious drama was seen not only as a means of promoting devotion but also as a means of refreshment. Insofar as the proponents of the plays thought of them as providing recreation, apparently in competition with "iapis" that had no religious motives, we can perhaps perceive, in addition to a general defense, one means of explaining the comic elements that form such a large and interesting part of the genre.

Further evidence of recreational or hygienic defenses of literary pleasure is not hard to find, nor is it difficult to think of other works or genres that must have implicitly or explicitly appealed to the ideas. Robert of Basevorn, in his manual on preaching, notes that a sermon, in order to sharpen the attention of an audience drifting off, may include—judiciously—jests that provoke laughter; other testimony, perhaps the most famous of which is in canto XXIX of the *Paradiso,* shows that preachers' employment of entertaining stories was not always as restricted as Robert urges.[33] Parodic forms like the *sotte chanson* are clearly meant for entertainment rather than edification, and, although the written evidence is Renaissance rather than

[33]Much has been written, notably by G.R. Owst and J.-Th. Welter, about *exempla* and entertaining stories in sermons and about the corresponding problems of disentangling motives of profit or pleasure. See most recently on the subject Siegfried Wenzel, "The Joyous Art of Preaching; or, The Preacher and the Fabliau," *Anglia,* 97 (1979), 304–25, who cites Robert and much other pertinent evidence. Particularly interesting is Jacques de Vitry's defense of using stories "not only for edification, but for recreation." Though he does not approve of tales without some moral usefulness, he seems to recognize as the principal value their psychological effect on the audience. In order to avoid excessive "sadness" or "fatigue," audiences may sometimes be recreated by pleasant stories, "so that afterward they are more alert to hear serious and useful words." Jacques then quotes line 343 of the *Ars poetica,* thinking not of the combination of pleasure and profit within *exempla,* even though such may exist, but of the role of principally entertaining stories within the more "utilia verba" of the sermon as a whole. *The Exempla or Illustrative Stories from the Sermones Vulgares of Jacques de Vitry,* ed. T. F. Crane (London, 1890), p. xlii. The *Dialogus creaturarum,* a collection of moralized dialogues between all sorts of natural phenomena, from the human to the inanimate, asserts its usefulness to preachers because it teaches morality in a way that avoids tediousness. In this case we can be sure that the claim to relieve weariness through "the delight of pleasing material" stems from medical thinking, for the author of the *Dialogus* is the physician Maino de' Maineri, whose *Regimen sanitatis,* cited in Chap. 2, recognizes that *gaudium temperatum* restores energy. Quoted in Welter, *L'exemplum dans la littérature religieuse et didactique du moyen âge* (1927; rpt. New York: AMS Press, 1973), p. 359.

medieval, so is the genre of the flyting: as the 1629 edition of Alexander Montgomerie's poems says, his flyting serves to "delight the itching eare," intends "Anger to asswage, make melancholy lesse."[34] Some Latin works defining themselves as *ridicula* point to a tradition of principally entertaining literature in the earlier Middle Ages.[35] I do not think we need to pursue these or other references further. As it is, we have a substantial body of evidence to demonstrate the pervasiveness of literary claims to recreate and refresh, ranging through a variety of secular forms—fabliau, romance, lyric—and representing literary endeavors of diverse intent, from the merest joke to serious attempts, like *Kyng Alisaunder* and the cycle drama, at providing both pleasure and profit. Though we have seen some writers who are uneasy with, and some who violently disapprove of, literature that can assert no other function, in general the values of entertainment and psychological restoration are stated with confidence. Some literature does more than recreate, and that is all to the good; but even to give pleasure by itself is a perfectly valid function, and much medieval literature does not hesitate to announce that as its goal and to affirm the resulting benefits.

Recreation in the *Canterbury Tales*

The single most important work to depend substantially on recreational and hygienic ideas is Boccaccio's *Decameron*, the principal subject of the next two chapters. This one closes with a short discussion of another literary enterprise of great complexity, Chaucer's *Canterbury Tales*, which, because of the way it uses ideas of entertainment, demands acknowledgment here yet

---

[34]Cited in part by Pritchett, pp. 267–68, who also notes that Bannatyne found the Dunbar-Kennedy flyting "Iocund and mirrie," and by David Lampe, "'Flyting no Reason Hath,' the Inverted Rhetoric of Abuse," *The Early Renaissance, Acta,* 4 (1978), 113–14, who discusses the genre as a rhetorical game.

[35]Peter Dronke, "The Rise of the Medieval Fabliau: Latin and Vernacular Evidence," *Romanische Forschungen,* 85 (1973), 275–97; Jürgen Beyer, *Schwank und Moral. Untersuchungen zum altfranzösischen Fabliau und verwandten Formen* (Heidelberg: Carl Winter, 1969), pp. 64–93. Beyer's views on the evolution of *Schwank* material are available in an English summary, "The Morality of the Amoral," in Cooke and Honeycutt, pp. 15–42. In the preface to his commentary on the *Anticlaudianus,* Radulphus de Longo Campo, enumerating his other compositions, claims to have written, along with grammatical and philosophical works, a "ridiculum" (p. 4). See above, Chap. 2, n. 47.

leads into criticism beyond the scope of this book. If the *Decameron* is the culmination of medieval recreational literature, the *Canterbury Tales* is the richest exploration of how all literary forms, those for profit as well as pleasure, may be used and abused. To pursue fully its view of storytelling would necessitate thorough consideration of all the dimensions of Chaucer's "poetics," a subject of much current critical interest.[36] I want only to look briefly at the recreational principle as the *Tales* articulates it and to suggest something of its importance to the work as a whole.

Although the fact is not often presented in such schematic terms, there are two framing devices in the *Canterbury Tales*, an outer frame which is the pilgrimage, and an inner frame which is the storytelling contest. Long ago, in a short but astute essay, H. S. V. Jones suggested that the structure of the *Canterbury Tales* was in effect an amalgam of *Piers Plowman* and Sercambi's *Novelle*,[37] and it is the function of the double frame to secure such a complex combination. Concerning the outer frame we have heard much: the pilgrimage to Canterbury was important to critics earlier in this century for its "realism," to many critics since the 1950s for its allegorical implications as the image of man traveling through this world to his heavenly destination. As Edmund Reiss has put it, "we cannot escape from the fact that he chose a pilgrimage. And that choice resulted in a certain tone and atmosphere. . . ."[38] But relatively few critics have

---

[36]See e.g. Robert W. Hanning, "The Theme of Art and Life in Chaucer's Poetry," in *Geoffrey Chaucer: A Collection of Original Articles*, ed. George D. Economou (New York: McGraw-Hill, 1975), pp. 15–36; Alfred David, *The Strumpet Muse: Art and Morals in Chaucer's Poetry* (Bloomington: Indiana University Press, 1976); Anne Middleton, "Chaucer's 'New Men' and the Good of Literature in the *Canterbury Tales*," in *Literature and Society* (English Institute Essays, 1978), ed. Edward Said (Baltimore: Johns Hopkins University Press, 1980), pp. 15–56, and her other exhilarating essays cited below.

[37]"The Plan of the 'Canterbury Tales,'" *Modern Philology*, 13 (1915–16), 45–48. Jones also noted the role of estates literature in shaping the *General Prologue*.

[38]"The Pilgrimage Narrative and the *Canterbury Tales*," SP, 67 (1970), 295. For a corrective to Reiss's attempt to ally the *Tales* with allegorical pilgrimage narratives, see Siegfried Wenzel, "The Pilgrimage of Life as a Late Medieval Genre," *Mediaeval Studies*, 35 (1973), 370–88. For affinities between the *Tales* and literal pilgrimage narratives, see Donald R. Howard, *Writers and Pilgrims* (Berkeley: University of California Press, 1980). My distinction between inner and outer frames should not be confused with Howard's more comprehensive approach to the work in terms of inner and outer form; see *The Idea of the Canterbury Tales* (Berkeley: University of California Press, 1976), pp. 134–209.

devoted attention to the inner frame, which is equally an artistic choice on Chaucer's part and which accordingly deserves the same sympathetic attention and consideration for the particular atmosphere it creates.

The inner frame is the game that the pilgrims agree to play on their way to Canterbury. Two articles have delineated the presence of the game structure throughout the *Tales*, making detailed citation of the evidence unnecessary here, but neither approaches the structure in terms of medieval ideas of play and recreation.[39] If we do, we find that the rationale of the Canterbury storytelling—at least as far as Harry Bailly and the pilgrims are concerned—depends on them:

> And wel I woot, as ye goon by the weye,
> Ye shapen yow to talen and to pleye;
> For trewely, confort ne myrthe is noon
> To ride by the weye doumb as a stoon;
> And therfore wol I maken yow disport,
> As I seyde erst, and doon yow som confort. [A 771–76]

The Host's construction of the game is the organization into rules of the impulse of the pilgrims to "pleye" along the way, to take what "confort," what *solatium*, and "myrthe" they can find. The storytelling contest he proposes has as its goal "to shorte with oure weye" (A 791), to make the time pass agreeably and thus more quickly, and the chief means to that end is "tales of best sentence and moost solaas" (A 798), with a prize for the pilgrim who can most effectively meet those demands. Although elsewhere Harry Bailly shows marked inclinations toward "solaas" rather than "sentence," here, as the rules of the game are explained, the Horatian ideal dominates. The best kind of entertainment is not trivial *joca* but substantial stories; the full literary enterprise, pleasure and profit, serves the end of "confort." The pilgrims assent to Harry's proposal "with ful glad herte" (A 811), agree to play by the announced rules, and the next morning it falls to the Knight to "bigynne the game" (A 853).

[39]G. D. Josipovici, "Fiction and Game in the *Canterbury Tales*," *Critical Quarterly*, 7 (1965), 185–97; Richard A. Lanham, "Game, Play, and High Seriousness in Chaucer's Poetry," *English Studies*, 48 (1967), 1–24. See also Stephen Manning, "Rhetoric, Game, Morality, and Geoffrey Chaucer," *Studies in the Age of Chaucer*, 1 (1979), 105–18. I am indebted as well to V. A. Kolve for ideas concerning play and game in the *Tales*.

It is important to see the relationship between this game, entered into for the perfectly valid pleasure of entertainment and the corresponding psychological solace that it promotes, and the pilgrimage. The agreement to engage in the recreation of storytelling occurs after we have read the portraits of the pilgrims and discovered the nature of their journey. Their human reality is part of the outer frame; the inner frame begins only when they agree to a set of arbitrary rules designed to create certain benefits within the limited time of their traveling. Hence there is, at least as far as the theory of recreation is concerned, no inherent conflict between the two. The game of telling tales is not indication per se of lack of seriousness; it is a social disport, serving specifically delimited goals. Toward the end of the game there are signs of the pilgrimage reasserting its claims, then an explicit rejection of fiction by the Parson, whose prologue and tale return the travelers to their most earnest concerns. For the company as a whole this transition, however abrupt the Parson's response to the Host may seem, is natural and evolutionary rather than disjunctive:

> Upon this word we han assented soone,
> For, as it seemed, it was for to doone,
> To enden in som vertuous sentence,
> And for to yeve hym space and audience;
> And bade oure Hoost he sholde to hym seye
> That alle we to telle his tale hym preye. [I 61–66]

The collective wisdom of the pilgrims recognizes that it is time to cease their social recreation, however satisfying it has been at its best, and to think of personal salvation, to move from the public delights of a "fable" to the private spiritual refreshment of a "meditacioun."

What Chaucer does in the course of the *Canterbury Tales* is to subject the theory of recreation, so comfortably announced and endorsed in the appropriately merry circumstances of after-dinner *confabulatio*, to the strains of human tension, to dramatize the difference between idea and motive. For all his apparently disinterested appreciation of proper play, the Host turns out to be perhaps excessively preoccupied with mirth and japes, and with the possibility of saying things in game that he could not otherwise. The Reeve, the Friar, and the Summoner are only the most obvious examples of people who turn the goal of communal pleasure to personal vindictive uses, who expose the problematic relationship between play and insult that Jean de Condé dealt with briefly in *Le sentier batu*. With the Wife of Bath and the Pardoner the line between private needs and public entertainment becomes deliberately difficult to draw. Yet the game remains an ideal, almost as much of one as the spiritual pilgrimage itself. Significantly, among its most vigorous defenders is the noble Knight. He not only begins it enthusiastically but interrupts the Monk when he perceives that the tragedies are creating a "hevynesse" (B² 3959) inconsistent with the goals of recreation— and, as R. E. Kaske has shown, unfaithful to a truly Boethian view of fortune.[40] Also, he keeps the game from disintegrating at the comic but terrible moment when the Host's vulgar insult silences the Pardoner, asserting that the company should again "laughe and pleye" (C 967). The Knight, who is often depicted as rather solemn, turns out to be not only a steadfast fighter for the faith but also a perfect example of Aristotelian *eutrapelia*. He is so pious that he will not take time to change his war garb before going on pilgrimage, but while on it he recognizes the value of "game" and attempts to ensure the success of such valid "pleye." For him, as for the Lollard knight Sir John Montagu, apparently, religious conviction and military pursuits do not entail rejection of the pleasures of moderate social amusement.[41]

The Clerk, too, accepts the principles of recreation, though with an edge in his response that alerts us to the reality that lies beyond the entertainment. In a masterly exchange, the Host asks him for a tale and, suspicious of what this threadbare, sober scholar might do to the game, reminds him of his obligations:

[40]"The Knight's Interruption of the *Monk's Tale*," *ELH*, 24 (1957), 249–68. Kaske also discusses a number of details that directly contrast Knight with Monk, to which may be added the Knight's proper *gaudium temperatum* as opposed to the Monk's cheerless tragedies and his subsequent lack of "lust to pleye" (B² 3996).

[41]I am thinking of the fact that the soldier Montagu also wrote fixed form lyrics, probably perceived in the context of gracious court entertainment. See Derek Brewer, *Chaucer in His Time* (London: Longman, 1973), pp. 63–66, and my article "Toward a Poetics of the Late Medieval Court Lyric."

> I trowe ye studie aboute som sophyme;
> But Salomon seith 'every thyng hath tyme.'
>   For Goddes sake, as beth of bettre cheere!
> It is no tyme for to studien heere.
> Telle us som myrie tale, by youre fey!
> For what man that is entred in a pley,
> He nedes moot unto the pley assent. [E 5–11]

These lines not only specify what the Clerk has agreed to but give a rationale for it from Ecclesiastes: *Omnia tempus habent*. This is not the time for the clerk to "studie" nor to preach (E 12–14), two activities most natural to a man who gladly learns and gladly teaches; rather, as manuals for students allow, it is time for the recreation that revivifies the capacity for study. The Host seems to feel the need to cite biblical wisdom in order to persuade one so committed to earnest intellectual endeavor. But the Clerk does not need to be prodded into participation:

> "Hooste," quod he, "I am under youre yerde;
> Ye han of us as now the governance,
> And therfore wol I do yow obeisance,
> As fer as resoun axeth, hardily." [E 22–25]

He admits, in language strong with terms of rulership, his part in the agreement made at the Tabard Inn. But the authority of the Host is merely "as now," during the special recreational time which the pilgrims have committed themselves to, and the Clerk need obey only as far as "resoun" demands. This line has a double resonance. First, it draws the distinction between the game itself and Harry Bailly's own inclinations. The Clerk complies fully with what is valid in the Host's request, but the choice of tale is his own, and the story of Griselda probably not what Harry was thinking of when he urged a "murie thyng of aventures" (E 15).[42] The appeal to "resoun" reminds us too of the larger ethical context of the storytelling game: the Clerk

---

[42]On the story as a source of humanist delight and recreation, and for more on this exchange between Host and Clerk, see Anne Middleton, "The Clerk and His Tale: Some Literary Contexts," *Studies in the Age of Chaucer*, 2 (1980), 121–50. On the varying uses of "myrie" in reference to literature, see Lois Ebin, "Chaucer, Lydgate, and the 'Myrie Tale,'" *Chaucer Review*, 13 (1979), 316–36.

need obey only as far as one of those books of Aristotle he so loves, the *Nicomachean Ethics*, reasons out the proper limits and nature of entertainment.

The Clerk sees, in a way that Harry Bailly does not, how restricted those limits really are. Against Harry's assertion of play instead of preaching he opposes a tale of profit by a "lauriat poete." To the easy "every thyng hath tyme," acceptable in itself but readily stretched to accommodate too much recreational indulgence, he opposes the reality that "alle shul we dye" (E 38), the final limit of man's allotted time on earth, the central fact that shocks us into remembrance that we are living in borrowed time, God-lent time, not in the free, self-determined time of games. Appropriately, he tells a tale of a marquis whose interest in his "lust present" must be sacrificed to the needs of preserving his realm from the disaster of the "deeth" of his "lynage," and of a woman whose chief attribute is patience, transcendence of the times for laughing and the times for crying that Fortune brings her. The prologue to the *Clerk's Tale* manages both to validate the Canterbury game and to remind us of the larger context in which it takes place; the tale itself, likewise, fulfills the agreement to provide a narrative that is "myrie" (at least in the Clerk's sense, if not the Host's) and as well leads us to reflect on matters that lie beyond the "lust present" of the storytelling game.

Most of the pilgrims, though, involve themselves more unequivocally in the entertainment, if not always for the proper motives. In general they participate willingly and respond congenially to the stories of others. Even some disruptions, like the Miller's butting in with a story of "harlotrie," can be absorbed into the recreation. The dominant mood is festive, and the entire inner frame can be seen as a manifestation of the special spirit of carnival, with Harry Bailly as a kind of Lord of Misrule.[43] This approach to certain types of literary comedy, best known through C. L. Barber's work on Shakespeare and Mikhail Bakhtin's on Rabelais, is complementary to the ideas of recreation I have been discussing. The analogy between literary celebration and the carnival world of the Feast of Fools and

[43]James R. Andreas, "Festive Liminality in Chaucerian Comedy," *The Chaucer Newsletter*, 1, no. 1 (Winter 1979), pp. 3–6; David, pp. 90–107.

other popular revels is valid in many respects; but in the case of the *Canterbury Tales* and other medieval works it tends to ignore their more self-conscious ethical justifications. Anthropological and psychological approaches to festive behavior tend to stress the oppositions themselves: everyday-holiday, repression-release, rule-misrule. The idea of recreation is in effect an effort to reach some kind of accommodation between these opposed tendencies, and as we have seen in this chapter, much comic and "festive" literature, rather than appearing purely as revelry, deliberately gives itself a recreational or hygienic context that works to legitimize the festivity by appealing to certain accepted workaday values.

Chaucer did not need to create a formal game in order to have his pilgrims tell tales or reveal their characters. In the *Roman de la rose* he had a model for the self-exposure of character; in a variety of earlier works, and in the contemporary *Confessio amantis,* he had collections where narratives arise more or less "naturally" within conversation to illustrate ideas or arguments. But he chose instead a structure like the *Decameron*'s, in which the tale-telling is made self-conscious. His establishment of the double frame, recreational time within pilgrimage time, indicates that his interest lay not solely in the presentation of fictions nor in the exposure of character but, also, in the relationship between the two. Anne Middleton has argued that this interest follows logically upon the *Legend of Good Women* and its prologue; the *Canterbury Tales* takes Chaucer's concerns with problems of interpretation and misinterpretation, the relationship between fiction and moral instruction, and gives them center stage.[44] Audience response becomes a part of the work itself; the twin frames of pilgrimage and game enable him to explore the complex relationships between life and literature.

Chaucer makes the recreational ideal a major element within his work—but not a justification for it. Unlike Boccaccio, who speaks of his intentions in the *Decameron* in his own voice, Chaucer invokes recreational ideas only within the context of a

---

[44]"The *Physician's Tale* and Love's Martyrs: 'Ensamples Mo Than Ten' as a Method in the *Canterbury Tales*," *Chaucer Review,* 8 (1973), 27–31. The relevance of the *Prologue* to *LGW* to Chaucer's poetics was first and most influentially argued by Robert O. Payne, *The Key of Remembrance* (New Haven: Yale University Press, 1963), pp. 91–111.

more inclusive framing structure. What happens to the principle of recreation in the hands of the Reeve, the Pardoner, the Canon's Yeoman, and the rest of the pilgrims is in one sense Chaucer's elaborate commentary on the difference between literary theory and reality. And since this book is about theory, it is time to return to literature that relies on ideas of entertainment in less complicated and ironic ways.

5

From Plague to Pleasure

The previous chapter gave evidence that a number of medieval works and genres rely on recreational and hygienic arguments. We turn now to further material, both fictional and nonfictional, that depends on those arguments, principally the medical ones. This material appears in the years following the Black Death, and it involves a relationship between plague and mental pleasure, usually in the form of a structural movement from a world riddled by pestilence to a happier, healthier environment dominated by repose and recreational enjoyment. It may seem surprising to associate entertainment with the catastrophe that had such terrible impact on late medieval society. But I hope to show that the relationship between the Black Death and certain literary and social recreations suggests a potent value to such mundane joys, and the evidence assembled here may help redress the natural tendency to dwell on only the most pessimistic kind of medieval responses to pestilence.

This is not the place to try to summarize the enormous impact of the Black Death on western Europe during 1348–50, nor of the subsequent outbreaks of plague that continued in the fourteenth century and beyond. The effects of the Black Death on late medieval literary and artistic expression are usually discussed in terms of increased preoccupation with the arbitrariness of life and the terrors of dying—the evidence from art is more abundant and convincing, but it is common to cite such written material as Chaucer's *Pardoner's Tale* and the appearance of the theme of the dance of death. Little attention has gone to less macabre responses, and the pattern of moving from plague to pleasure has not, to my knowledge, been treated per se in much detail. The *Decameron,* which is the most famous example of that movement, is of course immensely well known and is my principal subject. But it is not the only work to reveal the pattern, and some of its force and logic may be more fully appreciated if it is considered in the context of other works that also deal with the relationship of plague and pleasure. That relationship is predicated on the ideas about literature this book has been examining.

The *Decameron* and the Plague Tracts

Let us start with the *Decameron* and with its principal structural feature: the frame story that begins amidst the chaos of plague-torn Florence and moves into the orderly, gracious world of country estates and gardens. This pattern, as almost every critic of the work notes, provides dramatic contrast of the strongest order. But to leave the matter there is hardly sufficient, and most commentators try to answer the question of what purposes that contrast serves. Many have seen it as a device to allow the creation of a more or less ideal secular society. Charles S. Singleton's well-known explication of the frame interprets the contrast as a kind of escape, which produces a privileged, insulated world that can let the Augustinian journey go by and attend to literature for its own sake. More recently, some critics have taken the movement as indicative of other aesthetic concerns on Boccaccio's part: Giuseppe Mazzotta, in a provocative essay, discusses it as a structure that allows Boccaccio to probe the relationship between literature and history; and Guido Almansi sees it as part of the self-consciously artificial construction of the *Decameron,* an "artistic game" that keeps calling attention to itself as such.[1] All these

[1]For a recent summary of critical opinion on various aspects of the frame story, including the significance of the movement from plague to gardens, see P. L. Cerisola, "La questione della cornice del *Decameron,*" *Aevum,* 49 (1975), 137–56. For Singleton's views see "On *Meaning* in the *Decameron,*" *Italica,* 21 (1944), 117–24. Mazzotta, "The *Decameron:* The Marginality of Literature," *University of Toronto Quarterly,* 42 (1972), 64–81. Almansi, *The Writer as Liar: Narrative Technique in the* Decameron (London: Routledge & Kegan Paul, 1975), pp. 1–18. There is much in an essay by Carlo Ballerini that parallels the discussion to follow, but he does not explore texts other than the *Decameron;* see

views approach the movement as a literary device serving certain artistic purposes, and while I certainly do not dispute that premise, I do think that the relationship between plague and pleasure has a psychological and medical basis that has not been fully appreciated, that its medical logic suggests a therapeutic function for the *Decameron* fictions and by implication for other secular literature as well, and that, accordingly, these pragmatic values should raise some questions about interpretations that tend to read the work as if Boccaccio's aesthetics were Nabokov's.

The movement from plague to pleasure in the *Decameron* reflects in some way the fact of pestilence and people's responses to it. Petrarch, writing in 1373, did not comment on Boccaccio's introduction as a clever literary strategy; he admired rather the way his friend "accurately described and eloquently lamented the condition of our country during that siege of pestilence which forms so dark and melancholy a period in our century."[2] And modern historians of the Black Death seem to find the pages as reliable as chronicle testimony (not terribly accurate itself, to be sure), regardless of the fact that Boccaccio drew on earlier material for his description. If the depiction of the plague appears true to reality, perhaps there is a comparable fidelity in the movement at the center of the work, the flight from the chaotic and terrified city to gracious and jovial living in serene gardens. The chronicles tell of people fleeing the plague, of course, but the best sources for understanding the rationale of the *Decameron*'s frame narrative are the plague tracts, those manuals of advice on how to cope with the pestilence which appeared concurrent with its arrival and which, judging from their numbers, enjoyed widespread popularity throughout the later Middle Ages and Renaissance, surviving in fact as long as plague remained a serious epidemic threat in western Europe.[3]

"Il recupero della letizia dalla tragedia della peste alla libera vita di Bruno e di Buffalmacco," in *Atti del convegno di Nimega sul Boccaccio (28–29–30 ottobre 1975)*, ed. Carlo Ballerini (Bologna: Pàtron, 1976), pp. 51–203.

[2]Thompson, p. 233. For Boccaccio's loss of family and friends due to plague, see Vittore Branca, *Boccaccio: The Man and His Works*, trans. Richard Monges (New York: New York University Press, 1976), p. 76. On this translation of Branca see Piero Boitani in *Medium Aevum*, 47 (1978), 316–17.

[3]There are a few pages on the tracts in Philip Ziegler's *The Black Death* (New York: Harper & Row, 1971), which is a good survey of all the aspects of the

To discuss the plague tracts is to return to material much like that treated in the second chapter. Many a treatise calls itself a *consilium,* and the works are in essence generalized *consilia,* treating the subject of plague itself rather than one individual's malady. The most complete treatises generally contain three sections. The first deals with the nature and causes of the pestilence—the principal immediate cause was thought to be corrupted air, which entered the body and destroyed it, the principal remote cause, usually, a particularly malevolent conjunction of Saturn, Jupiter, and Mars in 1345. Although there was no official theory of contagion, some writers mention it as a contributing factor. The tracts also recognize varying degrees of susceptibility, depending on such matters as age, sex, regimen, and place of habitation.[4] The second section, directed to people who have not yet caught the disease, consists of a regimen to observe in order to minimize the chances of being stricken. The final section consists of specific remedies for those afflicted; here one finds directions on bloodletting and prescriptions for a variety of presumably curative potions. This kind of material often makes medieval medicine the butt of jokes and criticism, but even phlebotomy and lectuaries can be justified rationally given the theoretical understanding of the age, and it is important to remember that the writers of the plague tracts

plague. More substantial discussions are in C.-E. A. Winslow, *The Conquest of Epidemic Disease* (Princeton: Princeton University Press, 1943), pp. 98–114, and in Anna Montgomery Campbell, *The Black Death and Men of Learning* (New York: Columbia University Press, 1931), pp. 34–92, still the fundamental work on the early plague treatises. The chief source of texts is the collection edited over the years by Karl Sudhoff in *Archiv für Geschichte der Medizin,* 4–17 (1910–25), under the general title "Pestschriften aus den ersten 150 Jahren nach der Epidemie des 'schwarzen Todes.' " I will henceforth cite texts in *Archiv* by volume and page numbers. Essential for bibliography is Dorothea Waley Singer and Annie Anderson, *Catalogue of Latin and Vernacular Plague Texts in Great Britain and Eire in Manuscripts Written before the Sixteenth Century* (Paris: Académie Internationale d'Histoire des Sciences, and London: William Heinemann, 1950), as well as the works cited in Chap. 2, n. 12. For bibliography of incunabular tracts and facsimiles of some early printed French treatises, see A. C. Klebs and E. Droz, *Remedies against the Plague* (Paris: E. Droz, 1925). For a survey of plague tracts in England from the late Middle Ages on, see Charles F. Mullett, *The Bubonic Plague and England: An Essay in the History of Preventive Medicine* (Lexington: University of Kentucky Press, 1956).

[4]On all these ideas of causation see Séraphine Guerchberg, "The Controversy over the Alleged Sowers of the Black Death in the Contemporary Treatises on Plague," in *Change in Medieval Society,* ed. Sylvia L. Thrupp (New York: Appleton-Century-Crofts, 1964), pp. 208–24.

were not opportunists trying to mulct a desperate populace but were among the most eminent physicians of their time.

Not all the tracts are so neatly constructed, and many are much less complete. Some writers concern themselves with only one subject—an investigation of causes, a *regimen preservativum*, or a *regimen curativum*. Our interest lies in the material in the hygienic regimens, especially those which proceed according to the nonnaturals.[5] Their advice sometimes differs from that of the regimens discussed in Chapter 2 because of the particular problems the Black Death posed. For example, they are much more cautious about advocating exercise, and more strict in censuring sexual intercourse, because of their concern that physical exhaustion might render one more susceptible to the plague. (The ethical dimension of hygiene is nowhere more forcefully felt: overindulgence, by imbalancing the humors, lowers resistance to the plague and thus may have disastrous consequences.) Since the pestilence was attributed to contaminated air, the chapters on that nonnatural in the tracts are often quite extensive, with recommendations on how to purify the air, such as what woods to burn and what herbs to smell. A great deal of this material, like that dealing with the other nonnaturals, is thoroughly traditional. Concern with miasmic air goes back to Hippocrates, and the Middle Ages could find chapters on pestilential atmosphere long before the Black Death in such authorities as Avicenna and Rhazes.

In regard to the *accidentia animae,* the plague tracts do not so much alter the general principles of the regimens as make the recommendations a bit more pointed and sometimes more detailed. The most influential plague treatise of its time, the *Compendium de epidimia* of the Faculty of Medicine of the University of Paris, written in 1348 at the request of the King of France, offers a succinct guide to the disposition of the emotions which parallels much of the physiological material discussed in Chapter 2:

[5]The tracts composed in the tradition of John of Burgundy's (1365), which seem to have been especially popular in England, do not use the nonnaturals as an organizing principle, though in places they touch on similar ideas. On these works see David Murray, *John de Burdeus and the Pestilence* (Paisley and London, 1891), and Dorothea Waley Singer's informative "Some Plague Tractates (Fourteenth and Fifteenth Centuries)," *Proceedings of the Royal Society of Medicine,* Part II, Section of the History of Medicine, 9 (1916), 159–212.

... since bodily infirmity is sometimes related to the accidents of the soul, one should avoid anger, excessive sadness, and anxiety. Be of good hope and resolute mind; make peace with God, for death will be less fearsome as a result. Live in joy and gladness as much as possible, for although joy may sometimes moisten the body, it nevertheless comforts both spirit and body.[6]

Here the standard recommendation for cheerfulness carries with it an interesting concessive clause. The *Compendium* notes elsewhere that the plague is caused principally by Jupiter, a hot and moist planet, and that people whose humoral balance contains an excess of heat and moisture are most susceptible to it. Since *gaudium* promotes moisture and heat in the body (see the Middle English treatise quoted on p. 45), it would appear that happiness in time of plague might well cause a dangerous imbalance of qualities. But although the *Compendium* is aware of the theoretical problem, nevertheless it insists that the beneficial effects of cheerfulness outweigh the disadvantages of such alteration.

The Faculty's advice was soon available in the vernacular. A close French translation reproduces this passage exactly, and even an abridged translation, more practical in its concerns than the *Compendium* itself, recommends that one should "flee sadness and melancholy, and live as merrily and happily as possible (fouir tritesces et melencolies et uiure plus ioieusement et lieement que on puet)."[7] More interesting, because more expansive, is an adaptation of the *Compendium* dated 1425, which amplifies its wisdom into 3,500 lines of French verse. The chapter on the accidents of the soul explains in detail how the passions alter the body and how the "imaginative power" also has corporeal effects. It follows the original in arguing that

[6]"De accidentibus vero anime, est notandum quod quia nonnumquam ex accidentibus anime infirmitas corporis contingere potest, iram caveant et tristiciam nimiam, sollicitudinem; sint bone spei et fortis ymaginationis, cum Deo faciant pacem, quia inde mortem minus timebunt; in gaudio vero et leticia, quantum plus poterunt, vivant et, licet gaudium quandoque corpus humectet, spiritus tamen et cor confortat." Ed. H. Emile Rébouis, *Etude historique et critique sur la peste* (Paris, 1888), p. 114.
[7]Bibliothèque Nationale MS f. fr. 2001, f. 101; entire treatise on ff. 97–103v. The more accurate translation is in B.N. fr. 12323, ff. 135v–144; the passage on the accidents of the soul is on f. 140v. For discussion of the *Compendium* and these translations, see Alfred Coville in *Histoire littéraire de la France*, 37 (1936–38), pp. 336–59.

although the movement of joy ("action / De joie") may produce
moisture, it is nevertheless "natural in order to resist pestilence" because of the "comfort and lightness" it brings to the
heart and *spiritus*, enabling people to avoid "many dangers."[8]
Since the *Compendium*'s approach to the emotions is based on
the conventional wisdom concerning the *accidentia animae,* it is
difficult to know whether later treatises follow it directly or
simply rely on the standard ideas. In any case, recommendations to avoid fear and sadness and keep oneself cheerful appear in a variety of plague tracts from 1348 on. For purposes
of analysis, and for later applicability to the *Decameron,* we can
in some instances distinguish those more concerned with the
problem of fear from those dealing principally with the attainment of joy.

The earliest, and certainly one of the most interesting of the
plague treatises, is by Jacme d'Agramont, a Catalan physician
who wrote in April, 1348, to instruct the people of his city of
Lerida as the plague was approaching.[9] He discusses the nature
and causes of pestilence and presents a preventive regimen, but
he omits the section on cures since his work is for laymen and
he believes that treatment should remain in the hands of physicians. The regimen is organized according to the nonnaturals,
and in regard to the emotions Jacme begins by recommending
"gaiety and joyousness" as long as one's behavior is temperate.
He then turns immediately to the dangerous effects of "fear
and imagination. For from imagination alone, can come any
malady." He gives some examples of its power, including the
familiar assertion of prenatal influence on a baby's appearance.
Unlike Chaucer's Doctour of Phisik, Jacme apparently studied
both Galen and the Bible, for his next example is from Gen.30,
in which Jacob's sheep and goats conceive spotted offspring

[8]Olivier de la Haye, *Poëme sur la grande peste de 1348,* ed. Georges Guigue
(Lyon, 1888), pp. 108–11. Olivier's work is notable too for its glossary of
medical and psychological terms, which he added at the end of his poem so
that less educated readers could better understand the recommendations in
the text.

[9]"Regimen of Protection against Epidemics of Pestilence and Mortality,"
trans. M. L. Duran-Reynals and C.-E. A. Winslow, *BHM,* 23 (1949), 57–89; the
following quotations are from 84–85. For background see the same authors'
"Jacme d'Agramont and the First of the Plague Tractates," *BHM,* 22 (1948),
747–65.

because at the time of conception they were thinking of the
varied colors of the boughs he put before them.

> Another proof of this proposition can be made by the follow-
> ing experiment: When somebody stands on a level board on
> the flat floor he can go from one end to the other with noth-
> ing to hold on to, so as not to fall off, but when this same
> board is placed in a high and perilous position, no one would
> dare to try to pass over the said board. Evidently the differ-
> ence is due wholly to the imagination. In the first case there is
> no fear, and in the other there is. Thus, it is evidently very
> dangerous and perilous in times of pestilence to imagine
> death and to have fear. No one, therefore, should give up
> hope or despair, because such fear only does great damage
> and no good whatsoever.
>
> For this reason also it is to be recommended that in such
> times no chimes and bells should toll in case of death because
> the sick are subject to evil imaginings when they hear the
> death bells.

Later in the century the same concern with the evil effects
of fear appears in the tract of Nicholas de Burgo, a Florentine
physician who recommends that people avoid thinking and
speaking of the sick and the dead unless to report a recovery
(*Archiv*, 5: 356). The treatise on plague by the French physician Chalin de Vivario, dating from 1382 as does Nicholas's,
argues that fear and imagination are reasons why people do
not recover once they have contracted the plague, and it
paints a vivid picture of the debilitating effects of hearing
nothing but pestilence-induced sounds—ringing of bells, offices for the dead, transporting of the sick, morbid gossip.[10] A
fifteenth-century treatise notes approvingly the opinion that
"simply thinking about the plague makes a person infected"
(7: 92). As we will see later in this chapter, the fear of fear on
the part of physicians has relevance to details in the *Decameron*

---

[10]Partially edited by Robert Hoeniger as an appendix to his *Der Schwarze Tod
in Deutschland* (Berlin, 1882), p. 172: "alia racio quia tempore epidimiali plurimi
homines infirmantes sunt ac moriuntur ex continuis terroribus timoribus et
ymaginacionibus inductis ex pulsacione nimia campanorum et ex cantu mor-
tuorum per carrerias et audiendo corpus extra deportari ad communicandum
infirmos et audiendo eciam continue quod nunc Peter nunc Paulus moriatur."
See also *Archiv*, 17: 35–39, 87.

frame and to actions taken by some communities affected by plague.

What means of attaining *gaudium* do the plague treatises discuss? The *Compendium* offers no specific recommendation, though it is possible that one might interpret its advice to be happy in the context of the previous sentence about making peace with God. Certainly the joy that comes with the hope of celestial bliss would seem beneficial, and some tracts make *gaudium* explicitly religious.[11] But in general the ways to mental contentment are considerably more earthly. One says that cheerfulness comes by listening to "songs, stories, and melodies" (5: 390). Another recommends "gaudium temperatum," attained by associating with friends and by listening to "comforting talk, pleasing songs, and sweetly harmonious sounds" (6: 322). The standard trinity of delights—music, songs, and stories—appears in Gentile da Foligno and Pietro da Tussignano as well.[12] More extensive is the list of pleasures in Nicholas de Burgo, who mentions singing, dancing, proper companions, fine clothing, and who would have people enjoy themselves "through every means of moderate cheerfulness."[13] The advice of one treatise to be "continually merry and cheerful" (6: 336) epitomizes the prevailing attitude; but many tracts stress as well that merriment should be moderate, and for this the reasons are, as in the *Compendium* and the regimens discussed earlier, physical: excessive joy overextends the *spiritus* and natural heat (6: 365). A fif-

[11]*Archiv*, 5: 82: "Making peace with God will always bring joy, for one will not fear death." See also 11: 61 and the epistolary tract discussed by Singer, "Some Plague Tractates," 174–75.

[12]*Domini Gentilis fulginatis singulare consilium contra pestilentiam* [Salamanca, ca. 1515], f. 8v: "gaudeamus et delectemur in mellodiis, cantilenis, hystoriis et similibus delectationibus." Pietro's brief *Consilium pro peste euitanda* may be found in the facsimile edition of the Venice, 1491, text of *The* Fasciculus medicinae *of Johannes de Ketham*, intro. Karl Sudhoff, trans. Charles Singer, Monumenta Medica 1 (Milan: R. Lier, 1924), [f. 14v]: "congaudendum est et delectandum cum sono, cantu, historiis et his similibus."

[13]*Archiv*, 5: 356. For another extensive inventory of delights, including the recommendation to "hear pleasant things and attractive stories," see the Italian version of Giovanni de' Dondi's pest tract, ed. F. Carabellese, *La peste del 1348 e le condizioni della sanità pubblica in Toscana* (Rocca San Casciano, 1897), p. 74, a passage not in the Latin version in *Archiv*, 5: 352–54. Also the plague treatise of Maino de' Maineri, ed. R. Simonini, *Maino de Maineri ed il suo Libellus de preservatione ab epydimia* (Modena: Umberto Orlandini, 1923), p. 20 and n. pp. 43–44; cf. p. 26.

teenth-century physician sharply distinguishes between *gaudium temperatum* and *gaudium intensissimum;* the latter is dangerous, the former alone "impedes the plague and preserves people from it" (4: 218).

Dispensing medical advice was not the province of the plague tracts alone. Eustache Deschamps, who wrote lyric poems on almost every conceivable subject, produced some ballades and a virelay summarizing the established regimen to observe in times of pestilence, and his views may serve to indicate how the advice of learned physicians became available outside the tracts themselves.

> Qui veult son corps en santé maintenir
> Et resister a mort d'epidemie,
> Il doit courroux et tristesce fuir,
> Laissier le lieu ou est la maladie
> Et frequenter joieuse compaignie.[14]

> Whoever wishes to keep himself healthy and fight against death from pestilence should flee anger and sadness, leave the place where the sickness exists, and associate with cheerful companions.

Like many of the authors of the *Pestschriften,* Deschamps puts quite stringent limits on what is properly "joieuse," for he asserts a few lines later that one must lead a sober life and explicitly prohibits intercourse. As he puts it in another ballade, "Be cheerful without disturbing the heart" (VII: 41)—a conditional warning comparable to the *Compendium's* recognition that too much joy might create a dangerously large imbalance of qualities. But within this restriction he sanctions a fair amount of secular enjoyment, all with hygienic intent. His advice to wear "robes plaisans" derives from ideas we have seen in the *Secretum secretorum;* and when he tells his audience to "keep company with those whom you like," he is clearly reflecting medical views of the value of pleasant social *confabulatio.*

Not many years later John Lydgate offered the same kind of practical counsel in England. This is the first stanza of his bal-

---

[14]Deschamps, VI: 100. See also IV: 169–70, VII: 40–41, and VIII: 139–40. There is a longer regimen, not specifically for the plague, in VIII: 339–46.

lade on the pestilence, the opening lines of which are practically identical to Deschamps's:

> Who will been holle & kepe hym from sekenesse
> And resiste the strok of pestilence,
> Lat hym be glad, & voide al hevynesse,
> Flee wikkyd heires, eschew the presence
> Off infect placys, causyng the violence;
> Drynk good wyn, & holsom meetis take,
> Smelle swote thynges, & for his deffence
> Walk in cleene hei̇, eschewe mystis blake.

Although Lydgate makes no specific reference to the nonnaturals, his poem touches on all of them. This stanza alone involves four. It begins, significantly, with the *accidentia animae:* lightness of mind helps one resist the disease. Then follows the standard advice to flee the corrupted air and to eat and drink the proper substances. The recommendation to smell sweet things is part of the tracts' concern with rectifying the contaminated air, and the last line is also concerned with air, though the mention of walking implies the category of exercise and rest as well. The second stanza touches on repletion and evacuation, baths, coitus, and air again; the third deals with sleep and returns, in more detail, to food. In some manuscripts this poem is attached to Lydgate's famous *Dietary*, with no indication of a break in the text. That a poem specifically concerned with the plague could so readily fuse with a general regimen reveals both the pervasiveness of pestilence in fifteenth-century life and the widespread familiarity of the rules for dealing with it first announced in the plague *consilia.*[15]

---

[15]Text in Lydgate, II: 702; notes on the MSS in I: xv, though for a full list of MSS of the plague poem see the *Index of Middle English Verse* and *Supplement,* #4112. In addition to the MSS mentioned by MacCracken that do not distinguish the two poems, British Library Add. 10,099, ff. 211–211v, prints both under the single heading "Incipit doctrina sana." The first stanza of Lydgate's balade also found its way into his translation of the *Secretum secretorum,* where it appears as part of a prince's regimen of health. Ed. Robert Steele, *Lydgate and Burgh's Secrees of Old Philisoffres,* EETS e.s. 66 (1899; rpt. Millwood, N.Y.: Kraus Reprint, 1973), p. 41. For Lydgate's other references to the plague, usually more moralistic and religious than medical, see Charles F. Mullett, "John Lydgate: A Mirror of Medieval Medicine," *BHM,* 22 (1948), 403–15.

In the plague treatises I have seen, the most extensive discussion of how to dispose the accidents of the soul belongs to Dino del Garbo's son, Tommaso, himself a famous Florentine physician and a friend of Petrarch.

> Now we shall consider the means of bringing joy and pleasure into your hearts and minds during this time of pestilence. You should know that one of the best ways of doing this is to embrace cheerfulness in a reasonable way, following these precepts: do not occupy your mind with death, passion, or anything likely to sadden or grieve you, but give your thoughts over to delightful and pleasing things. Associate with happy and carefree people and avoid all melancholy. Spend your time in your house, but not with too many people, and at your leisure in gardens with fragrant plants, vines, and willows, when they are flowering. But you should not spend too much of the night in gardens or in other places out in the air, since the night air is always more harmful and dangerous than that of the day. And you should avoid associating with tipplers, loose women, gluttons, and drunkards; if you do not want to be thirsty, drink what is appropriate in a controlled way, as mentioned above. And make use of songs and minstrelsy and other pleasurable tales without tiring yourselves out, and all the delightful things that bring anyone comfort.[16]

[16]"Ora è da vedere del modo del prendere letizia e piacer in questo tal tenpo di pistolenza e nell'animo e nella mente tua. E sappi che una delle più perfette cose in questo caso è con ordine prendere allegrezza, nella quale si osservi questo ordine, cioè prima non pensare della morte, overo passione d'alcuno, overo di cosa t'abi a contristare, overo a dolere, ma i pensieri sieno sopra cose dilettevoli e piacevoli. L'usanze sieno con persone liete e gioconde, e fugasi ogni maninconia, e l'usanza sia co non molta gente nella casa ove tu ai a stare e abitare; e in giardini a tenpo loro ove sieno erbe odorifere, e come sono vite e salci, quando le vite fioriscono e simile cose. E non si vuole stare troppo la notte nè in giardini, ne' in altri luoghi all'aria, però che l'aria di notte senpre è più nociva e sospettosa che quella del dì. E vuolsi schifare d'usare con bevitori e con feminacciole co' mangiatori ingordamente e con ebri, avegna che non si vuole patire la sete, ma bei assai ordinatamente, come detto è di sopra. E usare canzone e giullerie e altre novelle piacevole sanza fatica di corpo, e tutte cose dilettevoli che confortino altrui." *Consiglio contro a pistolenza,* ed. Pietro Ferrato, Scelta di curiosità letterarie inedite or rare 74 (Bologna, 1866), pp. 40–41. On manuscripts and dating see also *Archiv* 5: 348–51 and 16: 134–35. Tommaso's attention to social rather than spiritual pleasures may reflect something of his own predilections; Filippo Villani, in his *Liber de civitatis Florentiae famosis civibus,* says that he was "refined, pleasant, and jovial, and he would very frequently enjoy himself in the company of other people." Ed. G. C. Galletti (Florence, 1847), p. 29.

Tommaso's tract undoubtedly postdates the *Decameron*, but if we take its recommendations as representative of a detailed regimen in regard to the *accidentia animae* and apply this medical perspective to the *Decameron* frame, the parallels are self-evident. What this and other plague treatises present in prescriptive form becomes the central dramatic movement of Boccaccio's frame narrative.

First of all, the *brigata* does what the treatises recommend if possible: they flee. The *Compendium de epidimia* advocates flight in its discussion of the first nonnatural, air, since moving to a new location is choosing the proper kind of air. It cites Haly Abbas as authority on this point.[17] Other treatises also advise flight, and a shorthand summary of this recommendation in three Latin adverbs became widely known: *cito, longe, tarde*—flee quickly to avoid exposure, go far away to escape the corrupted air, return slowly to insure that the disease is over (explained in *Archiv*, 4: 420–21). Some writers recognize complicating factors. Chalin de Vivario, in a medically sophisticated discussion, says that flight is advisable only if the corrupted air is regional rather than universal, and he is aware of the problem of people carrying the plague with them if they migrate (Hoeniger, p. 175). Olivier de la Haye, in his expansion of the *Compendium*, recognizes a moral problem: some people lack "charité" and abandon their nearest relatives, fleeing "like cowards." Nevertheless, he realizes that "Nature" ordains that everyone in danger wishes to save himself, and this natural instinct for self-preservation leads him to follow his source in approving flight from the plague (pp. 74–77). At times the advice takes on real urgency. In a fifteenth-century plague tract, Friar Thomas Multon begins the section on regimen by saying that the "first and principall" rule for preservation is "to gouerne the well and wisely and fore to fle al that may gender eny ffeuer or eny agewe." He follows with other hygienic precepts, and in regard to air repeats his first rule: "Also hit is good to fle the pestilence aier and go to an other contrey, for the sikenesse of the pestilence is contagious." Then follows a passage on bloodletting; Multon's conclusion to this section re-

[17]Rébouis, p. 96. The abridged translation, B. N. fr. 2001, f. 97v, attributes the advice to "flee the places and the cities where this mortality is rampant" to "wise men and ancient authorities."

turns with some forcefulness to that "principall" remedy: "And if thou rule the thus, as I haue told the, thou may bi the grace of god and by this gouernaunce preserue thiself fro the pestilence. But yit I sey, I rede the, fle the contrey be tyme that hit reynes, for hit is contagious."[18]

In light of these precepts, particularly Olivier's reflections on the problem of desertion, which are confirmed in chronicle accounts of the horrors of family members abandoning one another, we can see that Boccaccio is at pains to make the *brigata*'s flight from Florence as morally and medically justified as possible. In his long set piece on the ravages of the plague, he mentions disapprovingly those who, cruelly thinking only of themselves, abandoned city, home, and relatives in order to escape the pestilence. He elaborates on the dissolution of personal ties—people neglecting neighbors, even the closest relatives leaving each other, and, most terribly, parents forgetting children.[19] The members of the *brigata*, it turns out, are victims of precisely that kind of cruelty. These young men and women meet only when the city has been "almost emptied of its inhabitants" (p. 58); Pampinea notes that "we shall not be abandoning anyone by going away from here; on the contrary, we may fairly claim that we are the ones who have been abandoned, for our kinsfolk are either dead or fled, and have left us to fend for ourselves in the midst of all this affliction, as though disowning us completely" (p. 61). With reasoning that anticipates Olivier de la Haye, she argues that "every person born into this world has a natural right (natural ragione) to sustain, preserve, and defend his own life to the best of his ability" (p. 59; Branca, p. 29).

That right is the ultimate medical and moral justification for leaving Florence. It is not only the external danger that motivates Pampinea, however, but also awareness of her current emotional anguish and its causes:

> Here we linger for no other purpose, or so it seems to me, than to count the number of corpses being taken to burial . . .

[18]British Library MS Sloane 3489, ff. 46–49.
[19]*Decameron*, ed. Vittore Branca (Florence: Le Monnier, 1965), pp. 18–19. *The Decameron*, trans. G. H. McWilliam (Harmondsworth, Eng.: Penguin, 1972), pp. 53–54. Introduction, translation, and notes copyright © G. H. McWilliam, 1972. All subsequent references in the text will be to page numbers of these editions; any alteration of McWilliam's translation is indicated by italics.

> or to exhibit the quality and quantity of our sorrows, by
> means of the clothes we are wearing. . . . And if we go out-
> side, we shall see the dead and the sick being carried hither
> and thither . . . . Moreover, all we ever hear is "So-and-so's
> dead" and "So-and-so's dying"; and if there were anyone left
> to mourn, the whole place would be filled with sounds of
> wailing and weeping.
>
> And if we return to our homes, what happens? . . . now
> that there is no one left apart from my maid and myself, I am
> filled with foreboding and feel as if every hair on my head is
> standing on end. Wherever I go in the house, wherever I
> pause to rest, I seem to be haunted by the shades of the
> departed, whose faces no longer appear as I remember them
> but with strange and horribly twisted expressions that
> frighten me out of my senses. [Pp. 59–60]

Her speech catalogues all those things that Jacme d'Agramont,
Nicholas de Burgo, and other physicians caution against: the
depressing effects of seeing and hearing nothing except what
betokens death. The apparition of dead relatives appearing
"con una vista orribile" is precisely the kind of morbid *ymagina-
tio* that the plague tracts are concerned about. No wonder that
Pampinea says "mi sembra star male" (p. 31; McWilliam's "I
always feel ill at ease" [p. 60] understates the case); her fearful-
ness, dejection, and grotesque imaginings are not only a natural response to the plague but potentially a factor in her own
succumbing to it.

Another motive exists, this one more moral than psychological. Pampinea is distraught not only by what she sees of death
but also by what she sees of dissipation:

> And if we go outside . . . we shall see people, once con-
> demned to exile by the courts for their misdeeds, careering
> wildly about the streets in open defiance of the law . . . or else
> we shall find ourselves at the mercy of the scum of the city
> who . . . go prancing and bustling all over the place, singing
> bawdy songs that add insult to our injuries.
>
> . . . no one possessing private means and a place to retreat
> to is left here apart from ourselves. But even if such people
> are still to be found, they draw no distinction, as I have fre-
> quently heard and seen for myself, between what is honest
> and what is dishonest; and provided only that they are

prompted by their appetites, they will do whatever affords
them the greatest pleasure. . . . [Pp. 59–60]

She includes monks as well as laymen in this condemnation, for
they too "have broken the rules of obedience and given themselves over to carnal pleasures" (p. 60). Her recognition of the
difference between those who are "oneste" and those who are
not is a moral awareness like that of Tommaso del Garbo's,
who would have people pursue delight reasonably, "con ordine," drink "ordinatamente," and avoid associating with prof-
ligates.

This firm distinction between orderly and disorderly pleasure,
based ultimately on the ethical separation of proper recreation
from improper play, governs our understanding of the morality
of the events in the frame story. For not only does the *brigata*
leave Florence, it pursues the mental regimen most conducive to
resisting the plague and most likely to return its members to
mental and physical well-being. Pampinea's goal is to attain
cheerfulness ("allegrezza") without violation of reason ("ragione") (p. 33; Branca notes the parallel to Tommaso here),
precisely the kind of moderate pleasure the plague treatises recommend cultivating. The movement from the "afflicted city" to
a country estate with "delectable gardens" takes only a few sen-
tences, and Dioneo immediately proclaims that he has abandoned his "troubles" and has given himself over to "laughter,
song and merriment" (p. 64). As the most jovial and boisterous
member of the group, he is the quickest to make the mental shift
that the movement from plague to pleasure is meant to induce.
(He is, correspondingly, the one character whose appetite for
gaudium verges on the uncontrolled, and the fact that he has to
be restrained at times helps us understand the company's proper *gaudium temperatum* by presenting its limitations on his potential *gaudium intensissimum*.) Pampinea agrees that the *brigata*
has left Florence in order to flee "sorrows" and live "a merry
life" (p. 65) but notes the need to obey rules in order to preserve
their happy state. They will live with order and with pleasure
("con ordine e con piacere") (p. 41), thinking only of pleasant
things. Hence the servants have instructions "to bring us no
tidings of the world outside these walls unless they are tidings of
happiness" (p. 66), a restriction motivated not by indifference to

suffering but by the need to dispose one's feelings joyfully, and one that Nicholas de Burgo recommended some years later in his plague tract.

The hundred tales, it must be remembered, exist as part of a larger set of activities, all of which are designed to produce that orderly pleasure which Pampinea has established as an ideal. Their regimen includes a certain amount of exercise before the two daily meals, usually in the form of walks; music, songs, and dancing after meals; and of course a great deal of congenial conversation throughout. The choice of storytelling as a means of recreation occurs within the context of these other pleasures:

> . . . as you will observe, there are chessboards and other games here, and so we are free to amuse ourselves in whatever way we please. But if you were to follow my advice, this hotter part of the day would be spent, not in playing games (which inevitably bring anxiety to one of the players, without offering very much pleasure either to his opponent or to the spectators), but in telling stories—an activity that may afford some amusement both to the narrator and to the company at large. [P. 68]

Pampinea's concern about avoiding the anxiety that can come when a situation involves winning and losing is not trivial. Medieval games, even chess, often elicited violent reactions in the participants, and a civilized company would want to avoid, especially in the heat of the day, a circumstance in which tempers could flare.

Arnold of Villanova, in fact, recognizes this problem in his discussion of entertainment as a secondary nonnatural (see p. 42):

> Play in itself alters the body through exercise and the accidents of the soul (delight, sadness, anger, and intensity). In chess, dice games, and any other game in which loss or profit occurs, fear or hope is involved, and happiness or sadness follows. Even if a game is played only for the sake of winning, with no material loss to be feared, resentment and unhappiness still disturb the loser. Such effects are most clearly seen in certain dispositions: greedy and selfish people, if they lose something of value in a game, cannot escape sadness; irascible people, if they are beaten and, because of the presence of

others, dare not get angry, are immediately gnawed by frustration.[20]

The members of the *brigata* are surely neither greedy nor irascible, but since virtue involves in part avoiding the occasions of sin, there is good reason to make every effort to escape the potential ill effects of competition. Pampinea's solution is an excellent one: she chooses as principal entertainment something that is not a zero-sum game. In storytelling, all the participants gain "diletto."

It is in this context of pervasive but thoughtfully controlled disport that the narratives begin. At the end of the first day the "onesto diletto" of the *brigata* has been successful enough that the newly elected queen decides to continue with the same entertainment, but with the provision that the activities may later be abandoned should they·become annoying, "noiose" (pp. 116–17). Obviously they do not, but I suspect that a detailed survey of all the evidence showing the company's continued cheerfulness would. At the conclusion of the ten days' regimen of recreations, Dioneo, who first asserted the transformation from troubled to mirthful disposition, summarizes the purposes of the journey and explicitly links pleasure and health:

> Tomorrow, as you know, a fortnight will have elapsed since the day we departed from Florence to provide for our relaxation *in order to* preserve our health and our lives (per dovere alcun diporto pigliare a sostentamento della nostra sanità e della vita), and escape from the sadness, the suffering and the anguish continuously to be found in our city since this plague first descended·upon it. [P. 824; Branca, p. 1234]

The "diporto" is in the cause of health ("*a sostentamento . . .*"). The *brigata* has done what Tommaso del Garbo and other phy-

---

[20]"Ludus per se immutat corpus speciebus exercitii et accidentibus animi, scilicet delectatione, tristitia, ira, et studio, sicut in ludo scacorum et alearum et omnem quidem ludum quem sequitur amissio seu lucrum concomitatur timor aut spes et sequuntur letitia vel tristitia. Quod si tantummodo ludus ad victoriam fiat in quo rerum amissio non timetur, nihilominus indignatio atque displicentia victum conturbant et huiusmodi effectus manifestissimi sunt in dispositis. Nam auari et cupidi, si in ludo quicquam boni amiserint, non euadunt tristitiam. Iracundi vero, si victi fuerint vbi propter presentiam maioris irasci non audent, saltem displicentia corroduntur." Chap. 85, f. 32.

sicians recommend: they have avoided melancholy through
pleasant garden walks, music, and delightful *novelle,* and in so
doing they have kept themselves both physically and mentally
well.

It would be possible to cite other connections between the
plague *consilia* and the *Decameron* frame—Pampinea's reference
to the country air being "much more refreshing" (p. 61), for
example, is not just an ordinary detail in a conventional portrait of a *locus amoenus* but a significant medical observation. My
concern here, though, is only with the *accidentia animae.* This
much seems to me indisputable: the structural movement of
the *Decameron* from plague to pleasure involves a set of activities and dispositions which fourteenth-century medicine defines as hygienic, and the telling of stories is part of that regimen. What is the significance of this fact? I am not trying to
argue that the *Decameron* represents volunteer medical service
on Boccaccio's part, nor that a reading of the plague tracts
inspired his frame story. A parallel is not a cause, and the
medically sound activities of the *brigata* can be found in other
works of Boccaccio written before the plague. The parallel is
probably not so much a matter of direct influence as it is of a
shared response to the plague based on common assumptions
about the role of mental attitude in hygiene and about the
power of literary delight to affect mental attitude. I think it is
important for a number of reasons. First, it enriches our understanding of the logic and coherence of the *Decameron* frame,
giving the dramatic movement from plague-ridden Florence to
orderly gardens firm psychological and medical plausibility,
making it not merely escapist but therapeutic. Second, and
something to be taken up later in this chapter, is what the
pattern in both the tracts and the *Decameron* implies about fourteenth-century response to the Black Death. Third, and more
the focus of this book as a whole, is what the parallel suggests
about late medieval attitudes toward the function of nondidactic literature. Far from being seen in any kind of art-for-
art's-sake way, the *Decameron* fictions exist in a structure that
imputes to them beneficial hygienic effects on human beings.
That structure, however, consists not only of the frame story
but also of the author's own comments about his work and his
audience. I will discuss these matters in the next chapter, since

they take us too far away from the pattern that is the subject of this one.

The Pattern in Literature and Life

Let us turn now to the second major literary work based on the plague-to-pleasure pattern. About the same time that Boccaccio created the *Decameron,* in the years immediately following the arrival of the Black Death, Guillaume de Machaut, fourteenth-century France's greatest composer and probably its greatest poet as well, wrote the *Jugement dou roy de Navarre.*[21] Independently of Boccaccio he conceived the same structural movement, though his poem is quite different from the tale collection. It begins with summer passing into autumn, and with the colder season comes a corresponding tone; Machaut tells us that he was melancholy, musing alone in his room that the world governs itself "by the wisdom of the tavern" (39), that avarice and corruption reign, that nothing has order, "ordenance" (102). He tries to pull himself out of his brooding by reflecting on the wisdom of Ecclesiastes, that the world is "all vanity, and that there is nothing better to do than to be happy (liez) and to do good" (134–36).[22] But even more terrible thoughts assail him, of "horrible marvels" (143) that have never been seen before, signs of "war, agonies, and plagues" (154–55). He mentions a variety of ills—war, water poisoned by Jews, the hypocritical flagellants—which prompt Nature to send winds and to corrupt the air. Seeing all this "desordenance" (352), God lets loose death in vengeance, and Machaut describes vividly the ravages of plague. Fearful, he locks himself in his house, and leaves it only when spring comes, and with it the end of the epidemic.

---

[21]*Oeuvres de Guillaume de Machaut,* ed. Ernest Hoepffner, 3 vols., SATF (Paris: Firmin Didot, 1908–21), I: 137–282. References in the text are to line numbers of this edition.

[22]Eccles. 1:2 and 3:12. The significance of these allusions has been discussed by Margaret J. Ehrhart, "Machaut's *Jugement dou roy de Navarre* and the Book of Ecclesiastes," *Neuphilologische Mitteilungen,* 81 (1980), 318–25. She shows that Machaut's view of Ecclesiastes follows that of Nicholas of Lyra's commentary, which, influenced by the *Nicomachean Ethics,* stresses not contempt of the world but the moderate use of earthly pleasures according to right reason. We will see shortly what the poem offers as means of being happy.

This famous introduction constitutes only the first eighth of the poem. The rest of it is a love-debate. On one side is Machaut, whose previous debate poem, the *Jugement dou roy de Behaingne,* had decided that a man whose lover was unfaithful to him had greater grief than a woman whose lover had died. On the other side, arguing exactly the opposite, is Bonneürtez (Happiness), aided by other personifications such as Raison, Attemprance, Honnestez, Prudence, and Mesure. With a lineup like that there can be little doubt who will win, and at the end of the poem Charles of Navarre pronounces judgment in favor of Bonneürtez, telling Machaut that as penance he must write a lay, a chanson, and a ballade. Until recently it was commonplace to write the debate off as a routine court performance (Machaut changing his mind to please ladies offended by the decision in *Behaingne*) and to think of the introduction as a piece of interesting but excrescent realism, without thematic relevance. But Robertson has called attention to the fact that the plague is not only described with verisimilitude but personified and related to the "abstract reality" of God's order (in fact, Machaut even makes it a divinely ordered consequence of phenomena that historically followed it, not preceded it); William Calin and Margaret Ehrhart have argued a number of thematic connections between prologue and debate; and Douglas Kelly has found in the poem's reversal of *Behaingne*'s verdict evidence of an important evolutionary change in Machaut's conception of *fin amour.*[23] *Navarre* is a sophisticated and substantial poem, and I want only to consider briefly one pertinent aspect of it, the connection between the plague and the debate.

The plague itself is only one manifestation of a disordered, chaotic world. Whereas the introduction to the *Decameron* devotes all its time to the effects of the Black Death, *Navarre* treats the pestilence in the context of God's punishment for sinfulness and links it with other examples of disharmony, especially war. Machaut's "realistic" lines about people being thrown into pits and about fields lying uncultivated appear as part of a larger theme, what Calin calls "a traditional medieval motif, the universe upside-down" (p. 125). The poem uses the plague

[23]Robertson, *Preface to Chaucer,* pp. 235–36; William Calin, *A Poet at the Fountain: Essays on the Narrative Verse of Guillaume de Machaut* (Lexington: University of Kentucky Press, 1974), pp. 110–29; Kelly, pp. 137–44.

more for what it tells us *about* the world than for what it does *to* the world. This symbolic use of the Black Death was anticipated some months earlier by Jacme d'Agramont, who at the end of his plague tract has a fascinating chapter in which he allegorizes it on the level of tropology: "In this article the principle of pestilence is conceived as applicable in a moral, as well as a physical sense."[24]

Jacme begins by citing biblical parables that edify when morally understood. Similarly, "for those with clear and subtle understanding, all that has been said about pestilence in its natural sense, will apply equally clearly and truly to the moral pestilence." He defines moral pestilence as "a contra-natural change in the spirit and in the thoughts of men, from which come enmities, rancors, wars and robberies, destruction of places and deaths in certain definite regions beyond what is customary to the people living there." The rest of the chapter elaborates on this statement. Just as "natural pestilence" causes pathological changes in the body, so moral pestilence causes changes in the soul. The analogy between disease and sin has a long history in medieval thought, of course, and as John Alford has reminded us, it is not simply an analogy but a manifestation of an "essential connection."[25] Thus Jacme's allegorical finale to his scientifically scrupulous treatise should not come as a great surprise. He goes on to justify the other details in his definition, explaining how hatred, war, and other evils all evolve out of "the contra-natural thoughts above mentioned." He restricts moral pestilence to "certain definite regions" because it appears in different countries at different times; should it become universal, it "would be a great sign of the advent of the son of abomination, that is the Antichrist." Like the plague itself, moral pestilence "has causes, is announced by signs . . . and would respond to a regimen of prevention." But Jacme does not think his understanding adequate to work out all the details of his parallel, and so he closes with a prayer for protection to Christ, "who has preserved us from the pestilence, naturally or morally understood."

[24]*BHM*, 23 (1949), 87–89, for this and all the following quotations from Jacme. Augustine had long before analogized physical and moral pestilence, in *The City of God*, I, chap. 32.
[25]Alford, 388.

Machaut depicts the natural pestilence as a consequence of the moral pestilence of an avaricious age. Are we meant to see the debate as a response to that situation, containing perhaps elements that might belong to Jacme's hypothetical "regimen of prevention"? In *Navarre* the dramatic movement is sequential— spring comes, the plague disappears, Machaut ventures out of his "prison" (485) and into an encounter with Bonneürtez; in the *Decameron* it is causal—the *brigata* leaves the city in order to save itself. The weaker structural connection makes the link between plague and pleasure less integral in Machaut than in Boccaccio, yet it still implies, I think, a relationship much like that in the hundred tales. Machaut is out hunting rabbits, re- joicing in the now-healthy air, when Bonneürtez (though she is not named until later in the poem) sees him and sends her squire to tell him that she wants to debate. She accuses Machaut of wronging women and refers to the decision in *Behaingne;* he says he will defend himself, and they agree on the King of Navarre as judge. They enter a place of peace and beauty, "De deduit e de bon repos, / Ou uns cuers se puet reposer / Qui a point se vuet disposer" (1126–28)—a place of delight and tran- quillity, where a heart that wants to set itself right could take repose. The terminology here suggests the re-creative func- tions of delight and mental *quies.* In an elegant room where the debate will take place, Machaut meets Bonneürtez's compan- ions. They include Attemprance, who reveals no vice or "desor- denance" (1200) in her behavior; Pais, who says that a life of peace, happiness ("leësse"), and tranquillity ("repos") involves avoiding anger and vengeance (1207–18); Prudence, carrying Sapience in her heart, who knows the cause of all things in the firmament, including air and the other elements (1239–64); and Largesse, who reproves avarice as the worst sin (1277–78). Surely these virtues are meant to answer, in one way or another, the "desordenance" of the cupidity, aggression, and natural corruption depicted in the introduction.

That answer, though, by no means takes the form of a moral tract. The love-debate is first and foremost gracious social en- tertainment, something meant to give pleasure "to lovers" (1516). Calin has made a firm case for its large and equitable comic perspective, one capable of having fun at the expense of both Machaut-the-character and the occasionally overearnest female personifications.[26] Good humor permeates the poem; even as the judge and his counselors whisper among themselves before deciding Machaut's "penitence" (4047), he knows that their discussion is lighthearted, for he can hear them laughing (4056–57). But at the same time, the judge's "ordenance" (3755), which he arrives at with the help of Raison and Mesure, among others, clearly suggests a mode of secular behavior meant to be seen as admirable, one that would be a corrective to the moral pestilence that has led to the Black Death. Toward the end of the poem Raison delivers a long panegyric to Bonneürtez, and it entails, I think, an affirmation of the validity of well-ordered living, secular or sacred, one that implicitly offers a range of human experience that stands against the irrationality and destructiveness which the introduction portrays. Happiness, she says, transcends the vicissitudes of Fortune (3851–56) and appears in many places: between loyal lovers, in learning, in the contemplative life, even "in many recreations (esbanois), such as jousts and tournaments, for the purpose of advancing chivalry and making the deeds of good men known to women" (3909–13).

Properly motivated recreations, apparently, belong as much to the world of Raison and Mesure as true friendship and learning. Like Gace de la Buigne, whose hunting treatise we examined in Chapter 3, Machaut has a comfortably secular notion of moral "ordenance." His heart finds *quies* a lot nearer at hand than Augustine's does, and one suspects that he would wish us to add another domain of Bonneürtez to Raison's list: the satisfactions offered by an urbanely written love-debate that in the face of pestilential destruction asserts the value of properly ordered courtly pleasures. In late 1348 the Paris *Compendium* had told people, as the adaptation cited earlier puts it, to flee "melencolies" and to live as "ioieusement et lieement" as they could. Some months later, Machaut's response to the plague is to demonstrate that the movement from melancholy to happiness must involve a movement from avarice and rapacity to Charité and Mesure, and to embody that movement in the structure of a poem which itself will make people "ioieuse."

---

[26]James I. Wimsatt, *Chaucer and the French Love Poets* (Chapel Hill: University of North Carolina Press, 1968), pp. 94–102, also discusses the comic narrator and notes his relevance to Chaucer's poetic *personae*.

If the literary movement from plague to pleasure in Boccaccio and Machaut reveals a common medical and ethical response to the Black Death, one seen as well in Jacme's discussion of moral pestilence, it is reasonable to expect that other writers might use the plague thematically in their work. An obvious example is the rather perfunctory appearance of the pestilence in the love allegory known as the *Songe vert*,[27] where the interesting structural resonances of Boccaccio and Machaut have been reduced to a simple attempt at added pathos. The narrator has lost his beloved at the time of the "grant mortalite" that has caused so many men and women to grieve. He is melancholy, despairing, and, when he hears the bell ringing where her body lies, suicidal. Then he has a dream in which the Queen of Love leads him back from grief to interest in a new lady and to a renewed faith in love, a psychological movement symbolized by his change from black to green clothing. The plague here is the implicit cause of death, and the author interested in it only insofar as it helps establish plausibility and a suitably dolorous beginning. In another instance, religious rather than secular and moving not from plague to pleasure but from natural to moral pestilence, the *Somnium* of the Cistercian monk Peter Ceffons of Clairvaux is set in Paris as the plague is raging; then follows a dream vision in which Peter argues against a definition promulgated by the General Chapter which he thinks will do more damage than the Black Death because of its effects on men's souls.[28]

More elaborate, and more revealing of the literary and moral polarities of plague and pleasure, is the structural logic of a work that moves in the opposite direction from that of the *Decameron* and the *Jugement dou roy de Navarre*, from delight to pestilence. *Les livres du roy Modus et de la royne Ratio* consists of two loosely connected parts. The first is an elaborate hunting manual, the *Livre des deduis*, complete not only with instructions on hunting and hawking but with moralizations drawn from the animals and a debate on the relative merits of the "deduit de chiens" and the "deduit d'oisiaus." In Chapter 3 we saw its place in the development of hunting treatises in the fourteenth century. The second part is a moral tract, the *Songe du pesti-*

[27]Ed. Léopold Constans, *Romania*, 33 (1904), 490–539.
[28]The *Somnium* is discussed by Damasus Trapp, O.S.A., "Peter Ceffons of Clairvaux," *Recherches de théologie ancienne et médiévale*, 24 (1957), 109–14.

lence, about the evils present in the world, in the form of a dream vision and with such familiar conceptualizations as the three temptations, the three estates, and the battle of vices and virtues. Following the vision the author has a clerk interpret it, who supplies a set of prophecies (really written after the fact, of course) concerning the pestilence and war that will ravage France in the third quarter of the century.[29] At first glance the two parts appear unrelated, and their independence is further suggested by the fact that each appears alone in some manuscripts. Yet their author clearly saw them as connected in some way, and the logic of that relationship is, I think, very close to what we have seen in Boccaccio and Machaut.

The principal element that unifies the two parts is the presence of King Modus and Queen Ratio. In the *Livre des deduis,* Modus gives the rules for proper hunting behavior and Ratio the allegorical significance of the animals. The author, Henri de Ferrières, claims to be copying from an ancient book and asserts initially the harmony of that society where Modus and Ratio governed. Modus, we later find out, means "Bonne Maniere," and he is wedded to Reason because the two cannot exist without each other (I: 268). He represents more than just "good manners" in the modern sense; he manifests the properly ordered behavior of secular culture governed by reason. Together, says the author, they ruled over all human activity. Ratio's sphere was more theoretical: she gave basic rules for behavior that insured the "droit commun" (I: 5). Modus's authority involved more practical knowledge. He knew medicine and gave lawyers the skill to plead cases (I: 5). He was also in charge of "all games and entertainments," and his abilities as a musician enabled him to be "lord of peace" (I: 6). He hated idleness, and "he created all the hunts (deduis)—for red deer, boar, and fallow deer—so that we would not be idle" (I: 6). We have seen this argument for hunting previously; here too it works to give an ethical sanction to the sport and to the fact that Modus wrote a book about it. In all the instances depicting

---

[29]Ed. Gunnar Tilander, 2 vols. (Paris: SATF, 1932). Hereafter I will cite volume and page numbers of this edition. Whereas the hunting treatise is well known, the second part of the work has been generally ignored; according to Tilander, it was written in the mid-1370s, the first part sometime between 1354–76.

the rule of Modus we see the principle of orderly activity, disciplines with rules, a more precise meaning of *modus* as method, not just manner. Against such properly governed recreations as hunting stand the wicked ones, such as dicing and other "entertainments that promote war and conflict" (I: 7–8). As in the *Decameron* and in most of the theoretical material discussed in Chapter 3, the line is drawn not between sobriety and amusement but between proper and improper forms of play.

In the second part, Modus and Ratio no longer control society. We see them trying to win back mankind from Satan. We see them pleading before God that the World, the Flesh, and the Devil (the three temptations had been introduced in the *Livre des deduis* in some of Ratio's moralizations) have seduced people away from obedience to them. And finally we see precisely such things as "war and conflict" forecast for mankind as a result of people's not having followed Modus and Ratio. With these disasters goes "the pestilence to come," which will be sent by the Holy Spirit "in chastisement of the people for their great sins" (II: 199). The clerk supplies a description of the conjunction of Mars, Saturn, and Jupiter in 1345 as a sign of the epidemic to follow. We also discover at the end of the dream just why the author had set down the *Livre des deduis*, as he responds to a question from the clerk:

> Then he asked me if I had made the *Livre des deduis* which was based on Method and Reason, who had left the realm of France, which would for that reason experience great devastation from wars and plagues, and a great many people would die. "The reason that caused me to put the *deduis* in writing was that it seemed to me that few people remained who knew how to give them order (ordener), either in word or deed." Thus I told him that I had put down everything I knew, all of which was built on Method and Reason. [II: 192]

Reason and proper behavior have been lost, and no one in the present age knows how to arrange properly such noble recreations as hunting. Since the loss of Modus·and Ratio is the "cause" of plague and war, the author's attempt to reestablish their principles in the guidance of hunting can be seen as an effort to combat corruption and chaos, as can Boccaccio's *brigata*'s delineation of principles in the guidance of how to employ their leisure. Both storytelling and hunting are properly ordered secular activities which oppose idleness and license.

It seems obvious that the *Livre des deduis* and the *Songe du pestilence* were written essentially out of two quite different motives; one instructs in a sport, the other harrangues about a world gone bad. But the ethical aspects of recreation stressed so firmly in the hunting manual allowed Henri de Ferrières, when he later composed the *Songe*, to set the ideal of pleasure properly taken, with due regard to using that delight "according to reason" and remembering "always to serve God first" (I: 12), against the wicked kinds of indulgence that lead people to sin. In creating a structure that moves from pleasure to plague, *Les livres du roy Modus et de la royne Ratio* reverses the pattern we have been considering, but it intimates nevertheless that proper recreation may be one means of counteracting the disorder that caused the plague and that the plague in turn exacerbates.

I have been stressing the close connection between literature and life in works that involve movement from plague to pleasure. The pestilence, literally and tropologically, is disorder, chaos. Affirmation of secular order in the face of the Black Death is a moral and therapeutic response in itself, regardless of the particular form (storytelling, love-debate, hunting) that order takes. We have seen this shared response to the pestilence on the part of certain writers and physicians. Is there any evidence that their attitudes played a role in the society at large, that concerns for avoiding fear and attaining pleasure were historical as well as literary responses?

There is certainly a connection between the plague tracts' pronouncements on fear and actions that can be documented as social responses to the Black Death. We have seen Jacme d'Agramont's recommendation that bells not toll for the dead because of the dangers of instilling fear into the living, and we have seen Boccaccio's Pampinea give voice to just such fears. Chronicles reveal the same beliefs about fear that the physicians have. One Greek report of the plague in Constantinople, after a clinical account of its symptoms, moves on to psychological effects: "Most terrible was the discouragement. Whenever people felt sick there was no hope left for recovery, but by turning to despair, adding to their prostration and severely aggravating their sickness, they died at once." Because of the emotional damage done through the fear instilled by the tolling of the death bell, communities acted according to Jacme's advice. The sanitary ordinances of Pistoia issued to combat the plague in 1348 include, among a variety of rules for burial and mourning designed to minimize the omnipresent feeling of death, a provision that forbids the ringing of church bells at funerals, "so that the sound of the bells will not assault the sick, and fear not triumph over them." When the Sienese chronicler, Agnolo di Tura, reports that burials often took place without the proper offices, he adds that the death bell did not sound. There is no record of Sienese sanitary legislation in 1348 comparable to Pistoia's, but the absence of the bell might well suggest a common-sense, if not officially ordered, response to the dangers of fear. Similar efforts occurred farther north: Gilles le Muisit records that in Tournai the constant bell-ringings left the entire population afraid and that the clergy did not make any effort to change the situation because of its own financial interest. In response city officials issued legislation on a variety of moral matters, including some restrictions on burial services and mourning; later in 1349, as the plague grew worse, they issued further regulations, intended "for the benefit of the city," prohibiting entirely the ringing of bells for the dead and the wearing of black.[30]

Even more clearly tied to the plague tracts' advice on the *accidentia animae* is a law enacted in Venice on August 7, 1348. Taking note of the fact that many citizens were wearing mourning throughout the city, "which brings pain and sorrow to those who see it," the regulation forbids the populace to do so (with a few exceptions), for the reason that such garb would not do the souls of the dead any good and that "it would be

[30]Christos S. Bartsocas, "Two Fourteenth Century Greek Descriptions of the 'Black Death,'" *Journal of the History of Medicine and Allied Sciences*, 21 (1966), 396. Alberto Chiappelli, "Gli ordinamenti sanitari del comune di Pistoia contro la pestilenza del 1348," *Archivio storico italiano,* ser. 4, 20 (1887), 11. W. M. Bowsky, "The Impact of the Black Death upon Sienese Government and Society," *Speculum*, 39 (1964), 15. *Chronique et annales de Gilles le Muisit*, ed. Henri Lemaître (Paris: Renouard, 1906), pp. 255–57. I am not sure that it is fair to see these responses only as "petty acts," as does Stephen d'Irsay, "Defense Reactions during the Black Death, 1348–49," *Annals of Medical History*, 9 (1927), 175, though he is no doubt right that there was a greater concern for spiritual than for psychological relief.

more useful for the living to cast off such sadness and in its place introduce plenty of joy and feasting."[31] Here is a clear instance of cheerfulness perceived as a useful response to the plague—at least psychologically, one may infer, and perhaps hygienically. It is not necessary to prove that this and other legislation was directly due to the advice of physicians or the reading of plague tracts, though these possibilities are certainly likely. It is enough to recognize the correlation, to see that the ideas expressed in the treatises and the decisions of civic authorities reveal an identical attitude toward the proper disposition of emotions during the plague. The logic of the *Decameron* is to be found not only in medical advice but also in official public actions.

There is evidence as well that people entertained themselves out of motives similar to those of Boccaccio's *brigata*, though it is less clear-cut than community legislation designed to prevent destructive emotions. It is easy to infer from the Venice law or from the many chronicle accounts of people leaving plague-struck areas that citizens sought pleasure, but what they actually did or thought can only remain conjectural. Conjecture may have more foundation in the case of Giangaleazzo Visconti, who, when he left his palace in Pavia during outbreaks of plague in the years after the Black Death, would go to one of his country estates which he used principally for hunting.[32] Motives are much more explicit, however, in a story entered into the *Grandes chroniques de France*, which tells of two religious of Saint-Denis traveling on a visitation during the period of the Black Death. They passed en route through a village where the people were dancing and "making great revelry." When the two inquired about all this activity, the people told them that they were dancing because the epidemic had not yet entered their town, "nor do we expect that it will come because of the happiness that is in us (ne si n'avons pas esperance qu'elle y entre pour la leesce qui est en nous)." When the religious re-

---

[31]"... quia talis portatio non sit propterea suorum defunctorum liberacio animarum et pocius sit utile pro videntibus removere talem merronem [sic] et suo loco inducere plenum gaudium atque festum." Quoted in Mario Brunetti, "Venezia durante la peste del 1348," *L'ateneo Veneto*, 32 (1909), II: 16–17.

[32]D. M. Bueno de Mesquita, *Giangaleazzo Visconti, Duke of Milan (1351–1402)* (Cambridge: Cambridge University Press, 1941), pp. 177, 297.

turned to the village, having completed their visitation, they found "very few people, whose faces were very sad," and when the two asked about those who had previously been celebrating, they were told that God's anger had descended on the village, so that some had been killed, and others, because they did not know where to go to avoid the plague, "died of the fear they had."[33]

The story is told without commentary. It serves principally to show the sudden devastation caused by pestilence—one thinks of the youth at the beginning of the *Pardoner's Tale* who has, overnight, gone from carousing to coffin. But what of the villagers' emotions? Are we to believe that God has punished them for their revelry, or is their swing from "leesce" to "faces moult·tristes" simply designed to show the futility of thinking that one can have control over the spread of the disease? Obviously gaiety is no protection against the Black Death—though one might observe that it seems to be more *intensissimum* than *temperatum* here. Fear, however, seems to be taking its toll. Still, that fact that some people believed that joy could ward off plague (or, to be more cautious, the fact that a chronicle includes as history an anecdote in which people believe it) testifies to at least some acceptance of the physicians' contention that the *accidentia animae* play a role in one's susceptibility to pestilence.

Perhaps the most interesting historical case, though a complex one, is that of the famous court of love established in France at the beginning of the fifteenth century. Its avowed purpose was to honor and serve women, which it did through such means as poetic contests and love-debates. It is often mentioned by historians and literary scholars, usually as an example of the consuming interest taken by late medieval French court circles in splashy social pastimes.[34] But the charter of the court of love suggests a firm therapeutic reason for its existence: it claims that Philip of Burgundy and Louis of Bourbon requested that Charles VI establish it "during this displeasing and harmful epidemic of plague presently at large in the realm" in order to "pass part of the time more graciously and to create an awakening of

[33]*Les grandes chroniques de France,* ed. Jules Viard, IX (Paris: Champion, 1937), pp. 315–16.
[34]E.g. Huizinga, pp. 115–17.

new joy (affin de trouver esveil de nouvelle joye)."[35] Later the
charter specifies that the members of the court are to gather on
Valentine's Day "to dine in joyous recreation and amorous conversation" (209), and it indicates that visitors are to be given a
place at court should they wish "to enjoy themselves (esbattre)
to pass the time during the festivities of the *pui* or of other
worthy gatherings of our court of love" (217). These references
to passing the time, to "recréacion" and enjoyment, suggest
that whatever the court's claims may be to celebrate humility
and loyalty, its essential social and personal functions are comparable to the activities of Boccaccio's *brigata;* composing lyrics
and engaging in genteel conversation about love are gracious
entertainments that will, through their creation of "joye," alleviate the discomforts of the plague. Boccaccio is more explicit
about the nature of that alleviation, but it seems reasonable to
assume that a similar hygienic rationale underlies the pleasantries of French society as well.

Thus the charter of the *cour amoureuse*. That the court existed in some form is indisputable, for in addition to its
charter are various documents and references that testify to its
existence, and to an extensive membership, in the early fifteenth century. But Theodor Straub has shown that the
charter's statement about the court's origins cannot be true
and has raised questions about its historical reliability.[36] As it
turns out, the more accurate history of the establishment of
the court that he proposes does not entail rejecting its therapeutic motivation, for although the founding fathers could
not have been where the charter says they were on January 6,
1400, the founding mother was: Queen Isabeau of Bavaria
was at Mantes, waiting in the royal castle there, unable to
return to Paris because of an outbreak of plague. Straub has
shown that during this period Isabeau bought a copy of the

---

[35]Ed. C. Potvin, "La Charte de la Cour d'Amour de l'année 1401," *Bulletins
de l'Académie Royale des Sciences, des Lettres et des Beaux-Arts de Belgique*, 3d ser., 12
(1886), 202.

[36]For the contemporary evidence see Arthur Piaget, "La cour amoureuse,
dite de Charles VI," *Romania*, 20 (1891), 417–54, and "Un manuscrit de la *cour
amoureuse de Charles VI,*" *Romania*, 31 (1902), 597–603. Straub's argument is in
"Die Gründung des Pariser Minnehofs von 1400," *Zeitschrift für Romanische
Philologie*, 77 (1961), 1–14.

Cent balades, precisely the kind of elegant secular love poetry that the *cour amoureuse* sought to foster. He argues that the court must have been conceived at this time; though it is impossible to know how and why the history of its founding became altered, the inaccuracies of the charter as it survives in a late manuscript do not compel rejection of the existence of the court or of the motivation for its establishment. It was created as a pastime to bring joy during the plague, and if it seems as though we have life imitating Boccaccio's art, that is only because Boccaccio's art was so firmly based on medieval medical and psychological thinking.

A Response to the Black Death

I conclude this chapter with speculation on two principal points. The first has to do with the literary implications of the pattern of plague to pleasure. Its appearances in Boccaccio, the plague tracts, and the charter of the *cour amoureuse* point to a late medieval view of literary pleasure as therapeutic. This view would seem to be predicated on ideas discussed in the second chapter, ideas which, perhaps because of the impact of the Black Death, became sharpened enough to prompt literary creations that self-consciously embodied in their very structures what medieval medicine had been saying for centuries about the hygienic values of delight. How far ought this line of inquiry be pursued? Did Boccaccio really think that his work might have a physically beneficial effect on his readers or listeners? I believe he did. Not, of course, in the simple and extreme way that the villagers in the *Grandes chroniques* seem to have understood, but in the rationally plausible way of the regimens which recognizes cheerfulness as a factor in hygiene and hygiene as a factor in susceptibility to disease. The evidence of the plague treatises is firm on this point—they may debate questions of causes and technical medical remedies, but I am not aware of any controversy over or cynicism about the values of a good regimen, including the proper disposition of the *accidentia animae.* And the prevalence of the idea throughout subsequent waves of epidemic suggests its durability. In fact, when some of the early notions of how to deal with disease come into question, it is not the nonnaturals that are ridiculed but the faith in lectuaries and phlebotomy.[37]

Perhaps we are in a position today, after some years of popular interest in what is variously known as holistic medicine or alternative medicine, to acknowledge the powers attributed to mental attitude in the tracts as something more than silliness. There is certainly substantial documentation of a variety of ways in which the mind can affect bodily response, such as the correlation between meditative states and altered physiological patterns and the power of hypnosis to deal with pain. Clinical research has demonstrated psychosomatic factors in illness, but there has been much less controlled examination of their role in therapy or hygiene, the evidence for which tends to remain anecdotal, such as Norman Cousins's recent celebrated recovery from ankylosing spondylitis with a regimen of ascorbic acid and laughter.[38] This modern instance has a fifteenth-century parallel in the case of Alfonso V, who according to Jacques Amyot, after finding physicians useless in curing his sickness, decided to take "no mo medicines" but to have the deeds of Alexander read to him for his "recreacion," which created "so wonderfull pleasure, that nature gathered strength by it, and overcame the waywardness of his disease."[39] Nothing in this chapter, naturally, constitutes evidence that laughter at the *Decameron* increased people's resistance to the plague bacillus. But there is a great deal of evidence that educated people in the fourteenth century believed that enjoyment of music and fiction would decrease the likelihood of their being struck by

[37]See e.g. the opinions of the seventeenth-century physician Francesco Redi, as quoted in Carlo M. Cipolla, *Public Health and the Medical Profession in the Renaissance* (Cambridge: Cambridge University Press, 1976), pp. 110–11. In a delightful letter to a hypochondriac who has been trying every medicament he can get his hands on, Redi notes: "you will get well whenever you ignore ailments and do not fear them." Cf. Deschamps, VII: 249–50.

[38]First reported in the *New England Journal of Medicine*, 295 (1976), 1458–63; now available as part of a book, *Anatomy of an Illness as Perceived by the Patient* (New York: Norton, 1979). For related evidence see Raymond A. Moody, Jr., *Laugh after Laugh: The Healing Power of Humor* (Jacksonville, Fla.: Headwaters Press, 1978), pp. 17–40.

[39]Quoted, from Sir Thomas North's translation of the Preface to Amyot's translation of Plutarch's *Lives*, by Geoffrey Shepherd in his edition of Sidney's *Apology for Poetry* (London: Thomas Nelson, 1965), pp. 169–70.

plague. I am not suggesting that this hygienic function was the only or even the principal motive for the writing or the reading of the *Decameron* and the *Jugement dou roy de Navarre*, but it must have existed as one element in a complex of motives that produced those works.

At least in regard to the *Decameron*, some subsequent testimony points to its perceived medical value. As we will see in the next chapter, Laurent de Premierfait assumes that the work was written to give solace to the survivors of the Black Death still suffering from fear or sorrow. In a late fifteenth-century plague tract, Boninus Mombritius recommends the "book of the hundred tales" along with other "books of pleasure and delight" as works designed to dispel destructive accidents of the soul.[40] The therapeutic dimension of literary and conversational pleasure may also help account for the popularity of later *Decameron*-like structures of tale collections, beginning with Sercambi's direct imitation, in which a group of travelers leave plague-ravaged Lucca, and extending through all those Renaissance anthologies that feature what Clements and Gibaldi in *Anatomy of the Novella* call the "disaster cornice" (pp. 42–49).

A second concern of this chapter, and one more important to understanding Boccaccio's and Machaut's literary intentions, is what the movement from plague to pleasure says about fourteenth-century response to the Black Death. Most modern studies of the psychological effects of the plague stress the exaggerated reactions it produced: on the one hand, an intensified concern with sin and death which led to such bizarre religious phenomena as the flagellants; on the other, the dissolution of normal moral behavior into brigandage and profligacy. Boccaccio, Machaut, and the chroniclers testify to these polarities, which are in fact opposite sides of the same coin and which have parallels in the response of other eras to plague and similar cataclysmic events.[41] It would be absurd to deny that these

---

[40]*Una ignota opera sulla peste del medico umanista Bonino Mombrizio*, ed. Antonio di Giovanni, Scientia Veterum, XXXVI (Genoa, 1963), pp. 35–36. A scholar and editor of religious texts, Mombritius adds that such works are for a youthful world interested in pleasure and that "in regard to the soul" the best way to flee death is with the "pleasure and delight of spiritual consolation" provided by prayer and contemplation.

[41]Ziegler, pp. 270–79, gives a fairly typical summary, saying that if one had to "identify the hall-mark of the years which followed the Black Death, it would

extreme forms of behavior must loom very large in any assessment of the "mind" of the later Middle Ages after the plague,
however risky such generalizations may be considering the
need to deal with variables of time and place. And there is
certainly hard evidence, beyond the judgments of medieval
commentators and modern researchers into collective psychology, to show that the plague did occasion both increased religious fervor and increased immorality.[42]

But perhaps the conventional wisdom suffers from what
F. R. H. Du Boulay, in a different but related context, has
called the "overstatement of repetition."[43] Too often, I think,
more moderate responses to the pestilence have been drowned
out by the sounds of flagellations and orgies, and it is as part of
a more rational attitude that Boccaccio and Machaut, as well as
the plague treatises themselves, have a major place. For they
affirm the power of natural reason to deal with the plague;
they do not take refuge in either passionate religiosity or carnal
abandonment. Insofar as they acknowledge those extremes,
they do so only to reject them and seek a saner way. It seems to
me that the richest morality of the *Decameron* and the *Jugement*
(and, mutatis mutandis, of *Modus et Ratio*) lies not so much in
any particular assertions of value within the fictions as in the
implications of their structure: that in the face of chaos and
disintegration, it is possible for people to reassert civilization, to

---

be that of a neurotic and all-pervading gloom." For other psychological assess-
ments, see William L. Langer, "The Next Assignment," *American Historical Review*, 63 (1958), 283–304, and James Westfall Thompson, "The Aftermath of
the Black Death and the Aftermath of the Great War," *American Journal of
Sociology*, 26 (1920), 565–72. The most respected study of the artistic evidence
for a change in religious sensibility is Millard Meiss, *Painting in Florence and
Siena after the Black Death* (Princeton: Princeton University Press, 1951), which
includes a chapter on Boccaccio which argues that the plague did not affect
him deeply until after the writing of the *Decameron*. There is a strange article by
B. S. Gowen, "Some Aspects of Pestilences and Other Epidemics," *American
Journal of Psychology*, 18 (1907), 1–60, which begins as an assessment of the
Black Death's effects on people's minds (and includes, on 20–22, some consideration of pleasure as a preventative), but which evolves into a cross-cultural
survey of most anything the author considers mentally aberrant, from lycan-
thropy to the South Sea bubble.
[42]See e.g. Elisabeth Carpentier, *Une ville devant la peste: Orvieto et la peste noire
de 1348* (Paris: Ecole Pratique des Hautes Etudes, 1962), pp. 192–98, 220–21.
[43]*An Age of Ambition: English Society in the Late Middle Ages* (London: Thomas
Nelson, 1970), p. 12.

conduct their lives in an orderly manner, and to reaffirm the stability and worth of such secular virtues as polite discourse, wit, and even recreational pleasure.

Such a moderate, secular response is in no way antipathetic to religion. Boccaccio's *brigata,* after all, pauses on the weekends from its worldly entertainments for religious reasons, spending its time in prayer and meditation rather than storytelling. Taking earthly means to counteract the plague, even though it may be sent by God, is not incompatible with obedience to the divine will. The Paris *Compendium* notes that even though God sometimes sends pestilence and we must accept His judgment, that does not mean that we should neglect earthly remedies, since God created medicines.[44] Medieval and Renaissance plague tracts and regimens sometimes cite Ecclus. 38: 11–12 as justification: "give place to the physician. For the Lord created him: and let him not depart from thee, for his works are necessary." Jacme d'Agramont acknowledges that "if the corruption and putrefaction of the air has come because of our sins the remedies of the medical art are of little value, for only He who binds can unbind."[45] But if it comes from planetary conjunctions, he continues, or from the earth or water, there are things one can do about it. He does not deal with the thorny problem that since God works through natural things, divine chastisement and an unpropitious conjunction are not mutually exclusive causes, and perhaps his very failure to push further philosophically suggests the way in which religious orthodoxy and medical wisdom could coexist. The physician acknowledges God's power but does what he can, recognizes first causes but concentrates when possible on secondary ones, since they allow for practical response.

Of course there were other views on the relationship of secular and sacred remedies. Chaucer's Physician testifies to a tradition that perceived at least some discrepancy between medical and Biblical study. And in 1480, more than a hundred years after Gentile da Foligno wrote his plague treatises, the Bishop of Foligno, Antonio Bettini de' Gesuati di Siena, trying to stop desertion of the city during another wave of pestilence, felt the

---

[44]Rébouis, p. 92; cf. Olivier de la Haye, pp. 60–62.
[45]*BHM,* 23 (1949), 78.

need to attack Gentile's advice to flee the infected area. He argues that the physician's "natural and earthly remedies" deal only with the body, "having no regard for the health of the soul."[46] Since the soul is more important than the body, one must listen to the spiritual advice of the Church and look to the ultimate cause of the plague, which is God. Only charity, care for the sick, can finally save one's soul. The bishop's attack on Gentile's practical medical advice is not unique, and one can find similar oppositions throughout late medieval and Renaissance debates on how to deal with the pestilence.[47]

But such antagonisms are often the result of extreme positions, and they do not represent the more moderate course that seems to have been taken in the early diffusion of the plague tracts and in the immediate secular responses to the Black Death of Boccaccio and Machaut. It is simply not accurate enough to generalize, from evidence like the bishop's Christian fatalism, that "the Middle Ages, ignoring the teachings of the Greek physicians and relying entirely upon Scripture and the writings of the Church fathers, considered disease the scourge of God upon a sinful people" (Langer, 298–99). However much one can find this tendency in a lot of medieval medical thinking and in literary uses of disease, it does not reflect the governing spirit of the plague tracts, nor can it account for the secular plague-to-pleasure pattern discussed here. Sylvia Thrupp's conclusions seem to me much truer to the texts: "medieval men recognized the role of contagion in a plague-struck environment, advocated better sanitation and invented quarantine measures. Religious feelings did not hinder their efforts: no one would have suggested that prayer would clean up the streets or make dirty water pure."[48] This line of reasoning does not seek to deny medieval reliance on divine aid, merely to see it as part of a continuum of response. There is no inconsistency in John Lydgate's praying for relief from plague in one poem and delineating earthly remedies in another, nor in a sick person's turning to

[46]*Liber de diuina preordinatione uite et mortis humane* [Rome, 1485?], chap. xix, unpaginated.

[47]For England, see Mullett, passim; for Italy, Richard John Palmer, "The Control of Plague in Venice and Northern Italy 1348–1600," (Diss. University of Kent at Canterbury, 1978), pp. 280–314.

[48]"Plague Effects in Medieval Europe," *Comparative Studies in Society and History*, 8 (1966), 480.

faith-healing when other cures have failed.[49] As Paul H. Kocher has shown in regard to Elizabethan attitudes, the accommodations that existed between religion and medicine are too complex to be put in terms of simple opposition.[50] He argues that the Elizabethan view gave doctors sufficient intellectual room to think and practice, and it seems to me that the early plague tracts reveal a similar secular confidence.

It is precisely such secular confidence that Boccaccio and Machaut manifest. They saw the plague, and they saw the extremity of response it engendered, and they were more concerned about the latter. Both writers lend support to René Girard's thesis that the prevalence of the plague in Western literature reflects a greater interest in its metaphoric than in its medical impact. Pestilence, he says, disguises an even more terrible threat, the violence that destroys individual and social relationships.[51] This is the threat that Jacme d'Agramont attends to in the terminology of medieval allegory and that Boccaccio and Machaut respond to in their fictions. They see the plague principally in terms of what it does to (or reveals about) the human community, and they face the threat of disorder not by denying the values that have created community but by affirming the possibility of their reestablishment. In Machaut this affirmation centers principally on the figure of Bonneürtez and the other personified virtues; in Boccaccio it appears overtly in the secular virtues of wit, love, and magnanimity that are espoused in the tales themselves and implicitly in the decorum with which the *brigata* conducts itself.

The value of decorum becomes explicit in Dioneo's speech to the ladies after the hundredth tale has been told:

> For as far as I have been able to observe, albeit the tales
> related here have been amusing, perhaps of a sort to stimu-
> late carnal desire, and we have continually partaken of excel-
> lent food and drink, played music, and sung many songs, all

[49]For Lydgate, see p. 174. For the medical aspects of visits to shrines, see Ronald C. Finucane, *Miracles and Pilgrims: Popular Beliefs in Medieval England* (London: J. M. Dent, 1977), pp. 59–82.

[50]"The Idea of God in Elizabethan Medicine," *Journal of the History of Ideas*, 11 (1950), 3–29.

[51]"The Plague in Literature and Myth," *Texas Studies in Literature and Language*, 15 (1974), 833–50.

of which things may encourage unseemly behavior (cose meno oneste) among those who are feeble of mind, neither in word nor in deed nor in any other respect have I known either you or ourselves to be worthy of censure. On the contrary, from what I have seen and heard, it seems to me that our proceedings have been marked by a constant sense of propriety (continua onestà), an unfailing spirit of harmony, and a continual feeling of brotherly and sisterly amity. All of which pleases me greatly, as it surely redounds to our communal honour and credit. [P. 825; Branca, pp. 1234–35]

This is more than just self-congratulation, though admittedly Dioneo always seems quite pleased with himself. Here the line is drawn between the content of fiction and the deportment of morally responsible people, a distinction implicit from the beginning of the work when the *brigata* chose first to live "onestamente" in orderly cheerfulness, "fuggendo come la morte i disonesti essempli degli altri" (p. 33), and subsequently chose storytelling as one means of such living.[52] Vicious living is to be avoided like the plague—Boccaccio's phrase fuses the natural and moral pestilences. The journey into health and well-being is also a journey into "onestà"; as in the regimens, medical good sense has an ethical dimension. The company maintains decorum, refuses to overindulge itself even in a time of license, and uses storytelling properly, for pleasure and profit and their resulting benefits to mind and body. The very act of intelligent listening (and, by extension, reading) becomes part of the shared values of propriety, harmony, and amity. In this sophisticated work, as in the *Jugement dou roy de Navarre*, pleasure and profit blend in most interesting ways, as the taking of literary or conversational entertainment becomes a moral image of preserving social order even in the face of pestilence.

We tend to forget that the plague that swept over Europe in the fourteenth century did not receive the grim name of "Black Death" until centuries later, that the 1300s had earlier suffered through various disasters, especially famine, that in 1340 there was enough of a "pestilence of infirmities" to prompt Augustine of Trent to write a treatise that anticipates the later plague

---

[52]Cf. Branca, "Coerenza dell'introduzione al *Decameron:* Rispondenze strutturali e stilistiche," *Romance Philology,* 13 (1960), 357–58.

tracts,[53] and that waves of pestilence struck Europe throughout the rest of the century. Without wishing to minimize the devastation of the Black Death, I do think that the modern tendency to isolate it so extremely may make it appear to have been even more cataclysmic psychologically than it was. Boccaccio and Machaut are so often cited by historians for their initial pages on the horrors of the plague that it encourages neglect of their real concern, which is to transcend those horrors. At any rate, as I hope this chapter has shown, the Black Death did not promote only increased morbidity in literature. Amidst all the work that reflects the fear of death and that looks to last things, there is some, at least, that reflects the value of secular life and that looks to proximate things. For the living, singing songs and telling pleasant tales are important means of coping with the plague. The emphasis on order and measure in Boccaccio and Machaut reveals their concern for establishing an appropriate mode of behavior that in its moderate morality will guide reasonable people, those who wish to bruise neither body nor soul, through the pestilential time.

[53]Discussed by Thorndike, *History*, III: 224–32, with selections on 699–707. Though it makes no specific reference to the nonnaturals, Augustine's regimen recommends a number of after-dinner pleasures to preserve health (703).

6

The Decameron *and Its Early Critics*

The ten young men and women who tell the tales that constitute the *Decameron* do so in order to gain pleasure, which in turn promotes their well-being. We have looked at this reasoning as it appears in the introduction and at the end of the storytelling, but they are not the only places where the *brigata* discusses its motives. At the beginning of the fifth story of the ninth day, Neifile asserts that "we are assembled here for no other purpose than to rejoice and be merry" (p. 701). In an interesting passage located halfway through the hundred tales, Dioneo introduces the last story of the fifth day with a reference to the group's central concern:

> . . . we are more inclined to laugh at scandalous behaviour than virtuous deeds, especially when we ourselves are not directly involved. And since, as on previous occasions, the task I am about to perform has no other object than to dispel your melancholy, enamoured ladies, and provide you with laughter and merriment, I shall tell you the ensuing tale, for it may well afford enjoyment even though its subject matter is not altogether seemly. [P. 470]

He goes on to offer a summary of the responses he thinks his tale should elicit, including laughter at the wife's "amorous intrigues." Laughter and "allegrezza" are the goals of the storytelling, and they replace "malinconia" (p. 680). Dioneo does not directly mention the woes of the plague, which would be psychologically destructive; his allusion to their effects, the ladies' melancholy, is a sufficient and tactful reminder of the rationale for supplanting pestilence with pleasure.

Dioneo's theory of laughter helps illuminate the relationship between entertainment and morality in the *Decameron*. Although it is a human failing, nevertheless we laugh at "scandalous behaviour" rather than "virtuous deeds," especially when we are detached from it. Even this tale with material less than "onesta" will provide "diletto." In articulating this truth Dioneo establishes a moral frame of reference for evaluating the action of the tale; laughter at the wife's behavior entails some recognition that it is unworthy. Such comic detachment reinforces the distinction, quoted at the end of the previous chapter, that Dioneo draws at the conclusion of the journey between stories and morals, literature and life. Certain kinds of people might misunderstand the *Decameron* fictions, read them pornographically; but the *brigata*'s perspective is wiser, enjoying people's antics without becoming seduced by them. Throughout the work Boccaccio stresses the moral behavior of the company even though it listens to stories of immoral acts, and as we will see shortly he makes a similar point about reader responsibility in reference to the idle ladies for whom he composed the work. The book's playful but pointed subtitle reminds us of the moral value of reading it maturely and critically. The *Decameron* stories may be a Galeotto, a go-between, as Dante's Francesca called the book and author she read; but unlike her, the *brigata*, and by implication any wise reader, will find in its tales therapeutic rather than carnal stimulation.[1]

It will do so in great part by considering not just the content of the stories but also the skill with which they are told. The first narrative of the sixth day makes this principle clear: a knight's inept presentation of a good story elicits a subtle criticism from the well-bred and witty Madonna Oretta. This tale, at the center

[1]For more detailed discussion of this famous allusion see Hollander, *Boccaccio's Two Venuses*, pp. 102–6 and n. 44, which cites some exceptions to the company's usual detachment from the sexual *materia* of the tales; Millicent Joy Marcus, *An Allegory of Form: Literary Self-Consciousness in the* Decameron, Stanford French and Italian Studies 18 (Saratoga, Calif.: Anma Libri, 1979), pp. 20–21, which should be read in the context of her full thesis; Mazzotta, 68–69, and further in "The *Decameron*: The Literal and the Allegorical," *Italian Quarterly*, 72 (1975), 62–63, who stresses Boccaccio's concern with the pornographic potential inherent in fiction.

of the *Decameron* as are Dioneo's literary observations the day before, functions as a microcosm of the entire work, for the knight's performance occurs in the context of a company wandering around the countryside for their "recreation." His artistic disaster causes Oretta physical pain: "She began to perspire freely, and her heart missed several beats, as though she had fallen ill and was about to give up the ghost" (p. 484). As Franco Fido points out, the intense reaction—in addition to its value as humorous exaggeration—points to "the power of words over reality," suggests that the literary achievement of the *Decameron* is itself "an answer to the plague" in that good art can "salvage" what has been lost through fortune or error.[2] It also reveals a sly twist to one of the theories discussed in this book: the principle that literary delight confers physical benefits here gains reinforcement from an amusing vision of a negative instance in which literary displeasure produces sickness.

On one day, however, the *brigata*'s controlled merriment fades, and this "aberration" is worth attention for what it implies about the journey as a whole.[3] The ruler of the fourth day is Filostrato, who, as his name signifies, is desperately in love with one of the seven ladies and fearful that his passion will never be requited. Hence he chooses a topic "which applies most closely to myself, namely, *those whose love ended unhappily*" (p. 320). Fiammetta begins the storytelling by noting how "cruel" this subject is, "especially when you consider that, having come here to fortify our spirits (rallegrarci), we are obliged to recount people's woes, the telling of which cannot fail to arouse compassion in speaker and listener alike. Perhaps he has done it in order to temper in some degree the gaiety (temperare alquanto la leticia) of the previous days" (p. 332; Branca, p. 461). Stories that trigger feelings of pity will drive the blood and *spiritus* inward rather than outward; such a response might be warranted only, Fiammetta reasons, as a means of moderating extreme cheerfulness. She is thinking of the *accidentia animae* in the same way that Maino de' Maineri

---

[2]"Boccaccio's *Ars narrandi* in the Sixth Day of the *Decameron*," in *Italian Literature: Roots and Branches*, ed. Giose Rimanelli and Kenneth John Atchity (New Haven: Yale University Press, 1976), pp. 239–40; see his n. 15 for other criticism of this "metanovella."

[3]The word is Marcus's, who treats the fourth day on pp. 54–56, 121–22.

does when he recommends that excessive *gaudium* be regulated by occasional sadness (see p. 49). Filostrato's motives are in fact for personal amelioration rather than communal temperance: hearing tales related to his own "sorry state" will make him feel better, as he announces at the beginning of the day's second story. But its teller, Pampinea, knowing her "feelings" to be closer to the spirit of the company than his, chooses to "amuse (recrear)" her friends by telling a tale that fits the day's topic yet nevertheless will "make them laugh," that will "restore your spirits a little by persuading you to laugh and be merry" (pp. 342–43; Branca, pp. 478–79). Still, this narrative is only temporary relief; the mood remains somber until Dioneo exercises the option to make his story differ in theme from the day's assignment. The ladies laugh at it, alleviating the sadness induced by the others. Filostrato even apologizes for having forced everyone to treat "so disagreeable a theme" and turns the leadership over to Fiammetta to "restore the spirits" of the company after the harsh day of his rule (p. 401). On the following day he tells a humorous story to make up for his unpopular choice of theme (V, 4), and he delights the *brigata* so much that they no longer blame him for his decree. Most of the fourth day's stories are clearly counter to the prevailing spirit of the *Decameron*. They allow Boccaccio the writer to increase the scope of his work, but they can be integrated into the rationale of the storytelling only by creating a character whose emotions oppose the sentiments of the group as a whole. In focusing so intently upon the fourth day's theme as deviant, in having Fiammetta suggest that its only value to the company might be the hygienic one of insuring that their *letitia* remain *temperata,* and in reintegrating Filostrato into the merriment on the fifth day, Boccaccio reinforces our sense of the *Decameron* as a journey—save for this one detour—into delight.

But the storytellers are not Boccaccio's readers, and he frames their journey with three passages that point to his ostensible audience, idle ladies. Of these, the defense at the beginning of the fourth day is perhaps the best known and the richest source for critics who find in the work a naturalism or a "nuova etica" that heralds a Renaissance rather than medieval sensibility.[4] I am more concerned with the preface and the conclusion and with the ways in which Boccaccio's statements about how his stories serve the ladies enlarge the therapeutic and recreational meanings of the plague to pleasure pattern. In the preface, he directs his tales to women in love, who unlike men do not have a variety of ways of alleviating the "melancholy or ponderous thoughts (malinconia o gravezza di pensieri)" with which they are beset. As Branca notes, the distinction between men having many activities and women nothing to do but brood on love goes back to the beginning of Ovid's *Heroides,* XIX; but Ovid does not take Boccaccio's next step, which is to offer his work as an answer to the distress, the "noia," that results from such restricted opportunity. The hundred tales will be for the ladies what hunting, hawking, gambling, and other interests are for men in love: "succour and diversion" that will help ease their "noia" and, as the conclusion reaffirms, their "malinconia" (pp. 46–47; Branca, pp. 6–7, 1243). The parallels to the frame story are obvious and are reinforced by various verbal links: the *brigata* leaves all the "noie" present in the plague-stricken city (p. 33), detaches itself from the "malinconie" and "pensieri" that afflict people so exposed (pp. 1234, 39), and partakes of gracious entertainment for its own support, "sostentamento" (p. 1234), the same "sostentamento" that Boccaccio says he will provide for the ladies in need of it (p. 5). The medical parallel between the journey and proper regimen thus has at its base a more broadly conceived psychology of fiction which is applicable at any time. The frame story becomes a dramatized representation of the inner psychological movement from "noia" to "allegrezza" that Boccaccio intends his work to effect in his audience. Perhaps that is why there is no mention of the plague or the desolation of Florence when the *brigata* returns home; the narrative journey conforms to the envisaged mental journey of the young ladies, which will leave melancholy behind. Chronicle defers to comedy.

How, exactly, does fiction cause this psychological transformation? Its operation is defined in the *Decameron* as analogous

[4]Aldo D. Scaglione, *Nature and Love in the Late Middle Ages* (Berkeley: University of California Press, 1963), pp. 101–10; Raffaello Ramat, "L'introduzione alla quarta giornata," in *Scritti su Giovanni Boccaccio,* pref. Sergio Gensini (Florence: Leo S. Olschki, 1964), pp. 93–107.

to other recreations that restore mental balance. The crucial statements are in the preface, first in regard to the benefits which men in love gain from various distractions:

> Each of these pursuits has the power of engaging men's minds, either wholly or in part, and diverting them from their gloomy meditations, at least for a certain period: after which, some form of consolation will ensue, or the affliction will grow less intense. [P. 47]

> ... de' quali modi ciascuno ha forza di trarre, o in tutto o in parte, l'animo a sé e dal noioso pensiero rimuoverlo almeno per alcuno spazio di tempo, appresso il quale, o in un modo o in uno altro, o consolazion sopravviene o diventa la noia minore. [P. 6]

And then in regard to the similar effects of the *Decameron* stories:

> In reading them, the aforesaid ladies will be able to derive, not only pleasure from the entertaining matters therein set forth, but also some useful advice. For they will learn to recognize what should be avoided and likewise what should be pursued, and these things can only lead, in my opinion, to the removal of their affliction. [P. 47]

> ... delle quali le già dette donne, che quelle leggeranno, parimente diletto delle sollazzevoli cose in quelle mostrate e utile consiglio potranno pigliare, in quanto potranno cognoscere quello che sia da fuggire e che sia similmente da seguitare: le quali cose senza passamento di noia non credo che possano intervenire. [P. 7]

These passages are hedged with qualifying phrases, but there is some firm theorizing behind them. In turning to hunting or other distractions, a man draws his mind (trarre) to another subject, lessening the hold of the melancholy thought. Such action necessarily involves corresponding mental and physical changes, since, as discussed in Chapter 2, the body reacts favorably to emotions of joy and hope but poorly to sadness and fear. Hence some kind of consolation must follow; one's "noia" will be diminished through the restoration of proper bodily functioning and the consequent improvement of mental state. This is the logic that explains why physicians, as Dino del Garbo points out, "say that the best cure of [love] is to distract the man from thinking about his beloved so that he will forget it." Once the preoccupation that causes melancholy is lessened, the *virtus animalis* is no longer distracted ("distrahitur") and is able to resume its role in keeping the body well disposed.[5] Rather than thinking of recreations as superficial evasions, ineffective responses to a serious emotional problem, Boccaccio and Dino conceive of their power of distraction—etymologically a drawing away, a pulling apart—as a vigorous and effective force. To draw someone's mind from a consuming passion, which itself draws off natural energy, is to liberate him.

Reading fiction seems to involve a similar pattern of responses. Absorption in a story produces that Horatian duality of pleasure and profit; in becoming involved and gaining these ends, one's mind is necessarily drawn into the fiction and thus away from "noia." The gaining of pleasure and profit, Boccaccio says in the last clause, cannot happen without the passing away of distress. Does this mean, as McWilliam's translation has it, that reading causes distraction from distress, or, as Wesley Trimpi has read the passage, that the removal of "noia" is "a necessary psychological condition" for the full appreciation of the "useful advice" the *Decameron* offers?[6] Probably both. The parallel between men's and women's responses certainly means that removal of distress follows upon engagement with something delightful. And in the process of that engagement, as one is being delighted and advised, one's condition is returning to that optimum state that is the result of *gaudium temperatum;* the reader's mind is correspondingly sharpened, thus more ready to appreciate fully the pleasures and profits that fiction contains. Literature not only distracts one from "noia" but in doing so engenders a sensibility that is in turn able to gain greater pleasure and profit from it. In this medieval sense fiction creates (by recreating) its own audience.

To explore in any detail what kinds of profit the *Decameron* offers is to venture into areas far beyond the scope of this

[5]Bird, *Mediaeval Studies,* 2 (1940), 168; 3 (1941), 126–27.
[6]"The Quality of Fiction," 99, 117.

book. The reference to learning what to flee and what to pursue sounds very like the theory of literature as praise or blame, one that often appears in medieval statements about the purpose of poetry.[7] It is not hard to find values put forth in the tales for emulation or condemnation, and there has been influential critical discussion, notably by Ferdinando Neri and Vittore Branca, of the *Decameron*'s largest thematic concerns, leading to the final day's topic of the high secular virtue of magnanimity.[8] But surely many of the tales have few if any overt didactic intentions, and some, as Marcus and Mazzotta have argued, playfully subvert traditional readings of stories as morally exemplary. I share to a certain extent their tendency to find Boccaccio's "seriousness" to lie less in the specific content of his fictions (whether that content be interpreted either as "Christian" or "naturalistic") than in his exploration of a host of questions concerning the nature of literature and its reception by an audience. Significantly, when he returns in the conclusion to the idea of literary profit dealt with so briefly in the preface, he refers it back to the reader. Any verbal discourse, he says, may be rightly or wrongly used. One can find "evil counsel" in the *Decameron* stories if one tries. "And if anyone should study them for the usefulness and profit they may bring him, he will not be disappointed. Nor will they ever be thought of or described as anything but useful and seemly (utili e oneste), if they are read at the proper time by the people for whom they were written" (p. 831; Branca, p. 1241). But the proper time is one of idleness, the presumed audience melancholy ladies in need of diversion. In such a context the usefulness might well entail therapeutic as well as or rather than didactic benefits—*utilitas est delectatio*. In the prologue and the conclusion the complex question of pleasure and profit in literature is subordinated, as it is in other works we have seen, to the recreational claim. The reader must take responsibility for the proper or improper moral use of the *Decameron;* what Boccaccio asserts most forcefully is a context for its experience and the power of his work in that context to move minds from "noia" to "allegrezza."

[7]For example, Hermannus Alemannus, p. 7. See also Hollander, p. 224 n. 24, and Trimpi, 100. For the tradition as a whole, see O. B. Hardison, Jr., *The Enduring Monument* (Chapel Hill: University of North Carolina Press, 1962).
[8]Branca, *Boccaccio,* pp. 206–11.

That context, says Singleton, is Boccaccio's "effort to justify and protect a new art, an art which simply in order to be, to exist, required the moment free of all other cares, the willingness to stop *going anywhere* (either toward God or toward philosophical truth)," and he notes elsewhere that of course the author "is far more concerned with us, his readers, than with those ladies."[9] Both frames, the journey of the *brigata* from plague to pleasure and the envisaged journey of the idle ladies from melancholy to delight, exist to shape the reader's expectations. But although the art may be new, the justifications for it are not. Boccaccio does not ask us to enjoy the tales for their own sake; rather he incorporates them in frames that give them therapeutic value. The reader's journey may not be toward supreme truth, but he will be moving nevertheless, to the *quies* that is the result of literary *delectatio*.

Boccaccio adds another dimension to his frame that further illuminates the *Decameron*'s status as a work of recreation. The author who can give support to ladies in love was once himself in love, and he has the "power of making provision for their pleasures" (p. 47) only now that he has been freed from that condition. As he looks back to his own experience, he. remembers that while suffering from the "noia" induced by a passionate love stemming from his own "ill-restrained" appetite, relief came to him "from the agreeable conversation (piacevoli ragionamenti) and the admirable expressions of sympathy (laudevoli consolazioni) offered by friends, without which I am firmly convinced that I should have perished" (p. 45; Branca, p. 4). Nevertheless, in spite of their advice, his passion remained strong until finally it pleased God, who "decreed by immutable law that all earthly things should come to an end," that it "should in the course of time diminish of its own accord" (p. 45). Those friends who gave him pleasing and helpful conversation probably do not need the support ("sostentamento") of the *Decameron*, he says, but it is in gratitude for their help that he decides to aid in turn the "charming ladies" beset with love, idle, and thus prey to melancholy.

Robert Hollander, who has recently given these details the

[9]Singleton, "On *Meaning*," 119, and "The Uses of the *Decameron*," *MLN*, 79 (1964), 76.

attention they deserve, points out that Boccaccio's narrative pose here has a number of affinities "with those found in the *Fiammetta* and the *Corbaccio,* that is, with those narrators who warn against the dangers of carnal love."[10] Certainly the evaluation of passionate love is hardly adulatory; it is a source of "noia" and as such associated with the *noie* of the ladies and of the plague. But it is stretching things to say, as Hollander does, that "the narrator's express intent is to turn us away from love" (p. 108). His express intent is to provide some kind of relief for the women. His own past history suggests that the condition of passionate love is one not easily remedied, something one must live through until time takes its course. In such a situation, presented as a given for the ostensible audience of the *Decameron,* the best thing short of a lengthy "course of time" is the kind of friendly conversation that helped Boccaccio himself endure the throes of passion. That verbal sustenance, both pleasing ("piacevoli ragionamenti") and full of advice ("consiglio"), now takes shape in the narrator's hands as tales that offer both pleasure and profit ("diletto . . . et utile consiglio"). But for him *confabulatio* offered "relief from (rifrigerio)" the pangs of love, a desire that found "no proper respite (niuno convenevol termine)" (p. 45; Branca, p. 4). It ameliorated his condition, but it did not fundamentally change it. The analogy suggests that the *Decameron* too will be a comfort, a support, a refuge; it will not be a cure. It is written not to reprove people who find themselves in love but to sustain them. It will offer the limited *quies* of recreation rather than either the immediate "termine" of love satisfied or the permanent "termine" of Christian contemplation.

Yet Boccaccio implies—and I would stress that it is only an implication—that perhaps the *Decameron* may be able to do more. For if he was consoled but not cured by his friends, that is probably more a comment on his own ill-regulated appetite than on their intentions. It took the long passage of time for him to reach a state where the pains of love have diminished and in their place lies a certain kind of pleasure ("piacere") (p. 4). Insofar as the hundred tales correspond to diversions from love, they are recreational relief, and that is no mean goal. Insofar as they may lead to a complete abolishing of "noia,"

[10]*Boccaccio's Two Venuses,* p. 97; for details see 97–102, 141–42.

they would seem to function not only as the conversation of friends did for Boccaccio but as time itself did, so that the ladies' forthcoming pleasures ("piaceri"—the final word of the preface) seem to have some kind of affinity with the "piacere" of the man now freed from the chains of an excessive passion. The book's usefulness, then, would include its ability to give its audience (or at least those members of its audience whose "appetito" is not beyond regulation) the sort of insight which leads to a permanent liberation from mental distress. In this sense we can see the consolation offered by the *Decameron* as Boethian in the way that Marcus, in *An Allegory of Form*, has argued (pp. 112–25), though I think that the "therapeutic effects of fiction-making" (p. 114) which she recognizes are not exclusively or even primarily Boethian in implication but chiefly psychological in the secular tradition of recreational and hygienic thinking. The traditions are not mutually exclusive: implicit in the relief from "noia" is a mental balance that will permit rational assessment of one's experience. The *Decameron* gives us the means to that balance; it does not lecture us on what the assessment must be.

It should be clear that I have not tried to discuss the *Decameron* itself but instead the terms in which Boccaccio presents the hundred tales to his readers. Those terms suggest in places what Hollander calls "the attitudes of a Christian moralist" (p. 106) and in places, particularly at the beginning of the fourth day, what Scaglione calls "the attitude of conscious defense of the 'rights of nature'" (p. 104). But principally they suggest the power of fiction to alleviate psychological distress. The author of the work has already moved from "noia" to "piacere" (not through fiction, admittedly, but had he been more receptive he might have through talking with friends, one of the features of the *brigata*'s mental regimen); the work itself consists of stories that are part of a therapeutic design to move ten young men and women from "noia" to "piacere"; and the announced intention of the book is to effect a similar movement from "noia" to "piacere" in its audience of idle ladies. Boccaccio's framing devices focus less on the content of his stories than on their intended effects; together the pleasures and profits of the *Decameron* lead to *recreatio* in the fullest medieval sense, attainment of physical, psychological, and perhaps ultimately spiritual well-being.

Contemporary or near-contemporary criticism of a work does not guarantee accurate perception of it. But it may well be revealing, and not only of its author's own prejudices, especially when it comes from intelligent and sympathetic sources. The initial response to the *Decameron* recognizes it primarily as a great work of entertainment and in some cases justifies its pleasures on recreational and hygienic grounds. The evidence I will consider (certainly not a full inventory of all the early comments) involves three passages, each extensive enough to warrant being thought of as literary criticism: the anonymous prefatory material in an early fragmentary manuscript of the *Decameron;* Petrarch's remarks on the work in a letter written to Boccaccio in 1373; and Laurent de Premierfait's preface to his French translation completed in 1414. Of these, Laurent's text is the most detailed and explicit; I will begin with the earlier and shorter ones.

The anonymous preface in a *Decameron* manuscript written while Boccaccio was still alive is partial testimony to the excitement the work engendered in Florentine mercantile society during the 1360s and 1370s. There is much other evidence of this excitement, including Boccaccio's well-known letter to Mainardo Cavalcanti, all of which Branca has thoroughly documented and discussed, but none of it comes as close to full-scale literary commentary as do the paragraphs of this unknown admirer.[11] Although most of his comments relate not to Boccaccio but to women and the clergy, he does offer some consideration of the *Decameron* as a work of art. He sees it in the tradition of Boccaccio's other "beautiful and delightful books, in prose and in verse, in honor of those gracious ladies whose high-souled noblemindedness takes pleasure in occupying itself with pleasant and virtuous matters."[12] He summarizes its frame story of a "jovial company" that leaves Florence "during the time of pestilence" and spends its time disporting itself ("diportando") in delightful places (66). He does not discuss the values

[11]"Per il testo del Decameron—La prima diffusione del Decameron," *Studi di filologia italiana*, 8 (1950), 29–143, esp. 61–68, 134–42. The text of the anonymous preface is on 64–66, a description of the MS on 83–84. Branca summarizes this material in *Boccaccio*, pp. 197–200.

[12]*Boccaccio*, p. 198.

of such recreation at this point, but they appear at the beginning of his preface, where he praises writers and composers who bring pleasure and comfort to women. Such enterprise is praiseworthy because it enables the world to keep itself "in allegrezza," and such happiness is useful because it preserves youth ("lietamente vivendo fa lunga giovanezza mantenere"). The physical benefits of *gaudium* are apparent, and it follows that the "sommo piacere e diletto" which women find in reading Boccaccio serve to help sustain their spirits (64, 66). When the anonymous admirer asks, "Who can engage in more praiseworthy work than to keep a lovely lady cheerful during her youth?" he apparently considers the question rhetorical.[13] To what extent he has simply appropriated some of Boccaccio's own reasoning in the *Decameron*, to what relied on a more widespread secular poetics, is perhaps impossible to determine. It is clear at least that while he finds Boccaccio in general both pleasurable and profitable, his principal interest lies in the effects of literary delight on the women he finds so charming, and he defines those effects as physical and psychological benefits.

Petrarch is close to the author of this preface in time but not in literary milieu. Branca has pointed out the general neglect of the *Decameron* in early humanist circles, consistent with the late medieval perception of the book "not as a work adhering to literary tradition but as a book for agreeable, pleasant reading, as a work created not for the savoring of the refined men of letters but for the joy of the less-cultured readers."[14] Petrarch's view of the *Decameron*, as it emerges from the introductory remarks to his translation of the Griselda story in *Seniles* XVII, 3, contains a good deal of that humanist superiority to entertainment in the vulgar tongue, yet it also reveals an awareness of the circumstances and justifications of such literary endeavor.

He acknowledges the variety of stories to be found in his friend's collection, but he indicates clearly what predominates: "Along with much that was light and amusing (iocosa et levia), I

---

[13]"E chi può fare più lodevole operazione che mantenere una vaga donna lieta nella sua giovanezza?" (64). He may be drawing on Boccaccio's own question in the preface, where, defending his offer of comfort to those who need it, he asks, "And who will deny that such encouragement, however small, should much rather be offered to the charming ladies than to men?" (p. 46).

[14]*Boccaccio*, pp. 200–2; see also "La prima diffusione," 54–61, 134–35.

discovered some serious and edifying things (pia et gravia) as well, but I can pass no definite judgment upon them, since I have not examined the work thoroughly."[15] Apparently only those stories "pia et gravia" warrant careful reading and judgment, and they appear much less often than humorous and "light" material. In fact, Petrarch rather pointedly comments that the tale of Griselda, which so pleased him that he decided to translate it, making explicit at the end its moral significance, "differs entirely from most that precede it." The *Decameron*, then, is primarily a collection of amusing stories, and with this understanding Petrarch discusses his response to the work as a whole:

> My hasty perusal afforded me much pleasure. If the humor is a little too free at times, this may be excused in view of the age at which you wrote, the style and language which you employ, and the frivolity of the subjects, and of the persons who are likely to read such tales. It is important to know for whom we are writing, and a difference in the characters of one's listeners justifies a difference in style. [P. 233]

> Delectatus sum ipso in transitu; et si quid lascivie liberioris occurreret, excusabat etas tunc tua dum id scriberes, stilus, ydioma, ipsa quoque rerum levitas et eorum qui lecturi talia videbantur. Refert enim largiter quibus scribas, morumque varietate stili varietas excusatur. [P. 290]

Petrarch specifies four characteristics: (1) the *Decameron* is a work of Boccaccio's youth, a fact he assumes at the beginning of the letter; (2) its subject matter is light ("rerum levitas"); (3) its audience is also light ("levitas . . . eorum qui lecturi talia videbantur"); (4) its style corresponds to the *mores* of its audience, as is fitting. Petrarch adduces these four considerations to excuse whatever excesses in *lascivia* occur throughout the work, but they are obviously conditions which pertain to the *Decameron* as a whole, not just to its questionable passages. To what kind of literary situation do they refer?

There is a striking parallel to this set of characteristics in

---

[15]Trans. in Thompson, p. 233. Text in J. Burke Severs, *The Literary Relationships of Chaucer's Clerkes Tale* (New Haven: Yale University Press, 1942), p. 290.

Geoffrey of Vinsauf's discussion of comic material in the *Poetria nova*. After giving an example of a comic story, he explains the qualities and circumstances of such literature:

> A comic discourse is marked with the character of lightness in the following ways: levity of spirit is the source of comedy; comedy is an immature form, attractive to green years. Moreover, the subject of comedy is light; to such a subject the sportive period of youth readily devotes itself. See to it that the third element is light. Let all aspects, then, be light: the whole is in perfect harmony if the spirit is light, and the subject light, and the expression light.

> Hac ratione levis signatur sermo jocosus:
> Ex animi levitate jocus procedit. Et est res
> Immatura jocus et amica virentibus annis;
> Et leve quid jocus est, cui se jocundior aetas
> Applicat ex facili. Res tertia sit levis. Ergo
> Omnia sint levia. Sibi consonat undique totum
> Si levis est animus, et res levis, et leve verbum.[16]

This passage, a theoretical background to Petrarch's remarks, enumerates the precise characteristics he attributes to the *Decameron:* youthful authorship, lightness of subject matter, lightness of style, and lightness of spirit on the part of author and audience. The appropriateness of style to subject and audience is familiar enough as a topic in all the medieval arts of discourse; however, Geoffrey is not discussing here one of the conventional triad of styles, which he deals with elsewhere, but the special attributes of a kind of speech which is light rather than serious, *sermo jocosus,* a particular mode of expression which he associates with youthful frivolity.

We are in a position to see some of the resonance of Petrarch's and Geoffrey's references to lightness of mind. *Levitas* is often associated with interest in jokes and other trifling discourse, sometimes quite negatively, as in Bishop Ralph of Walpole's monastic statutes that condemn using words that are "light" to others, sometimes more neutrally, as in Antoninus of Florence's discussion of lying, which says that there is no mortal

---

[16]*Poetria Nova of Geoffrey of Vinsauf,* trans. Margaret F. Nims (Toronto: Pontifical Institute of Mediaeval Studies, 1967), p. 85. Latin in Faral, *Les arts poétiques,* pp. 255–56.

sin "in a joking lie" because the purpose is "some light delight (aliqua levis delectatio)" rather than deceit.[17] On the more positive side, insofar as lightness of mind may be thought of as the opposite of Lydgate's undesirable "hevynesse," it may well carry some implication of hygienic value. The imputation of lightness to both work and audience suggests the kind of circumstances described at the beginning of the fabliau *Du chevalier qui fit les cons parler*, which claims to bring "confortement" to the "oiseus," that is, to satisfy the recreational needs of people looking for something agreeable to pass the time.[18] The perception of the *Decameron* as a work of "levitas" is thus true to its express intentions of inducing cheerfulness in an idle audience through delightful fictions, and Petrarch's initial "Delectatus sum" signals his own pleasure in the work even in spite of its excesses of *lascivia*. Of course, as Anne Middleton has pointed out, the story of Griselda pleased him even more, offering a kind of delight more suitable to his literary tastes, one meriting translation into Latin so that people unfamiliar with Italian "might be pleased with so charming a story."[19]

Petrarch is, then, certainly not unfair to the *Decameron;* yet he is not at all inclined to aggrandize its status, and what he does not say is as interesting as what he does. He does not seize on remarks that might lead to a more respectful view of the work's moral or artistic seriousness, such as Boccaccio's reference to profit in the *Decameron* preface or his observation in the fourth day defense that in writing the *novelle* "I am not straying as far from Mount Parnassus or from the Muses as many people might be led to believe" (McWilliam, p. 330). Petrarch's arch observation early in his letter that the book was written "and published, I presume, during your early years (iuvenis)" (Thompson, p. 232; Severs, p. 290) may be chronologically legitimate, since Boccaccio probably wrote the *Decameron* in his mid- to late thirties and *juventus* extends at least to forty in some medieval

[17]Evans, p. 13; *Summa theologica*, Pars II, tit. X, c. 1, col. 1054.

[18]Cited above, Chap. 4. See also the prefatory remarks in the German fabliau *Irregang und Girregar*, which addresses itself to a youthful audience looking for pleasing entertainment as a time filler; text and translation in *The Literary Context of Chaucer's Fabliaux*, ed. Larry D. Benson and Theodore M. Andersson (Indianapolis: Bobbs-Merrill, 1971), pp. 124–27.

[19]Thompson, p. 233. Middleton, "The Clerk and His Tale: Some Literary Contexts," *Studies in the Age of Chaucer*, 2 (1980), 125–36.

classifications of the ages of man. But it hardly seems respon-
sive to Boccaccio's narrative pose, which, as we have seen, is
that of a man whose ardors have been diminished by the passage of time, who allies himself in the fourth day defense with
other men who "in their old age" continued to pay tribute to
women (McWilliam, p. 329). Petrarch suggests that the author
was essentially like his envisaged audience, not a maturer and
wiser counselor. And, of course, he does not deal with the
question of the validity of natural desire raised at the start of
the fourth day; nor does he rehearse any of the more extended
recreational arguments, preferring instead to imply them only
with the more ambivalent reference to "levitas."

Petrarch does not judge the *Decameron* to be substantially different from what Florentine mercantile society found it to be; he
differs rather in the value he places on a work whose primary
aims are recreational. The one group may have been "light"
enough to relish an elegant diversion like the *Decameron,* but
Petrarch's attitude toward recreation, though tolerant, is less
sanguine. He sometimes admits its usefulness, as in the letter
cited at the beginning of Chapter 4 and in this one to Francesco
Nelli: "I have nothing of importance to tell you today. But as
overworked fields profit by lying fallow, and as busy minds need
an occasional respite, I will ask you to forget your serious concerns for a bit and listen to a silly story."[20] But in other contexts
he is conscious of the possible dangers to the mind in relaxation,
and he can invoke the same agricultural image (which goes back
to Seneca's *De tranquillitate animi*) to somewhat different effect:
"The holiday which I ordain is for the body, not for the mind; I
do not allow the intellect to lie fallow (veto in otio ingenium
quiescere) except that it may revive and become more fertile by a
period of rest. For a rest benefits the brain just as it benefits the
soul."[21] *Quies* is justified only to the extent that it leads to greater
productivity. Throughout the *De vita solitaria,* and in other
works as well, Petrarch stresses the close relationship between
rest and work. Even recreative woods and fields enable one not

[20]*Epistolae variae* 44, trans. Morris Bishop, *Letters from Petrarch* (Bloomington:
Indiana University Press, 1966), p. 217.
[21]*The Life of Solitude,* trans. Jacob Zeitlin (n.p.: University of Illinois Press,
1924), p. 291. Text in Francesco Petrarca, *Prose,* ed. G. Martellotti et al. (Milan:
R. Ricciardi, 1955), p. 556.

only to recuperate from the weariness of mental labor but also "to sow the seeds of new projects in the field of his genius, and in the very interval of rest and recuperation prepare matter for the labor to come." The result is a state of "an active rest and a restful work (actuosa requies et quietus labor)."[22] Petrarch's sense of "temporal urgency"[23] leads him here virtually to negate relaxation as a factor in one's mental life; he is thinking about leisure and contemplation, not recreation and play. One hundred stories, even though some of them be "pia et gravia," would be too extensive an offering of entertainment to be completely acceptable to a man whose ideal is that "not a moment of time will pass with any waste or loss to the student."[24] However ready to be charitable to his friend's work and to take what serious matter he could find there, Petrarch is, ultimately, far more like "students, who endeavour to use their time profitably rather than while it away" (McWilliam, p. 832), than like young ladies with time on their hands. And the *Decameron* addresses itself only to the latter.

Petrarch could look on the *Decameron* as the youthful work of a friend and admirer. Two generations later another humanist, Laurent de Premierfait, came to it as an admirer of Boccaccio's learning and wisdom. He was a scholar and translator, one of that group of early French humanists who absorbed Italian influence at the papal court in Avignon. He had already translated Cicero's *De senectute* and *De amicitia* and had twice, in 1400 and again in 1409, put Boccaccio's *De casibus virorum illustrium* into French, the second version proving highly popular throughout the century. Some of the manuscripts of it include a Latin poem in praise of Boccaccio, which, along with its French translation that may also be by Laurent, shows great respect for Boccaccio's Latin works and no awareness of his vernacular efforts except the *Decameron*, which it does not represent very accurately and seems to value mainly for the story of Griselda. In short, until he began to translate the *Decameron*, Laurent knew Boccaccio as

---

[22]Zeitlin, p. 157; Petrarca, *Prose*, p. 366.

[23]The phrase is Ricardo J. Quinones's; see his discussion of Petrarch's sense of time in *The Renaissance Discovery of Time* (Cambridge, Mass.: Harvard University Press, 1972), pp. 106–71, esp. 135–52.

[24]Zeitlin, p. 157.

most of the rest of Europe did: as the author of important humanist scholarship.[25]

In 1411 Laurent became aware of another side to Boccaccio's genius. For three years he worked on a translation of the *Decameron*, completing it in June, 1414, with a dedicatory letter to Jean, Duke of Berry, for whom he had also produced the second, much expanded, translation of *De casibus*. The circumstances of Laurent's translation, which he explains in the letter, are well known: since he did not know Italian, he worked with a Franciscan friar, Antonio of Arezzo, who turned the hundred tales into Latin in order for Laurent to be able to put them into French. His translation is, for good reason, usually discussed in terms of the ways it alters Boccaccio's text, for example, its greater concern for circumstantial detail, its occasional tendency to moralize or add sententious material. Similarly, the only substantial critical study of his prefatory letter stresses the greater didactic weight he gives to the *Decameron*.[26] But Laurent's preface is also a major statement of the recreational justification of literature, and it marks a fitting end both to an analysis of the early understanding of the *Decameron* and to this book as a whole. Although Norton has looked closely at some important elements of this text, another detailed reading from a different perspective is warranted.

The preface begins with the fall of man, as had the one to

[25]The best brief introduction to Laurent may still be G. S. Purkis, "Laurent de Premierfait, First French Translator of the *Decameron*," *Italian Studies*, 4 (1949), 22–36. The only full-length work on him is Henri Hauvette's thesis, *De Laurentio de Primofato* (Paris: Hachette, 1903). On his translations see also Patricia M. Gathercole, "Fifteenth-Century Translation: The Development of Laurent de Premierfait," *Modern Language Quarterly*, 21 (1960), 365–70. For details on his connections with French and Italian humanists, see Ezio Ornato, *Jean Muret et ses amis Nicolas de Clamanges et Jean de Montreuil* (Geneva: Droz, 1969), passim. The most recent edition of his verses on Boccaccio is by Gathercole, "A Frenchman's Praise of Boccaccio," *Italica*, 40 (1963), 225–30; see also Hauvette, pp. 24–25, for the headnote to them in one MS. On the knowledge of Boccaccio in late medieval France, see the first three essays in *Il Boccaccio nella cultura francese*, ed. Carlo Pelligrini (Florence: Leo S. Olschki, 1971).

[26]Glyn P. Norton, "Laurent de Premierfait and the Fifteenth-Century French Assimilation of the *Decameron*: A Study in Tonal Transformation," *Comparative Literature Studies*, 9 (1972), 376–91. On the nature of the translation see, most recently and thoroughly, Paolo M. Cucchi, "The First French Decameron: Laurent de Premierfait's Translation and the Early French *Nouvelle*," *French Literature Series* (University of South Carolina), 2 (1975), 1–14.

the *De casibus* translation. The sin of Adam and Eve issues in the world of fortune, turns love into hate, joy into sadness, and, most interestingly, idleness into care ("oysiuetez en cusancons").[27] Idleness, here used positively to denote prelapsarian self-sufficiency and contentment, turns into fretfulness. Man has become "ignorant, worrying, brooding, grieving, and subjected to the vagaries of fortune." But only foolish people let themselves be moved by such changes; fortune cannot destroy the calm of the wise. Moreover, it appears that wise men have a way of making ordinary people bear with fortune more easily: it is proper for them, in order to aid the distraught, to write books, especially stories, which will bring solace and happiness ("soulaz et leesse") to them, removing their troubles.[28] As an example Laurent cites Terence, whose comedies brought "great delight and joy" to their listeners and on holidays gave relief from continuously enervating work. By listening to his "narratives representing the true mirror of the ways of human life," citizens not only became comforted in spirit ("solaciez en courage") but were exposed to "the significant manners of all estates of lower- and middle-class people." It is clear that Laurent is thinking within the Horatian framework: the solace that beguiles troubles is delight, "delectacion"; Terence as well offers some kind of profit by revealing the nature of various types of people.

At this point Laurent shifts focus rather abruptly. He notes that "noble and exalted poets" were honored publicly and supported financially in order that they might try to surpass their competitors. He approves of such virtuous competition, adding that the noblest spirit tries to excel "not in fiction but in more

---

[27]Bibliothèque Nationale MS f. fr. 129, f. 1, checked against Bodleian Library MS Douce 213, f. 1, the only other MS to include Laurent's preface. Ed. Hortis, p. 743. Cf. Chap. 2, n. 56. All subsequent quotations are from B.N. fr. 129, ff. 1–3v. For a full inventory of all the MSS, see Paolo Cucchi and Norris J. Lacy, "La tradition manuscrite des *Cent nouvelles* de Laurent de Premierfait," *Le Moyen Age*, 80 (1974), 483–502, which supersedes the earlier work of Purkis and Gathercole.

[28]"Pour secourir doncques aux turbacions et mouuemens des folz hommes, jadiz fu et est licite et permis aux sages hommes de faire mesmement soubz fiction aucuns liures en quelconque honneste langaige, parquoy les hommes perturbez et esmeuz pour aucuns cas prengnent en lisant ou en escoutant aucun soulaz et leesse pour hors chasser du courage les pensemens qui troublent et empeschent les cueurs humains." F. 1v; Hortis, p. 744.

explicit [nonfictional] work (non pas par fiction mais par oeuure tresclere)." Now Boccaccio appears. He was in his time expert in "divine and human learning and history." He also recognized the ills that fallen man is heir to, especially "fear and sadness, through which all other worldly goods are erased and destroyed." These emotions cannot be eradicated, since they are part of our fallen state, but they can be deflected or diminished by decent pleasures and joys ("souspenduz ou admoindriz par quelconques honnestes delectations et joies"). Witnessing the effects of the plague, the "grant mortalite," Boccaccio wrote the *Decameron* "for the comfort and solace of the survivors," for those who lived through the plague still continued to exist in fear of death and in sadness for their lost friends and relatives. Laurent then turns from *intentio* to *utilitas*. Although some readers may think that the *Decameron* is mainly for entertainment, one who reflects on each story will find more profit than pleasure, for Boccaccio delineates and criticizes vices and commends virtues in a variety of ways.[29] What distinguishes the book from the "stories of poets" is its greater social scope; ancient poetry tended to delight or profit only the common people or to reprove only the higher or middle classes. But the hundred tales include men and women of all estates, pagan as well as Christian, clerical as well as lay.

Norton is certainly right to point out (390 n. 17) the parallel between Laurent's treatment of the *Decameron* and Boccaccio's discussion, in the *Genealogy of the Gods,* of the third kind of fiction. The translator seems to have come to terms with the stories by treating them more or less as Boccaccio treated Terence and Plautus. Like them, Boccaccio seems to be principally offering *delectatio.* But they all reveal human behavior and thus can be read in exemplary ways. Laurent goes further, though, arguing that the *Decameron* is really more for profit than for pleasure, that one learns from it not "incidentally" but pur-

---

[29]"Et combien que selon le hastif jugement de celui ou de ceulx qui sans precedente et longue consideracion dient et prononcent leur sentence, les Cent nouuelles semblent plus seruir a delectacion que au commun ou particulier prouffit, neantmoins l'escouteur ou liseur qui longuement et meurement aduisera le compte de chacune nouuelle, il trouuera es histoires racomptees plus profit que delict; car illec sont tous vices morsillez et reprins, et les vertus et bonnes meurs y sont admonnestees et loees en autant et plus de manieres comme est le nombre des nouuelles." F. 2; Hortis, p. 745.

posefully and consistently. He had read in Boccaccio's preface that the idle ladies would learn what to avoid and what to pursue, and he takes that idea and restates it more forcefully in his own, a natural emphasis, perhaps, given the familiarity of the poetics of praise and blame. If we focus only on this sentence, we might well find his interpretation far too categorically moralistic.

But he has given us more. The analogy to Terence is in fact helpful in regard to the nature of Boccaccio's stories, and Laurent is not alone in finding the closest rapprochement between the *Decameron* and the *Genealogy* to lie in that third kind of fiction.[30] He also appreciates the great social range of the work. But principally he thinks of the text as one of "delectacion," an attempt to beguile fear and sadness, two of the principal *accidentia animae* that regimens and *consilia* recommend avoiding. He thinks of the *Decameron*'s audience as profoundly affected by the plague and Boccaccio's immediate purpose as alleviating their grief. This reasoning is an extension of the logic of the plague to pleasure structure. Laurent does not speak directly of the idle ladies, whose immediate cause of sadness is love, not pestilence, but they are perhaps implicitly included, along with the survivors of the Black Death, in his remarks about wise men writing for more ordinary people disturbed by events of fortune. He may be thinking of Boccaccio's narrative pose at the beginning of the *Decameron*, that of a man who has transcended passionate love, who through time has emerged from its "noia" into a state that seems to bear some of the detachment from worldly cares that Laurent imputes to those "sages" who have ceased to involve themselves with the transitory goods of a fallen world. If so, his perspective is not the "simplistic moral dichotomy" argued by Norton, who assumes a "fundamental discontinuity between the youthful and the mature Boccaccio" (378–9) and attributes the distinction between wise and foolish people only to Laurent's carrying over an idea from his preface to the *De casibus* translation. It is a rather more sympathetic reading, one anticipating Hollander's in some respects, of part of the *Decameron*'s complex structure of framing material. Boccaccio, a man learned in di-

---

[30]See e.g. Branca, *Boccaccio*, p. 211; Tateo, esp. 325 n. 2, 332–39.

vine and human knowledge, realizing that emotional relief comes especially through narrative ("mesmement soubz fiction"), ceases to pursue the "noble labour" of writing the most excellent "tresclere" works (one of which Laurent had translated twice) and turns instead to pleasing "fiction" as a response to the widespread grief he sees around him. This view may be reading Boccaccio backwards chronologically, moving from the later Latin scholarship to the *Decameron;* but it has a basis in the text, Boccaccio's own narrative posture, and it has not led to any serious distortions of the recreational purposes the author emphasizes in the framing structures.

In fact, the rest of Laurent's preface, except for those passages where he discusses the genesis of the work and his efforts to obey the desires of the Duke of Berry, is wholly concerned with the value of the *Decameron* as solace. He specifies the various profits that arise from pleasure, beginning with a simple Cato-like statement about the need to mix entertainment with one's worldly cares ("cusancons mondaines") and continuing with more distinctly medical arguments concerning the value of joy, which we examined in Chapter 2. He next anticipates the potential objection of detractors that material from the Bible would offer greater "delectacion." This he admits, but biblical mysteries should not be translated, whereas translating purely literal narratives such as the hundred tales is permissible. Besides, one cannot read the Bible continually, for everyone feels the need to take time out occasionally in order to "bring solace and comfort to one's intellect, one's spirits, and one's pursuit of learning (soulacer et conforter son engin, ses esperiz, et aussi son estude)."

To support his claim that such recuperation is necessary and legitimate, Laurent brings forth a number of arguments. First he cites the bent bow analogy, which he applies to academic experience: teachers intersperse "some fables or tales" in their lessons, thus enabling their readers or listeners to refresh themselves and renew their capacity to follow diligently the rest of the instruction. Then he appeals to the evidence of animal behavior: birds fly, but not always; beasts are not constantly in motion but at times rest and recuperate. "Car chose longuement ne dure qui n'a repoz, delict, pasture" (f. 3); nothing can live for long without rest, delight, sustenance—that collection of physical and psychological needs which the Middle Ages embodied in the term *recreatio*. Then comes another analogy, significantly a hygienic one, this time focusing on variety rather than on relaxation: a change in food refreshes one's appetite. And finally: although gold and silver are the most precious metals, nevertheless lead and tin "are not to be condemned or disparaged"; each has its value. Or as a more vigorous defender of the imperfect put it,

> For wel ye knowe, a lord in his houshold,
> He nath nat every vessel al of gold;
> Somme been of tree, and doon hir lord servyse.
> God clepeth folk to hym in sondry wyse,
> And everich hath of God a propre yifte,
> Some this, som that, as hym liketh shifte.

When a learned humanist begins to appropriate some of the Wife of Bath's arguments, it is time to stop and take stock. Laurent's last analogy probably tells us more about his attitude toward the *Decameron* than he would have cared to admit publicly. For all his attempts at justification, the fact is that Boccaccio's work, as far as he is concerned, is not literary gold. But he spent three years of labor on it, and he is determined to make it as noble an enterprise as he can. He pulls out every argument for legitimate recreation he can think of, and by couching it all in the context of fallen man, gives, as Norton has argued, a more "ponderous" and moralistic view of the *Decameron* than the work probably warrants. Yet although he claims that the hundred tales offer "more profit than delight," he does not really argue this point at length; one doubts that—even allowing for his tendency (or perhaps Antonio's?) to moralize a few of the stories—he would be comfortable explicating the ethical lessons of some of Boccaccio's more ribald tales. As in the *Decameron* itself, there is a claim to profit as well as to please, yet the more extended defense appeals not to didactic but to psychological and physical benefits. If Laurent had not perceived the work as fundamentally intended to recreate he would not have devoted most of his preface to rehearsing the standard justifications of literary entertainment.

The letter defends recreation thoroughly, yet reveals an undertone of defensiveness. Laurent tries hard, awfully hard, to make enjoyment respectable, but the more he works at it the more we realize the differences between the *Decameron* and what he really values. It does not, unlike *De casibus,* contain "only authoritative histories and serious matters"; it is not the Bible; it is lead, not gold or silver. When Laurent says to the Duke, "I give over its defense to you" because in the future there may be people more inclined to attack or condemn him and his work than to excuse its failings, one suspects that more than a conventional modesty topos is at work. Laurent's prefatory letter to the *De casibus* translation contains an appeal for protection against detractors, but a shorter and more traditional one.[31] And although three years of work is admittedly substantial, Laurent's references to "the long and burdensome work of translation" and "the load on my shoulders" make the enterprise sound much more like duty than pleasure. Unlike Petrarch, he could not just glance through this *levis* collection in his moments of leisure; a book meant for recreation, addressed to idle ladies rather than serious scholars, became an assignment. Laurent correspondingly makes it more serious, and at the same time intimates some slight uneasiness about the ultimate value of the work. Yet he never loses sight of its central purposes; and like other early critics of the *Decameron,* he thinks of those purposes in terms of the psychological and hygienic values of literary pleasure.

Laurent's preface makes an appropriate end to this book for two reasons. First, it is a capstone to many of the arguments and images that appeared throughout the Middle Ages to defend literary pleasure. It is one of the period's most vigorous and thorough affirmations of the value of recreational reading. As such, it epitomizes my central concern, to articulate some later medieval literary ideas that accept and justify reading or hearing stories for the pleasure they bring. As we have seen, these justifications tend, implicitly or explicitly, to operate within the Horatian context of pleasure and profit. But to affirm the value of literary pleasure is certainly not to deny the value of literary profit. The ideas I have explored are perfectly

[31]Ed. Hortis, pp. 731–40.

compatible with medieval ethical and allegorical theories, and may in fact help lead to a more rounded, sympathetic understanding of medieval literary thought that acknowledges the mutual and interacting roles of pleasure and learning without devaluing either.[32]

Yet it is true that the defenses of pleasure examined here occur much more frequently in connection with nondidactic literature than with narratives of explicit moral intent. In this sense the recreational argument associates itself with the rise of secular fiction in the later Middle Ages, a rise that can be linked to various social, intellectual, and technological developments between the twelfth and fourteenth centuries. To explore all these developments is far beyond the scope of this book; but I believe that the acceptance of literary pleasure in theory is part of the distinctive cultural climate of the later Middle Ages, a period that saw the emergence of what Donald R. Howard calls "fiction" as opposed to "myth" or "legend"—a body of narrative told principally not as an illustration of exemplary or allegorical truth, and not as a recounting of historical events, but as an imaginative construction interesting and significant in itself.[33] The presence of such fictions—fabliaux, romances, Boccaccian *novelle*, Chaucerian tales—is itself evidence of a growing secular sensibility; and justifications of literary pleasure are correlative to that material and that sensibility. They open up from the standpoint of theory the possibility, even the desirability, of taking pleasure in literature. For many people in the later Middle Ages that possibility, that ethical space in which delight could flourish, must have been exciting and liberating.

But it would be wrong to think that the defenses celebrate pure aesthetic pleasure or that they promote literary enjoyment as an end in itself. As I have stressed, the justifications are pragmatic, claiming physical or psychological or ethical benefits that make the gaining of pleasure from stories rationally acceptable. That acceptability presumes that recreative values are limited, not ultimate. And for all the increasing secularity of the later Middle Ages, those ultimate Christian values still per-

---

[32]Salman's "Instruction and Delight" is a pioneering effort in this direction.
[33]"Fiction and Religion in Boccaccio and Chaucer," *Journal of the American Academy of Religion*, 47, Supplement (1979), 307–28, esp. 310–11.

meate the culture. To Dante and Deguileville the recreational argument must have seemed to endorse only distraction from what is really worth attending to. And, from a different perspective, to early humanists the argument must have appeared to trivialize the importance of literary studies. Here is the second reason why Laurent's preface is such a suitable concluding text, for beneath its extended affirmation of the value of recreation lies, I think, a slightly ambivalent undertone. He and Petrarch believed that the best literature did more than refresh physically or psychologically, and neither would have wanted to spend prolonged time with fictions that offered only *levis* pleasures. The recreational argument makes literary delight acceptable, but in a context that gives that delight only certain restorative rather than contemplative functions. And it insists that delight be useful. In *Anatomy of the Novella* (pp. 48–49) Clements and Gibaldi argue that the evolution of Renaissance tale collections points to an increasing willingness to accept fiction simply for the pleasure it provides without feeling the need to articulate or imply recreational benefits. That kind of sensibility does not appear often in the Middle Ages.

The idea of recreation is, of course, not uniquely medieval. As a literary defense it can be found in Greek romance and in many Renaissance works; it is familiar today, though almost always in the restricted context of sports activities. What seems to me most distinctive about its place in late medieval culture is the implicit tension between the affirmative and the defensive aspects of the argument. Recreational and hygienic ideas reveal both a tolerance of the purely entertaining, one based on the conviction that pleasure promotes well-being, and at the same time a feeling that such experience cannot stand by itself, that without constant reassertion of its acknowledged values and limits vacation becomes too much like truancy. The discrepancy between enjoyment and the need to justify enjoyment becomes most apparent in the later fourteenth century, as we see traditional recreational arguments being used to explain secular experiences—the joys of hunting, the joys of the *Decameron*—that seem far too rich, far too significant culturally, to be satisfactorily contained within notions of proper play. We can see the ideas under strain as they have to encompass a more extended secular vision than they had to before. The principles that Aristotle invoked to discuss the role of jests in casual conversation now become stretched to accommodate many different forms of activity and a wide range of literary endeavor. The expanded secular culture of the later Middle Ages still relies heavily on the recreational idea to understand and justify its interest in worldly pleasures. It does not yet give those pleasures independent status as goods in themselves.

As this summary implies, my approach has been principally historical. But I think that the recreational theories and applications presented here may reveal more than the accommodations worked out in the later Middle Ages between a Christian culture and the impulse to be entertained. They reflect as well some perennial concerns in people's thinking about fiction—the relationship between literature and life, the ways in which artistic delight affects an audience. In the later Middle Ages a number of writers—physicians, philosophers, and poets—dealt with those concerns in terms of recreational and hygienic ideas, affirmed the very significant power of fiction and entertainment to revitalize. Their recognition and understanding of that power may well help illuminate the pleasure that every age has taken in storytelling. For we know that, in mind and body, literary delight makes something happen.

Index of Sources

Index

Literature as Recreation
in the Later Middle Ages

Designed by Richard E. Rosenbaum.
Composed by Huron Valley Graphics
in 10 point Linotron 202 Baskerville, 2 points leaded,
with display lines in Baskerville.
Printed offset by Braun-Brumfield on
Warren's Number 66 Antique Offset, 50 pound basis.
Bound by John H. Dekker & Sons, Inc.
in Joanna book cloth
and stamped in Kurz-Hastings foil.